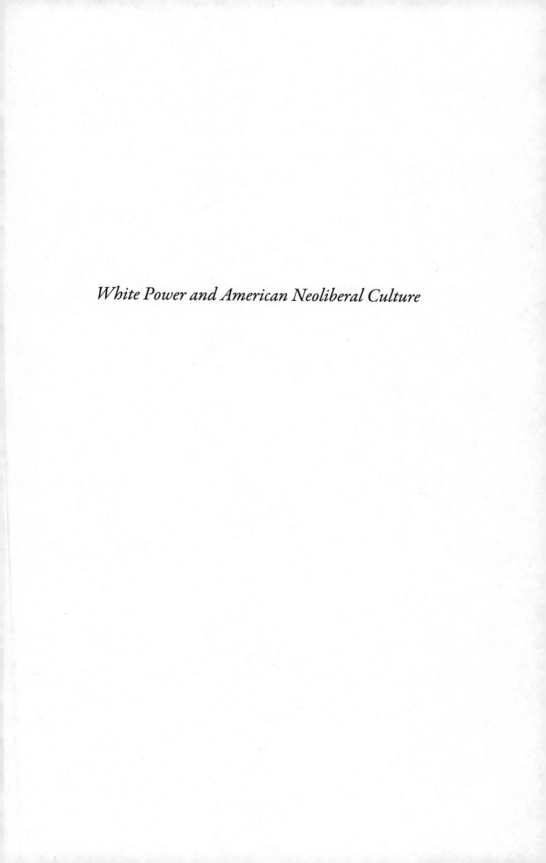

White Power and American Neoliberal Culture

White Power and American Neoliberal Culture

Patricia Ventura and Edward K. Chan

UNIVERSITY OF CALIFORNIA PRESS

University of California Press
Oakland, California

© 2023 by Edward Chan and Patricia Ventura

Library of Congress Cataloging-in-Publication Data

Names: Ventura, Patricia, 1968– author. | Chan, Edward K., 1967– author.
Title: White power and American neoliberal culture / Patricia Ventura and
    Edward K. Chan.
Description: Oakland, California : University of California Press, [2023] |
    Includes bibliographical references and index.
Identifiers: LCCN 2022024988 (print) | LCCN 2022024989 (ebook) |
    ISBN 9780520392793 (cloth ; alk. paper) | ISBN 9780520392809 (ebook)
Subjects: LCSH: White nationalism—United States—21st century. |
    Neoliberalism—United States—21st century.
Classification: LCC E184.A1 V46 2023 (print) | LCC E184.A1 (ebook) |
    DDC 320.54089/09—dc23/eng/20220629
LC record available at https://lccn.loc.gov/2022024988
LC ebook record available at https://lccn.loc.gov/2022024989

Manufactured in the United States of America

32 31 30 29 28 27 26 25 24 23
10 9 8 7 6 5 4 3 2 1

CONTENTS

ACKNOWLEDGMENTS

There are so many people to thank for this project that it is hard to know where to start, but a partial list begins with our colleagues at Spelman and Waseda and the following people, who read parts of this manuscript in its various stages of development: Lee Bebout, Maricela deMirjyn, Silvia Dominguez, Gabrielle Halko, Susan Hegeman, Rebecca Hill, Stephen Knadler, Deanna Koretsky, Sequoia Maner, Jeffrey Allen Tucker, Phillip Wegner, and the editors, anonymous readers, and board members at UC Press. Errors in this publication are all ours, of course, but this book is stronger for their brilliant contributions and suggestions. Finally, we would like to acknowledge our sisters and their families, our in-laws, and our friends. Special appreciation, of course, goes to Yuri, Glenn, and Max, as well as to coffee and wine, all of which got us through this project.

Introduction

DISASTER WHITENESS

THIS BOOK STARTED AS A TONGUE-IN-CHEEK discussion of a question way back in 2019: Was Donald Trump the epitome of neoliberalism or the harbinger of its demise? But, of course, much has transpired since then and talking through that question led us down a grim path that brings together white power—which we see as the current extremist form of white supremacy—and neoliberal culture—as the current form of racial capitalism—in an exploration of topics much larger than any one individual. Indeed, our question became an entry point into the long history of American white ethnonationalism and white supremacy and their love-hate relationship with democracy of which Trump is merely a particular iteration, an expression of the patriarchal racial capitalism at the deep core of American neoliberal culture. Our work led us to analyze the violence of white power, which we investigate through sadistic novels and manifestos written by a range of figures with some connection to white power ideology. At the same time, we study the racist, misogynist core at the center of American neoliberal culture and the fundamental role of patriarchal family values in both white power and neoliberalism.

To stay with Trump for another minute, we may well ask what makes him so relevant to neoliberalism. As a self-styled pussy-grabbing businessman and huckster "billionaire" who emerged from bankruptcy by playing the character of a sensationalist dealmaker on his own reality television show, Trump personified neoliberalism's entrepreneurial and emotional priorities. However, when we consider many of Trump's other positions, a more complicated story emerges. For instance, when he promised, with a stunning lack of success, to overturn the Affordable Care Act (ACA), he did not reject the idea of publicly funded alternatives, even though neoliberal ideology firmly opposes the social safety net, but instead said he would replace the ACA with "great health care." So too, he expressed opposition to the neoliberal shibboleths of "globalism" and free trade as evidenced by his launching of a costly trade war with China.[1] Unencumbered by the technocratic expertise neoliberalism is known for, his policy pronouncements were not supported by thought-through political programs as much as vaguely sketched out far-right populist ideologies.

Such policies and pronouncements show that Trump and many on the far right are not motivated by the belief in the free market and small government that are assumed to be the central tenets of neoliberal ideology. They are driven by commitment to a principle much older than neoliberalism. They are motivated by a 150-year-old antidemocratic "white rage"—as historian Carol Anderson terms it—that has been simmering since the Civil War and flares up seemingly every time that people who are not white men achieve important milestones.[2] From this perspective Trump is less the leader of any movement and more the repudiation of Black Lives Matter and the negation of the first Black president, not to mention the would-be first woman president, of the United States. Reaching back further into U.S. history, Trump links us back to the founding of the United States on colonized land reshaped with the labor of stolen people. Seeing U.S. history from this viewpoint not only emphasizes this settler-colonial past, but it also redefines the most potent ideologies in U.S. life, such as the American dream. From here, the American dream as ideology and birthright shows that white power nationalism is only the latest version of an older ideology based on the twinning not just of racism and imperialism, but also of white supremacy and capitalist accumulation. From this long view, Trump can be seen as merely the latest spokesman for a crusade trafficking in the ressentiment of white heterosexist patriarchy. He is a personification of an ideology promoting economic, political, cultural, and social domination by those defined as white and male.

So, to understand the complexities of American neoliberalism, we examine the sources of that rage and of the white power affect that desires to "Make America Great Again." We analyze the social conservatism at the heart of neoliberalism and of the writings of white power ideologues and ethnonationalists. We argue that neoliberal capitalism's aims to eliminate barriers, strip regulations on economic activity, and enable the free flow of capital result in economic oscillations that are themselves a microcosm of the extremes that characterize the ethno-racism within American neoliberal culture, and ultimately within American capitalism itself.

Neoliberalism has been beset by wildly destabilizing oscillations, the Trump presidency marking only one of many moments of crisis and contradiction in the American neoliberal era. A quick scan of book titles from 2019 reveals that many scholars see neoliberalism as a catastrophe. Titles such as *In the Ruins of Neoliberalism* to *Mutant Neoliberalism* to *Never-Ending Nightmare* suggest a level of alarm that, to be fair, had predated Trump but that in his wake raises several questions, not least of which is why has neoliberalism been so successful ideologically if it is such a nightmare? We will address that question in the pages to come.

But first we should take a step back to consider a larger point that has dogged scholars for decades. If neoliberalism has been a dominant cultural force since the 1970s, we may well ask if it remains a relevant framework given the many changes the world has since undergone. Stuart Hall asked that question himself in the wake of the globally destructive Great Recession of 2007–2010, and in answering it he saw the recession as marking a moment within "that conjuncture which we can define as 'the long march of the Neoliberal Revolution.'" For Hall, the *conjuncture* is a "social configuration" that results from a period of crisis. It arises "when a number of contradictions at work in different key practices and sites come together—or 'con-join'—in the same moment and political space."[3] So as we acknowledge the hesitation of some scholars to use the framework of neoliberalism at all, ostensibly because it is overused or too sprawling, we follow Hall, who maintained that the "neoliberal revolution" is nowhere near over.[4] He determined that neoliberal ideas have proliferated throughout the world, reorganizing whole economies, governments, and societies.[5]

Today, as we write these words in a season of democratic crisis, it remains the case as Hall said that "naming neoliberalism is *politically* necessary to give resistance content, focus and a cutting edge."[6] In short, we can mobilize the tools that have been developed over these past decades to understand neoliberalism, and we can do our part to keep those tools updated in order to contribute to the resistance. Analyzing the targets of these policies and ideas has led us to explore the contemporary imbrication of white power racism and neoliberal culture in the United States. This leads to the second point that dogs scholarship on the issues we are discussing. Focusing on white power can seem to be disconnected from everyday racism, or even let the latter off the hook under the rationale that at least it is not as bad as the extremists' kind. Focusing on extremism does not erase the daily, relentless racism of microaggressions, color-blind rhetoric, dog whistles, and institutional racism that shapes quotidian lived experience and white fragilities. Indeed, it is deeply relevant that Trump, who has acted as a spark for the white extremist resurgence in the United States, was elected by a majority of white Americans who would not endorse the radical extremism we study in this book. But all of these "brands" of racism are tied together. Indeed, it is also relevant that some white liberals who would never vote for Trump have endorsed a system of overcorrection to white fragility that results in exoticizing racism.[7] These positions result in a racism that enters from another door, and it too is an ever-present danger in Trump-inflected American culture.

In this book we try to find a space between the racial-neoliberalism-is-everywhere approach and the real-racism-exists-only-in-a-few-locations position, just as we reject the idea that being anti-racist is fundamentally about calling out racist personal attitudes or individuals. Our goal here is to analyze a deeply dangerous and growing threat to democracy and people's lives that is installed at the fundamental level of capitalism. We do this by building on our previous separate scholarship that analyzes white power utopias (Chan) and American neoliberal culture (Ventura).[8] We examine here the relation between the two in order to locate the white power resurgence we see around us in the context of the "neoliberal revolution."

To contextualize that revolution, we argue that Trump embodies the white power moment that reconnects us to American neoliberalism's misty prehistory as a market-obsessed "theoretical utopianism" of economic freedom against centralized planning.[9] As it was put by Friedrich Hayek, one of the early theorists of neoliberalism, supporting the system of private property "is the most important guarantee of freedom."[10] As a result, freedom becomes the stated rationale for opposing the social service state with its required taxation and regulation. We argue that this rationale is only part of a regime that is fundamentally opposed to equality and democracy themselves, that opposes the social service state because it requires society as a whole rather than isolated individuals to bear the costs of social reproduction.

At least two forces have been operating at the core of American neoliberalism: fear of losing the cultural dominance of the patriarchal family and an economic motivation to shrink the social-welfare and regulatory state in order to funnel wealth upward to the super-rich. Examining the foundational roles of whiteness and the system of racial capitalism is crucial for understanding both forces. As neoliberal theorists position the white patriarchal family to take the place of the state in its governmental functions, white power groups prioritize reproducing more white people and constructing a collective consciousness that begins with the traditional nuclear family and enlarges to encompass whiteness as a tribal family. We study this crucial nexus between white ethnonationalist ideology and neoliberalism in the form of the white heteronormative patriarchal family that extends seamlessly out to incorporate white people generally as a racial family.

Filling in what is left out of too many analyses of neoliberalism begins here at the intersection of white power and capitalism, in which race and family are not epiphenomena but constitutive categories. To critically analyze neoliberalism from the perspective that capitalism is necessarily raced means that analyzing the history of neoliberal politics, policy, and theory opens a space for us to make the unlikely connections between white power and neoliberalism's founding generation of professors and politicos, many of whom would never have explicitly supported white supremacy but whose actions created the conditions for its resurgence as white power—in the name of affirming family values.

In the United States, understanding the rise of neoliberalism and the perpetuation of white supremacy from this nexus of influences requires analyzing the political power of whiteness as a "gravitational force" and grasping that "the core contradiction of neoliberal society is race" with its production of the "possessive investment in whiteness."[11] This strategy of converting whiteness into cultural, and consequently economic, capital has been successful when it has targeted white people who deeply resent the efforts to democratize American life more fully. In the United States of the neoliberal era, the targeting has taken many approaches, including, most notably for our analysis, the "long Southern Strategy" that according to political scientists Angie Maxwell and Todd Shields works like a triptych connecting religious fundamentalism and patriarchy as "separate hinged panels that can be folded inward—bent to cover or reinforce white supremacy."[12] From this perspective we examine the rhetoric and politics of white patriarchal entitlement mobilized to build a future that deflects the gnawing fear of millions of white people that their racial identity has lost its value in a globalized and multicultural world.

And so we circle back to the question we started with. We know that Trump is a product of neoliberal culture, but he is hardly its apotheosis. We argue that the more significant development of the Trump years is the revitalization of white power that accompanied Trump's rise to the presidency through a campaign appealing to whiteness, which we study here through utopian novels and in the manifestos of white power actants and would-be actants. By providing a larger context, we hope to add insight that helps in the effort at resistance. To that end, we maintain that studies of neoliberal culture should acknowledge what W. E. B. Du Bois and, after him, David Roediger have definitively shown: whiteness has historically been a value added to white people's paid wage.[13] While some white people have never been positioned to use that wage to access wealth-building institutions such as favorable housing and well-funded schools, nearly all whites enjoy the relative freedom of a presumption of innocence in the face of overzealous policing and the dark powers of the carceral state. It is certain that for many white people, whiteness is a cultural wage that can but doesn't always link to actual material wealth, especially as evidenced by the deep poverty plaguing those states historically linked to the most extreme versions of white supremacy. However, the stories offered by the various agents of whiteness, from the political establishments to the ethnonationalist extremes, allow white people to maintain a tenuous grasp on the historic promises of guilt-free supremacy and exception offered to them for centuries.

The racially motivated violence by white power extremists in the years since the election of Barack Obama illustrates their effort to highlight the color line in the United States, and this is not even taking into account the murder and violence perpetrated against Black and Brown people by police that brought forth and continue to feed the Black Lives Matter movement. In 2008, the Southern Poverty Law Center (SPLC) described more than two hundred hate-related incidents as triggered by Obama's election.[14] David Duke, of Ku Klux Klan fame, identified him as a "visual aid" to inspire white racial unity.[15] After the 2016 election of Trump, the SPLC reported a spike in the number of hate groups, this time presumably inspired by Trump's frequent xenophobic and racist pronouncements.[16] Thus, for different reasons, the elections of Obama and Trump fed a wide-ranging and insidious white identity politics as well as the more extreme cases of white racial terror. As we will argue, the violence of white power erodes the goal of striving toward a pluralistic society and reveals a bleak reality articulated by philosopher Cedric Robinson: "The purpose of racism is to control the behavior of white people, not Black people. For Blacks, guns and tanks are sufficient."[17] This white power racism links easily with neoliberal ideology and governmentality to undermine the idea of society itself and thus the validity of the entire social service state. To take its place, both white power and neoliberalism offer the heteropatriarchal family as a replacement.

TERMINOLOGY: NEOLIBERALISM AND
NEOLIBERAL CULTURE

To begin our study, we need to define the terminology that forms the parameters of this project. For starters, *neoliberalism* is a sprawling term traditionally naming a set of capitalist economic approaches favoring financialization, business deregulation, minimal taxation, globalization, free trade, and market fundamentalism supported by states dedicated to corporate interests. Neoliberalism develops from racial capitalism as a program to promote institutions and ideologies that protect private property and wealth. As a critical analytical approach, racial capitalism acknowledges the fundamentally racist, colonial, and thus racially exploitative nature of capitalism itself, which separates people from each other in order to, in lay terms, make the rich richer.[18] Neoliberal racial capitalism enables tremendous economic inequality, which it reframes as a social good that rewards hard work and a sign that the system is operating correctly.

Neoliberal culture is the name for the massive infrastructure shaping everyday life under neoliberal racial capitalism. It is like an ecosystem in which contemporary life is lived and emotions are felt. American neoliberalism is hegemonic in the United States, and American neoliberal culture is a kind of atmosphere for daily existence in the United States. We see American neoliberal culture as having taken root as a reaction against the social movement activism of the civil rights / Vietnam / anti-colonialism era and established itself as a result of neoliberal and post-Fordist capitalism, subsumed under the larger category of racial capitalism. In the United States we see it coming to fruition with the end of the Cold War in 1989 and lasting through our present moment.

Neoliberalism's priority is to erode the notions of society and the commons (public goods and resources), and in this way it erodes the validity of the social welfare state. From another perspective it is a rationality, governmentality, and ideology that when taken together place capitalist economics at the center of existence as an element of nature, almost like the earth or water. It explicitly rejects the idea of society and social obligation, in some iterations positioning agency in the hands of the self-responsible individual and for many adherents endorsing a strong state to direct the actions of those responsible individuals. As a mode of subjectivity it is often said to produce *homo economicus,* the individualist who is supposed to be a rational evaluator of the economic landscape, who sees the self as human capital and as a product to be maximized by making the "right" consumer choices and regulated through a rigid program of self-surveillance and self-discipline.[19] But it also produces an additional idealized subject, less discussed in the literature about neoliberal subjectivity but who is proving exceptionally important in these times. This subject, *homo affectus,* whose existence centers on an affective mode, draws a sharp contrast with the economic rationality of the classic neoliberal subject but is a central figure in the emotional economy of the neoliberal workforce, especially as contemporary industries increasingly center on feelings, care, emotions, and service to others—a development that those operating in a stereotypically masculinist vein bristle against.[20] According to sociologist Birgit Sauer, the affective citizen is a product of a neoliberal governmentality that perpetuates fear resulting in a right-wing discourse in which people "are given the right to be furious and passionate, they are freed from caring about others (as they have always been), from feelings of solidarity; and men are encouraged to modulate fear into anger and direct this anger towards 'Others.'"[21] White power mobilizes this affective mechanism in order to recruit white people to its ranks and rationalize its ideology, such that the only solidarity allowed is with the white race.

TERMINOLOGY: WHITE POWER AND THE FAR WHITE

We have chosen to use the term *white power* to refer to the loose but parallel, and at times connected, conglomeration of ideologies and activities commonly designated as *white supremacy, white nationalism, white separatism, (white) ethnonationalism,* and *the far right,* as well as the relatively short-lived *alt-right.* These other terms, though similar, designate specific aspects of an overall regime of white power, a term that was also used in 1966 as a call to action responding to Black Power in the title of a manifesto of sorts by George Lincoln Rockwell, who had also founded the American Nazi Party in 1959. It is also used in the single most influential white supremacist novel— *The Turner Diaries* (1978), by William Pierce using the pseudonym Andrew Macdonald—as a call to arms.[22] Our use of the term *white power* is influenced by C. Richard King and David J. Leonard and by Kathleen Belew, the latter referring to "the social movement that brought together members of the Klan, militias, radical tax resisters, white separatists, neo-Nazis, and proponents of white theologies such as Christian Identity, Odinism, and Dualism between 1975 and 1995."[23] However, we extend the period through to our own present, the years after Trump's dismal presidency, and Belew has also recently referred to the resurgence of the white power movement.[24]

It is important to employ such terms with awareness of their diverse meanings and the palimpsest-like way they have evolved. From the outside, all these groups are sometimes loosely conglomerated to the degree that they can be called a "movement," and yet they often work disconnectedly and at odds and without clear leaders. Moreover, white supremacists are not necessarily white nationalists desiring a white-only nation, and white separatists might claim they are not white supremacists, only that they want to exist apart from nonwhites who are not necessarily racially inferior. Of course, the various manifestations of racism in the recent mainstreaming of the far right, the vociferousness of more openly white supremacist groups, and acts of white domestic terror are not unrelated, and each encourages the other in a larger framework of white power, envisioned here not only as a subject position but also as a set of ideologies.

In this regard we develop the additional term *far white* to capture the spectrum of white identity politics and ideologies, especially as they influence the estimated twenty-one million Americans who are not members of any white power group but who endorse the use of political violence. Politically, the belief that most commonly unites them is a fear of replacement, of white people losing their demographic and social position in U.S. society.[25] The term names those who invest in whiteness as a distinct identity but are not active in white supremacist groups; it captures a sometimes fuzzy overlap between far-right politics and white power extremism. The far white becomes a particularly dangerous identity when mainstream politicians and pundits express these racially extremist views and positions, whether genuinely or cynically. So while the far white are not willing to actually join a group that we would identify as white power, they nevertheless buy into some part of the ideology and are in some way sympathetic to the political ideals displayed in the August 11–12, 2017, Unite the Right rally in Charlottesville, Virginia, and the U.S. Capitol insurrection of January 6, 2021, and they might even engage in violence like some of the shooters we discuss in chapter 1.

For the far white, as for white power, rights can only be understood as a quantity: advancements in civil rights for others requires a loss of rights for them. These violent ideologies may originate on the fringes with extremists who fear the loss of white status and privilege—and the material wealth and resources that accrue to those—but it seeps into the mainstream through conduits like Trumpism or the Tea Party, where it interacts with and reinforces already long-held assumptions, even if subconscious, about the structure of whiteness baked into the foundation and legacy of race relations in the United States through ideologies like Manifest Destiny, racial hierarchies, and so on. Although these ideologies may have been attenuated to some degree by struggles for racial equality, the inertia carries over into the present and reemerges in fears that white people will become vastly outnumbered by racial "others." Indeed, the violence in incidents such as the U.S. Capitol insurrection, which was racially motivated to a significant degree,[26] speaks to the fact that the founding notion of "America" as a white country never really disappeared.

Central to both the far white and white power is a white identity politics that has been trading on notions of victimization since at least the 1970s but certainly has connections to the Reconstruction era. In its extreme form, it calls for outspoken racism in a time when dominant culture maintains that bigotry is no longer supposed to be open and pluralism is to be the modus operandi. As we discuss in chapters 2 and 3, neoliberal culture created a space for white people, particularly white men, to embrace a malignant racist politics that gained social acceptability by removing support for the New Deal big government programs that they had previously supported. Key to their support had been the exclusion of Black people from the benefits of the social service state. What changed was the reframing of society to no longer exclude Black people. When those neoliberal strategies that had used white ressentiment to successfully erode the social service state and increase the wealth of the nation's 1 percent had been played out, Trump arrived to make America great again by embracing a masculinized alternative position that allowed white people to at least rhetorically reclaim the social service state by endorsing the kinds of exclusions that had been built into its original and more-popular-with-white-folks New Deal–era iteration. Thus, whiteness could find its identity in the far-right racist/xenophobic populism that helped propel Trump into office without him having to reject the social service state in principle or practice. Indeed, we see that an activist state, in the service of whiteness, is encouraged in the white power utopias we discuss in chapter 4. White power ideology doesn't necessarily eschew the idea of the social embodied in the state as long as it doesn't benefit those outside the white tribe.

We see white power as distinct from the mundane *white privilege,* important in its own way, which also assumes a version of racial supremacy and has existed as a foundational part of racial capitalism. However, one place we can now see the effort to put racially extremist views back into the mainstream is the khaki- and polo-wearing white men (and some women) who carried tiki torches down the streets of Charlottesville chanting "You will not replace us!" and "Jews will not replace us!" Contrasting the stereotypical image of the white supremacist as the hood-and-robe-wearing white man, these "regular Joes" follow in the footsteps of people like David Duke, who "cleaned up" the image of the KKK, and Richard Spencer, who put a well-dressed, pretty-boy face on the racism of the alt-right. The Fox News Channel, always unabashedly right-wing, now flirts with the discourse of white power ideology through two of its most popular figures, Tucker Carlson and Laura Ingraham, who stoke anxiety over the supposed decline of the United States' white population. That Fox has been the most-watched cable news network since 2002 suggests that a great number of Americans welcome these ideas.[27]

As the discussion above suggests, what we are referring to as white power and the far white differ from earlier forms of white supremacy / nationalism / separatism while continuing to draw on the historical notions of racial privilege the latter also espouse. The presumption of white superiority in the European colonization of North America and the early colonies that became the republic in the eighteenth century largely goes unremarked because it was an unquestioned part of the European worldview at the time, part of the formation that philosopher Charles W. Mills calls the racial contract that perpetuates the racial exploitation of nonwhite people as a central event at the origins of modernity and continuing virtually unabated to the present.[28] Later, the popularity of the eugenics movement and the rise of racial science from the nineteenth century and into the twentieth in a very mainstream way further codified notions of white supremacy. Then there are the actions and movements that arose in response to various versions of the "race problem": the first incarnation of the Ku Klux Klan in response to the Reconstruction era's audacity to, if only nominally, put Black people on the same plane of political equality as southern white people. The KKK would then recede as white supremacism was reconstructed in mainstream society, only to rise again in the 1910s and 1920s in the face of increased immigration of Jewish people and other Europeans from countries like Italy, who were considered to be of suspect whiteness. After ebbing again, the KKK rose again in its third incarnation in response to the civil rights movement of the 1950s and 1960s.

The KKK, however, never completely represented those who could be considered white supremacists. And although the various KKK groups do play a role in what we are calling white power today, they are mixed with other streams of white supremacist ideology, such as neo-Nazism, Christian Identity, and ultra-nationalism, and they can and do intersect with less extreme white identity politics. In short, white power and the far white are the current radicalized forms of a white supremacy whose lineage goes back to the racial contract as explicated by Mills. In the United States, while neoliberalism became the cultural dominant, white power ideology also became the primary expression of violent white supremacy responding to the same set of historical events as neoliberalism: the gains achieved by the civil rights movement (such as they are), the immeasurable blow to white American masculinity by the Vietnam War (both from not being able to defeat a racialized enemy and the anti-war protests in the United States), the progress fought for by gender and sexual liberation movements, and the changing demographic makeup of the United States after the reform of racist immigration restrictions in the 1960s.

Neoliberal capitalism and neoliberal culture were profoundly impacted by the same energies that marked this moment. The movement activism and great social struggles of the 1960s and 1970s led to and corresponded with the rising mistrust by the populace in the U.S. federal government, which was seen as too interventionist and suspect. The tenor of the interventionism and nature of the mistrust were of course relative to one's position. From a white patriarchal "traditionalist" perspective, the federal government was seen as abandoning white patriarchy by extending to single mothers and people of color the protections and benefits that white males had guarded jealously. Once these protections and benefits were extended to nonwhites, the taxation required to fund them was recharacterized as government oppression, with white men repositioned as victims.

However, feelings of white victimization have actually been a common part of American white racial consciousness. For an example, one need only consider the victim status claimed by southern white men since the loss of the Civil War.[29] Claims harkening back to the mythical "Lost Cause" of the Civil War were cast repeatedly across the decades. Importantly here, they were recast in the wake of the equality and peace movements of the Vietnam / New Left era and came together as the Southern Strategy— discussed in chapter 3—which used anti-government rhetoric to cover for racism and aimed to roll back gains in racial equity by promoting a seemingly race-neutral offer of meritocracy and cuts in big-government spending.[30] These tactics lie at the center of neoliberalism's anti-government / anti-social-service-state rhetoric.[31] They may well have found their most potent form in the famous proclamation by Ronald Reagan, "Government is not the solution to our problem; government is the problem."[32]

Today, as the white heteropatriarchal family emerges as the point at which neoliberalism and white power ideology converge, the common enemy is not actually big government in the form of the social welfare state, but rather a state that would attend to the needs of nonwhite people and women who live outside the patriarchal family. This far-right perspective resists the austerity policies that dominated U.S. politics throughout the neoliberal era. Indeed, the far right's anti-capitalist posture can actually be enfolded into neoliberalism by emphasizing the state's ability to support the white family, while the stance against democracy evidenced in white power rhetoric ties it back to autocratic tendencies within neoliberal government that does not honor all people's right to have rights.[33]

As white power radicalizes untold numbers online, support of "accelerationism" (i.e., fomenting a race war) has made a particular impact in the internet's subterranean worlds of which white power terrorists are denizens. The online and global ethnonationalist community is a dizzying and rapidly changing sphere.[34] We review it through white power manifestos, and we dive deeper into it through our reading of white power utopian novels. We well know that novels are a singular aspect of a significantly larger conversation, but these texts give us a way to approach the larger foundational questions we are asking, while attempting to tread lightly in the minefield of unrelenting social media shitposting, most of it ironic trolling aimed to provoke liberal and leftist readers who are not part of the white supremacist world.[35] In our work we try to represent the scope of white racial acts of terror in the United States while acknowledging two key ethical concerns: the dangers of naming and thus publicizing white terrorists and their ideas, and letting everyday acts of white supremacy somehow off the hook because they do not rise to the violent brutality of white power terrorism. What is most important for our purposes is to look at the violence in the context of white power ideology and neoliberalism to show a particular danger in our historical moment.

We claim that both American neoliberal culture and white power would be better understood if we think of each as enabling the other at key moments in U.S. history when Americans who identify with whiteness reckoned with events such as the civil rights movement and the loss of the Vietnam War, the election of the first Black president with Obama, and the Trump era.

Analyzing such historical moments are the goals of chapters 2 and 3. We argue that white power and neoliberalism support each other, that their priorities align in ways that supercharge the power of both, and that they work together to shape the contemporary United States. Nowhere is this connection clearer than in the investments both make in the white heteropatriarchal family.

The family becomes the preferred rationale for the extreme violence and ideological tendencies of white power in the United States, which we maintain can be more fully understood within the context of American neoliberal culture. Neoliberalism shifts the obligations of social reproduction onto existing patriarchal structures to promote its radical economic and social agenda that reinforces inequalities and corrodes institutions and policies working toward justice and equity. So too American neoliberal ideology fits organically into the United States' institutions and traditions of racism; indeed, white power aligns with and supports neoliberalism's goals not by happenstance but by their shared roots in racial patriarchal capitalism. Thus, the eruptions of violence we see in the acts of white terror considered in this book inevitably result from the intertwining of white power and neoliberalism.

ONE

Starting Points

WHITE POWER NEOLIBERALISM / NEOLIBERAL WHITE POWER

WHITE POWER IN/AND THE NEOLIBERAL ERA

Ethnonationalism has entered into popular consciousness in the United States because of the confluence of several events, including the ascendance of a variety of far-right populist leaders domestically and across the globe— Jair Bolsonaro in Brazil, Jarosław Kaczyński in Poland, Narendra Modi in India, Viktor Orbán in Hungary, Donald Trump in the United States—the toxic proliferation of radicalized white supremacist groups, and the dramatic rise in spectacles of white racist mass violence. In the case of mass-violence incidents, they garner widespread attention in part because of their explicit ties to white power ideologies that are perceived around the world, accurately, as a threat to justice and democracy.[1] Spread in mainstream media as well as in the dark corners of relatively unregulated message boards like 8chan/8kun, these ideologies circulate globally in privately coded ways as well, speaking directly to those who have been "red-pilled" and choose to learn what white power ideologues and their fellow travelers push as the true story of the oppression of the white man whose story and viability are being erased by liberal multicultural political correctness.[2] A few touchstones have emerged, and we reflect on them in this chapter as a way to contextualize our larger study of the sphere where white power and neoliberalism come together. Indeed, this sphere paradoxically spans the globe and yet remains insular, operating within the bounds of community, nation, and race while key ideas, artifacts, and figures circulate broadly and emerge interconnectedly through-out the world.

A major example here is the manifesto written by notorious Norwegian mass murderer Anders Breivik, *2083: A European Declaration of Independence*

(2011). The manifesto literalizes this paradoxically global insularity by featuring over 1,500 (ranting) pages that largely plagiarize or paraphrase many existing texts: the Unabomber manifesto, the paleoconservative William S. Lind's *"Political Correctness": A Short History of an Ideology,* the anti-Islamic writings of conspiracy theorist Robert Spencer on his Jihad Watch website, and the "Eurabia" conspiracy theory alleging Muslim immigrants are intentionally colonizing Europe with help from the European Union, which is mostly associated with Bat Ye'or (aka Gisèle Littman), a notorious Egyptian-British conspiracy theorist who propagates Islamophobia. Breivik also targets Marxist cultural theory, especially from the Frankfurt School, as part of the plot to Islamize Europe. Indeed, Breivik's manifesto touches on all the biggest hits from the far right and white power, but the pervasive "white extinction anxiety" occupies the heart of the text, bound up in a fear of "the great replacement"—the white ethnonationalist belief that white European and European-descended people around the world are being replaced by nonwhite non-Europeans in their home countries, now envisioned as imagined communities of a vanishing whiteness. Reacting against shifting demographics and overstated in demagogic ways, these fears represent a reaction formation against movements for a more racially just and inclusive society.

Breivik's long list of threats to white people illustrates an essential contradiction at the heart of white power. It maintains an intense opposition to globalism and yet encompasses a vision of white Western civilization globally. On the economic front, Breivik, like many white power advocates, blames contemporary corporate capitalism and its foundation in consumerism for the deterioration of Western societies. He opposes "US-style laissez-faire capitalism" with which neoliberalism is so profoundly tied, and yet he supports free markets within the context of a strong authoritarian state.[3] Because capitalism in its current form lends itself to nonwhite immigration into the ostensible homelands of white people in both settler colonies and Europe itself, white power ideologues oppose the singular desire for capital accumulation, which necessarily promotes globalization. Indeed, Breivik blames corporate capitalism and its foundation in consumerism for the deterioration of Western societies. And yet, as with fascism generally, the strong state never replaces the private interests of the powerful. As anthropologist Sindre Bangstad claims, Breivik's manifesto is really a hodgepodge filled with countless contradictions and non sequiturs that "reflect a profoundly instrumentalist and neoliberal idea of politics," in which neoliberalism has become the reigning logic of all social spheres.[4] The ideologies espoused by

Breivik and other white power ideologues and terrorists may run counter to neoliberal economics in the latter's foundation in global financialization. However, white power activities are funded online increasingly through the global trade in cryptocurrencies, and their ideas can only circulate through dark global media channels that allow these figures to avoid the state and corporate controls placed locally in nearly all Western nations.[5] So again the connections between white power and neoliberal ideologies contain many contradictions given that resisting globalization is central to white power, even though it is a global movement. As Stuart Hall has argued, the work of ideologies is to stitch together social contradictions that involve powerful affective energies; indeed, ideologies thrive on them.[6]

The confluence of neoliberalism and white power today underlies the alarming growth of both white ethnonationalist authoritarianism as well as extreme violence perpetrated within the at times indistinct but pervasive fog of white power ideology. As we will argue in this chapter and in this book as a whole, the anti-society (not to mention antisocial) ideologies shaping American neoliberalism expose the white supremacism at its core and play to many white people's fears that whiteness has lost some of its symbolic and real capital in the contemporary globalized, multiculturalized world. In the United States, this white panic results from American neoliberalism's foundation in racial capitalism.[7] In its social form, it is shaped by a patriarchal infrastructure (which we discuss in chapter 2). In its political form, it takes such shapes as the erosion of the welfare state (which we discuss in chapter 3). In all its forms, it produces violence and a sense of "aggrieved entitlement"[8] in which people who identify with whiteness as being necessarily dominant feel they are being unjustly replaced by inferior people taking the jobs and status to which the dominants believe they are naturally entitled, as we shall see throughout this chapter.[9]

In the United States, white ethnonationalism and white supremacy may not represent popularly articulated or always explicit perspectives, but they are foundational features of American culture in general. Their blossoming into white power in the neoliberal era has been pushed along by what we can think of as a "disaster whiteness," to adapt Naomi Klein's term "disaster capitalism," which describes the neoliberal strategy of capitalizing on major changes and catastrophic events. Disaster capitalism is an accumulation strategy of "orchestrated raids on the public sphere in the wake of catastrophic events" pioneered by neoliberal totem Milton Friedman, who felt "only a crisis—actual or perceived—produces real change."[10] With disaster whiteness, neoliberal forces take advantage of the feeling of affective catastrophe experienced by many white people at pivotal historical moments since the 1960s. To understand disaster whiteness in practice we need only consult the words of master GOP strategist Lee Atwater responding to these changes in 1981:

> You can't say [the N-word]—that hurts you, backfires. So you say stuff like, uh, forced busing, states' rights, and all that stuff, and you're getting so abstract. Now you're talking about cutting taxes, and all these things you're talking about are totally economic things and a byproduct of them is, blacks get hurt worse than whites. . . . "We want to cut this" is much more abstract than even the busing thing and a hell of a lot more abstract than [the N-word].[11]

In twenty-first-century electoral politics, one particularly contentious site of disaster whiteness has been the struggle among competing white folks as they organize around issues of gender. Consider, for instance, sociologist Theda Skocpol's work on the fights between the women-centered, liberal #Resistance that arose after the 2016 election and the white reactionary Tea Party, in which women also play a prominent role, that arose after Obama's 2008 election and morphed into Trump's base; both groups are organized around issues of national identity whether related to governmental treatment of those with little institutional power or racialized concern for immigration.[12] To overturn the social progress made by people of color, women of all races, and LGBTQ+ communities, the American far-right populist political strategy, informed as it is by long-held beliefs of white patriarchal supremacy, has been to bring in white voters not by addressing their policy concerns but simply by centering ethnic whiteness and heteropatriarchy.[13] This approach pivots on a deeply affective appeal to an unspecified American past that was presumably "great" and can be made great again.

For their part, white power terrorists do not see returning to the old ways as the most effective strategy. They envision a project for an ethnonationalist patriarchal *future* built on a new generation of white children born to women required to be mothers and men who embrace the role of warrior-protector. As William Pierce, the deceased leader of the white power group National Alliance, wrote in *The Turner Diaries* (under his pseudonym Andrew Macdonald), "The path to our goal cannot be a retracing of our course to some earlier stage in our history, but must instead be an overcoming of the present and a forging ahead into the future."[14] White extremists like Pierce offer a brutally potent vision of monoracial wholeness that stokes white fears of becoming subordinate and irrelevant in a zero-sum game.[15] As one writer put it, "These individuals are entirely serious about achieving a transnational white nation through violent revolution. Think of it as a globalized white supremacist version of the ISIS caliphate, but with worse food."[16]

RACISM, NEOLIBERALISM, CAPITALISM

These white power janissaries are operating out of what they think is a natural, if not scientific, hierarchical definition of various races with whiteness on top, even though the meaning of the very term *white* itself has changed through the centuries and is not even agreed upon by white supremacists today. If whiteness has morphed over time, it has always adapted to the racial politics of the day. In the United States generally, the Irish, Italians, and white-skinned Jewish people, for instance, had to work their way into whiteness.[17] Even within the ranks of white power where anti-Semitic racial ideologies predominate, some figures (e.g., Dylann Roof) see Jews as white.

For us, *race* is not a description of people but an action done to people within a system of inclusion and exclusion, privileging some and perpetrating violence on others. Whiteness in the United States developed as a racial category to, at least in part, prevent economic class solidarity by ushering poor European Americans into honorary alliance with wealthy European Americans as a control stratum over enslaved African Americans; the enemy becomes the proverbial racial other.[18] For Cedric Robinson, this racializing is "rooted not in a particular era but in [Western] civilization itself." In the context of capitalism, this active racializing creates and sustains the conditions that Robinson calls *racial capitalism,* a term that encapsulates how capitalism came into being and thrived in Europe through already existing, deeply racialized forms. What he calls "racialism"—a more expansive notion than what people generally designate as "race"—is a material force that is inextricably ingrained in the social structure created by capitalism.[19] For our purposes, what is important is Robinson's revision of Marxism, which traces racialism back to the origins of European civilization. Capitalism *later* took root, following the preexisting logic of racialization in determining social formations. In other words, capitalism emerged in a soil fertilized by racialism.[20] In U.S. history, racial capitalism cloaks national identity in the ideal of liberty while perpetrating violent practices like race-based slavery and genocide.[21] Operating from the perspective of racial capitalist critique means seeing that wealth not only flows into a few hands but that it does so through the exploitation of people who are racialized and othered through processes such as colonialism (in all its forms) and slavery. W. E. B. Du Bois talks about this kind of exploitation as "using the land and labor of the majority of mankind mainly for the benefit of the European world and not for the benefit of most men, who happen to be colored."[22]

We can only agree with Robinson that capitalism has always been racial capitalism. By extension, neoliberal capitalism is thus neoliberal racial capitalism. Articulating the racial in neoliberal capitalism spotlights the ways in which capitalist accumulation strategies produce and reproduce particular racial identities, which are then made material and commodified, monetized, and marketed.[23] And while dominant rhetorics surrounding race make it easier to see *homo affectus* as raced, racial neoliberal capitalism highlights the way *homo economicus*—the purely rational and self-interested entrepreneurial ideal—also has a race, even though dominant culture rarely makes that race explicit. For examples, here we need only think of the unspoken racism in neoliberalism's paradigmatic accumulation-by-dispossession strategy as evidenced in any number of ways, including spectacularly in the subprime mortgage crisis at the heart of the 2008 global financial collapse, during which foreclosure rates and racial status were unambiguously connected. That is to say, Black and Latinx homeowners suffered excessive rates of foreclosure in part because they were forced into nearly usurious subprime home loans in a process some have called reverse redlining.[24] By 2020, the ratio of Black-to-white home ownership equaled that of 1890.[25] For sociologist Randolph Hohle, the recoding of the term "public" as Black and "private" as white was crucial in enabling the rise of neoliberalism as it vilified taxation and justified minimizing public services and business regulation.[26] As he concludes, "There was no rational or economic reason for whites to embrace neoliberalism. There was only race."[27]

So too seeing neoliberalism through the framework of racial capitalism helps to explain the operations of what theorists of race around the early twenty-first century such as Eduardo Bonilla-Silva, Patricia Hill Collins, and David Theo Goldberg convincingly showed was a color-blind racism where the dominant ideology moves from explicitly articulating racial separatism to brazenly pretending that race does not exist at all.[28] This "racism without racists" framework sees the existence of inequality as massive individual failures and justifies racist reactions by using dog-whistle terms (think "thug" as a term for Black men expressing anger, for instance).[29] But each passing year of the Obama era left the analysis of the rhetoric of neoliberal color blindness that much more incomplete as conditions on the ground changed. The particular form of racialized politics that emerged is not necessarily a negation of previous understandings but is in many cases a layering of more explicit Eurocentric terminology onto the rhetoric of color blindness—think of the rise of the term "Western chauvinist" instead of "white supremacist." In the years after the 2020 global Black Lives Matter protests, Republican legislatures found a successful version of these racialized politics by passing "anti-woke acts" that restrict public schools and institutions from providing training to deal with inequality or from teaching histories and ideas that might make (white/straight/male) learners feel guilty or upset, including discussions of LGBTQ+ issues, sexual discrimination, and significant parts of Black history.[30]

Under the guise of helping all children to feel positive about their backgrounds—or, as one governor put it, to "protect our students from divisive ideologies like critical race theory that pits [sic] kids against each other"—such laws operate in the tradition of neoliberal policies that seem to deploy liberal and multicultural terms of inclusion as the core of their valuation strategies.[31] But neoliberalism has always hinged on the old patriarchal white supremacist framework, and when Trump was elected, it became clear that many Americans deeply desired an outspoken figurehead instead of a quieter white identity politics. The Trump backlash showed that the forces of white supremacy never were satiated by that racism-without-racists strategy: they had grown accustomed to seeing their race as the most valuable part of their holdings. But whether we think of whiteness as a wage or whiteness as property, to use two of the most powerful theorizations, the Trump conjuncture shows that neoliberalism is now wrapped up in a more explicit conception of racial capitalism.[32]

Certainly, Donald Trump as president embodied the breadth of American neoliberal culture as a dominant racial rationality, racial ideology, and racial governmentality. From this perspective, it is easier to see how he also became a powerful container of explosive affects, seen indelibly in the January 6, 2021, insurrection at the U.S. Capitol. Just what had been at stake in his mad, middle-of-the-night tweets that illustrated his paranoia, justified his venality, endorsed his cruelty, and milked popular resentment? From the perspective of the ideas we are considering here, Trump embodied the more general neoliberal affect built on a litany of racial and sexual resentments that themselves revolve around fear, horror, insecurity, anger, loneliness, and an expressed need to be desired.[33]

And yet Trump did not go far enough to satisfy the white power extremist movements to whom he gave a new life. For instance, John Earnest, who attacked a synagogue in Poway, California, rhetorically asks in his 2019 manifesto whether he is a Trump supporter or not, to which he replies, "That Zionist, Jew-loving, anti-White, traitorous cocksucker? Don't make me laugh." As to whether Earnest himself is a conservative, he clarified, "I am not a useless, spineless coward so no—I am not a conservative." Proving his commitment to a radical racial politics, he followed the advice of the novel *The Turner Diaries* (discussed in chapter 4) and its ominous enticement to fight "the System" in a murder orgy called The Day of the Rope. In his manifesto, Earnest addresses his fellow "anons," writing,

> Some of you have been waiting for The Day of the Rope for years. Well, The Day of the Rope is here right now—that is if you have the gnads to keep the ball rolling. Every anon reading this must attack a target while doing his best to avoid getting caught. Every anon must play his part in this revolution and no man can be pulling his punches. This momentum we currently have may very well be the last chance that the European man has to spark a revolution.

How can we understand such horror? Susan Searls Giroux articulates a stark vision of neoliberal culture's daily diet of profound violence upon the human body and mind as reproducing a Sadean kind of savagery and sovereignty that helps us understand the brutal spectacles we are considering here: "The essential plot ingredients of Sade's malevolent, imaginary universe are uncannily recapitulated in the hard realities of a racially driven neoliberalized society . . .; the exercise of force and domination that quickly betrays itself as masochistic self-destruction."[34] Neoliberalism, like Sadism, results in nihilism when followed to its inevitable conclusion. On the way to that conclusion, the politics that emerge facilitate the aggrieved whiteness evidenced in the dominant strands of contemporary conservatism within American neoliberal culture as much as in today's white power extremism.[35] That is, American capitalism historically promised a society that unabashedly works in the interests of white men and in the service of the white heteropatriarchal family headed by the father/husband.

The popularization of the far right and the radicalization of the center right show that many Americans saw and continue to see steps toward racial and gender equality as the loss of their status in a zero-sum game. For them, being stripped of the social acceptability of acting out on racial and gender hierarchies in polite society was a deprivation—one that apparently never affected Trump, which was partly why he was so popular. To put it another way, it was as if it was not enough to own the base and the superstructure as it were; the racial and gendered grounds of that ownership had to be explicit. This nostalgic reiteration of clear racial and gender hierarchies is manifestly present in the white power novels we discuss later and in what political theorist Wendy Brown identifies as neoliberal racism's "unrestrained will to power." Brown maintains that this "desublimated force, tinged by the pain of a wound (dethroned white masculinity) courses through traditional values politics today."[36]

According to the Southern Poverty Law Center, 6 percent of America's approximately 198 million non-Latinx white people have beliefs consistent with at least aspects of the white power worldview.[37] One poll taken in August 2017 after the Charlottesville Unite the Right rally, when white power activists violently attacked opponents of a Confederate monument, suggested almost 10 percent of the U.S. population think it is "strongly or somewhat acceptable to hold neo-Nazi or white supremacist views."[38] The openness of the racist rhetoric in Charlottesville announced an outspoken fraternity between neoliberal figures like Trump and white power figures like alt-right activist Richard Spencer desperate for the legitimacy the former president's indirect shout-outs gave them, such as when he told the hate group–cum–fight club Proud Boys to "stand back and stand by" when asked to denounce white supremacist groups during a presidential debate.

This mainstreaming of white power is evidenced not only in the structures of inequality that we discuss throughout the book but even in the mundane elements of white power life. Think here of something as simple as the white power "uniform" of khaki pants and white polo shirts worn by fascists in Charlottesville.[39] Think of the common backyard tiki torches they wielded as if they were going to a suburban backyard luau. Or think even of the Hawaiian shirts of the boogaloo bois that developed as an inside joke come to life (since the members refer to the second civil war that they see as imminent as "the Big Luau," which itself derived from a long series of jokes and memes evolving from the cheesy 1980s movie *Breakin' 2: Electric Boogaloo*). Now these items stand in for the white ethnonationalist claim of the normality of whiteness itself; they are the artifacts of a white supremacy that has historically been the *racially legislated* norm in suburbia.[40] In this regard it is worth noting that the demographic norm of the Capitol Hill rioter was a middle-aged white man with a job, often white-collar, with no ties to existing far-right militias or gangs but who willingly joined in common cause with these groups to form "a new kind of violent mass movement" motivated by fear of "white replacement."[41]

The theme of racial anxiety and white population loss, often referred to as "white genocide," "white replacement," or, most histrionically, *"le grand remplacement"* by French writer Renaud Camus, has now become a prominent notion for white power advocates and is promulgated by far white politicians and media personalities.[42] So too it is said to be a motivator for this new coalition of white power as it meets the far white, mobilized by what they perceive as a world moving away from its greatness that needs a radical restructuring to be made great—and white—again. Their story is part of this larger story of white power ideology that is the most prevalent motivator of terrorist violence in the United States today. Its centrality for white supremacists came into stark relief for the many Americans who had not been paying attention to this discourse after an anti-Black mass shooting at a Tops Friendly Markets grocery store in a predominantly Black part of Buffalo, New York, on May 14, 2022. Just before the assault, the gunman, Payton S. Gendron, posted a white supremacist, anti-Semitic manifesto as part of his stated goal to "spread awareness to my fellow Whites about the real problems the West is facing, and to encourage further attacks that will eventually start the war that will save the Western world, save the White race and allow for humanity to progress into more advanced civilizations."

His unabashed version of replacement has helped to draw larger attention to another more palatable version of the conspiracy that, post-2020, became an obsession of the era's highest-rated cable news program, *Tucker Carlson Tonight,* which none other than Viktor Orbán says should be broadcast "24/7."[43] In this version, race is not explicitly mentioned except when dismissing the idea that replacement theory has anything to do with racism. Instead, Carlson couches his version of "great replacement" (shamelessly) in the language of voting rights. Thus, "obedient voters from the Third World" are being imported by Democrats to "disenfranchise" "legacy Americans," whom he address directly: "[Your power] to control your own life disappeared with the arrival of new people who diluted your vote.... As your state swelled with foreign voters your views became irrelevant."[44]

Here, Carlson promotes what we might call "far white democracy," using less the language of race than of politics and place. But whether in this euphemistic version or in the very blunt one, geography becomes a proxy for the larger forces of racial capitalism itself. Thus, it was the location of the Buffalo attack that illustrates the ironies of the replacement conspiracy. Aimed to stop the ostensible persecution of white people, the shooting took place in a neighborhood that is actually a product of a long-established anti-Black ghettoization. The area was predominantly Black because decades of segregation through redlining and racially motivated disinvestment had guaranteed it would be. And, like many predominantly Black working-class neighborhoods, this area was a food desert with the exception of this one store. The killer had done research and traveled some two hundred miles from his predominantly white hometown in Conklin, New York, to execute an attack that would strike the soul of the Black community and get the attention of white people everywhere.[45] And that is the point: the great replacement theory is a conspiracy used to encourage white people to action—to protest, to vote, to kill—in an attempt to maintain and expand the practices of inequality—colonialism, exploitation, preferred status. Ultimately, its function is that of all racisms, which, as historian Achille Mbembe puts it, is "to regulate the distribution of death."[46]

WHITE POWER AND FAR WHITE ACTS OF TERROR AND ACCELERATIONISM

Fueled by the global reach of social media and necessitated by the restrictions of national law and corporate policies, the Buffalo massacre is itself a product of white power ideology, which is profoundly transnational as it operates in the murky spheres of the internet and social media, beneath and outside many local controls.[47] For adherents like the Buffalo shooter, the idea of "accelerationism," the belief that social chaos should be encouraged in order to bring about political change, is offered as a part of the solution.[48] In white power contexts, accelerationism includes instigating racial holy war, or RaHoWa, by sowing chaos without overtly taking a political or ideological stand in order to create a social instability that will destroy societies around the world. As the Australian white power terrorist Brenton Tarrant, who perpetrated the deadliest mass shooting in New Zealand, writes in his manifesto,

> It is far better to encourage radical, violent change regardless of its origins. As only in times of radical change and social discomfort can great and terrific

change occur. These tumultuous times can be brought about through action. For example, actions such as voting for political candidates that radically change or challenge entrenched systems, radicalizing public discourse by both supporting, attacking, vilifying, radicalizing and exaggerating all societal conflicts and attacking or even assassinating weak or less radical leaders/influencers on either side of social conflicts. A vote for a radical candidate that opposes your values and incites agitation or anxiety in your own people works far more in your favour than a vote for a milquetoast political candidate that has no ability or wish to enact radical change. Canvas public areas in support of radical positions, even if they are not your own. Incite conflict. Place posters near public parks calling for sharia law, then in the next week place posters over such posters calling for the expulsion of all immigrants, repeat in every area of public life until the crisis arises. Destabilize, then take control. If we want to radically and fundamentally change society, then we need to radicalize society as much as possible.

Tarrant, styling himself a race warrior, sees the United States as a prime location for accelerating RaHoWa. Not only are there clear and deeply rooted racial divisions there, but the fanaticism attached to the Second Amendment is an easy tool to rile white people to strike back against the government: "Civil war in the so called 'Melting pot' that is the United States should be a major aim in overthrowing the global power structure and the West's egalitarian, individualist, globalist dominant culture."

The work of starting this civil war has already exacted a high price. Below we call attention to the horrific human toll it has taken by listing some of the specific acts of terror committed in a string of high-profile as well as less-visible mass shootings by proponents or sympathizers of various forms of white power ideology in the last ten years.[49] Most of the acts we discuss here were committed in the United States, but some were carried out in other predominantly white countries. These acts have not been isolated efforts, as accompanying manifestos often refer to past shootings as inspirations; even if the perpetrators are working alone and not as part of any particular group or militia, they are often connected within the vast web of white racist radicals who have been extraordinarily active on the internet and social media since their early days. While we include this material to establish the scope and extent of white terror, readers are encouraged to skip the final section of this chapter if they do not want to read about the violence exacted by white power terrorists.

. . .

Although the 1995 Oklahoma City bombing has been the deadliest white power terrorist act, and its inspiration has been directly tied to *The Turner Diaries,* acts of white power terrorism actually diminished until the election of Barack Obama before becoming increasingly regular events in the 2010s. We may well start our discussion with the events of July 22, 2011, with the first of several high-profile acts of white terror in recent years. On that day Anders Behring Breivik set off a car bomb outside the offices of the Norwegian prime minister in Oslo, killing eight people. Later that afternoon he went to the island of Utøya and killed sixty-nine more at a summer camp for Norwegian Labour Party youths. The Breivik attack became an iconic instance of mass violence related to white power ideology.

Almost four years later, on June 17, 2015, Dylann Roof shot and killed nine Black worshippers at the Emanuel African Methodist Episcopal Church in Charleston, South Carolina. In his worldview, the media and American popular consciousness showed sympathy for the wrong party in the infamous murder of Trayvon Martin by self-styled vigilante George Zimmerman in 2012 by ignoring what Roof called "black on white crime." Roof came to believe that someone—indeed, he, himself—needed to take "drastic action" to fight for the preservation of the white Aryan race.[50]

In this regard he was not alone; from 2015 to 2021 right-wing extremists were involved in some 267 terrorist plots and 91 fatalities,[51] but most of these were not the attention-grabbing horror of Roof's attack or the infamous mass shooting at Marjory Stoneman Douglas High School in Parkland, Florida, on February 14, 2018, when student Nikolas Cruz killed seventeen people and injured seventeen more. Cruz had decorated his ammunition with Nazi symbols. Moreover, "His mother told investigators that she made her son remove [hate] symbols, including a Nazi symbol and the words 'I hate N------' that were drawn on his book bag,"[52] and he reportedly used the term "white power."[53]

On October 22 of the same year, the "MAGA bomber" (part-Filipino Cesar Sayoc), a Trump loyalist, sent what turned out to be faulty mail bombs to a number of Trump's perceived enemies (including George Soros, Hillary Clinton, Barack Obama, and the current president and vice president, Joe Biden and Kamala Harris); *Washingtonian* magazine claims Trump magnified Sayoc's racist beliefs against Mexicans and African Americans.[54] A few days later, on October 27, Robert Bowers shot and killed eleven Jewish congregants and wounded six more at the Tree of Life Synagogue in Pittsburgh, Pennsylvania, which was "the deadliest attack on Jews on American soil."[55]

Although he didn't leave a manifesto, Bowers reportedly circulated information about the racist "religion" Christian Identity, and his social media posts included the "1488" white power symbology referencing the "14 Words" slogan (which we discuss in chapter 2) and "Heil Hitler" ("8" representing the eighth letter in the alphabet). He criticized Trump as a globalist taking orders from Jewish people and invoked the white power refrain that immigrants are invading the United States and will eventually dominate and replace white people.[56]

In this fear he was like the Australian Brenton Tarrant, who wrote a manifesto entitled "The Great Replacement," which he released on March 15, 2019, the day he shot and killed fifty-one people and injured forty at two different mosques in Christchurch, New Zealand. In his white genocide screed, he tied his actions directly to Breivik.[57] Other shooters motivated by white power beliefs in the United States, in turn, referenced Tarrant. One example is John Earnest, who shot and killed one woman and injured three others at a synagogue in Poway, California, on April 27, 2019. On August 3, 2019, Patrick Crusius shot and killed twenty-two people and injured another two dozen at a Walmart in El Paso, Texas, in the deadliest attack on Latinx people, his targets, in U.S. history. And on May 14, 2022, eighteen-year-old Payton S. Gendron livestreamed himself armed with an assault rifle as he killed ten people and injured three, almost all of whom were Black, in Buffalo, New York. His manifesto, written in the style of Brenton Tarrant, name-checks Tarrant along with other so-called ethno-soldiers Bowers, Earnest, and Roof in an attempt to become infamous, and to become a meme like them.

Apart from these well-publicized shootings, there were many others that are lesser known but have some connection to racism, misogyny, anti-Semitism, and/or Nazism, and thus, we would argue, are aligned at least in some way with white power ideas. Though some of these other killings seem to have been more personally motivated, all still reference some aspect of the white racism that is central to the well-publicized shootings and deserve to be noted to show the widespread reach of white power ideology, even if only in fragments of racist thinking. On August 5, 2012, Wade Michael Page—"a noted white supremacist"—shot and killed six people at the Sikh Temple of Wisconsin in Oak Creek, likely believing it was a Muslim mosque (a conflation of perhaps unsurprising idiocy that has occurred more than once in the United States, including in the killing of Balbir Singh Sodhi four days after 9/11 in Mesa, Arizona, by Frank Silva Roque).[58] Page was part of several white power music groups and is thought to have been radicalized at Fort Bragg in

North Carolina, tied to instances of white supremacy and neo-Nazi activity.[59] On April 14, 2014, Frazier Glenn Cross shot and killed three people at Jewish facilities close to Kansas City, Kansas. According to the *New York Times,* "The gunman founded the Carolina Knights, a chapter of the Ku Klux Klan, and used anti-Semitic language in earlier political campaigns."[60] Page and Cross's mass shootings reflect the racialization of religion—the latter as part of a long-standing anti-Semitism around the world and the former a more contemporary version of anti-Islamic sentiment that has clearly taken root in Europe but also occurs in the United States.

Disgruntled twenty-six-year-old Chris Harper-Mercer shot and killed nine people and injured eight others at Umpqua Community College near Roseburg, Oregon, on October 1, 2015. He left a manifesto on a USB drive that he gave to a student.[61] Harper-Mercer identifies himself as 40 percent Black (which "didn't come from a man"), and his six-page manifesto rails against Black men, who are described as "thugs" whose "brain power has been submerged into their penis." He further claims that "everyone lives in fear of the black man." He also disparages Latinx people, but they "can be put into remedial education and be made smart." Asians, like whites, are sanctified: "The Asian and Indian [presumably referring to South Asian] women are traditional and good. So are the men. I have always respected them. They will rule America in the inner city and the world." Rather than connecting his deed and ideas to white power, however, he instead connects himself to occult Satanism; nevertheless, his motivations exhibit the broader racism espoused in white power ideology. On July 23, 2015, John Russell Houser shot and killed two people at a movie theater in Lafayette, Louisiana. The *New York Times* notes he "praised anti-gay and anti-Semitic figures on messaging boards and social media."[62]

Veteran Dionisio Garza wounded nine people in a Houston-area strip mall on September 26, 2016, while wearing Nazi military insignia, more of which the police also found at his house.[63] Next, the strange case of Devon Arthurs and his roommate Brandon Russell, a National Guardsman; they along with their other two roommates were supposedly part of the neo-Nazi group Atomwaffen. Arthurs killed two of his roommates on May 19, 2017, after converting to Islam. This case is not classified as domestic terrorism because the conflict was mostly internal to the group; however, the case points to the volatile nature and irrationality of those involved in contemporary racist ideas that feed into white power.

On November 1, 2017, Scott Ostrem shot and killed three Latinx people at a Walmart in a suburb of Denver, Colorado, anticipating Crusius's 2019 attack. "Neighbors described the suspect as 'verbally abusive' toward Hispanics."[64] The following year, at a high school outside Houston in Santa Fe, Texas, a student named Dimitrios Pagourtzis shot and killed two teachers and eight students and injured thirteen others on May 18, 2018; his internet postings revealed Nazi insignia on his coat.[65] On November 2, 2018, Scott Beierle, a man with a history of misogyny, shot and killed two women and injured five others at a yoga studio in Tallahassee, Florida. Previous to his attack he had posted videos on YouTube railing against illegal immigration, interracial couples, and racial diversity.[66] Three days later, Gregory Bush shot two Black people at a Kroger supermarket in Jeffersontown, Kentucky, after trying to enter a Black church; he is said to have "a history of mental illness, made racist threats and repeatedly called his ex-wife the N-word."[67]

And finally, in 2020, the unrelenting pressures of COVID-19 shutdowns combined with the tensions of a brutal presidential election that played out on television as melodrama and the heinous police killings of unarmed Black people created the perfect conditions for white power violence. This included plots against government leaders and violence perpetrated by individual vigilantes and meme-inspired groups organized through social media such as the self-styled boogaloo bois, who celebrated the social unrest in order to accelerate the new civil war they are trying to encourage, and far white forces like the Groypers, who use "America first" rhetoric to promote the United States as a pro–white Christian nation.[68] Indeed, as the Black Lives Matter protests in the wake of the 2020 murders of George Floyd, Breonna Taylor, and others played out, these "ultra-libertarians and white supremacists"[69] rose to prominence in the media ecosystem and have been linked to the January 6, 2021, insurrection at the U.S. Capitol, to which we now turn.[70]

We see the insurrection as singularly important because of the threat it posed to the U.S. Constitution as the foundation of American democracy and the guarantee of a peaceful transfer of power. On that day a horde of insurrectionist Trump supporters breached the U.S. Capitol building: QAnon conspirators wearing Viking horns and animal pelts appeared alongside MAGA hat–wearing looters who vandalized the Capitol with human feces and painted violent messages like "murder the media" on doors. They waved flags for the QAnon-favored presidential ticket of Trump and John F. Kennedy Jr. (who died in 1999 but who they believe is alive and in hiding). Others took down the U.S. flag posted outside the building to hoist a Trump banner while still others carried the Confederate battle flag into the building. Rioters displayed white power signs and paraphernalia, including shirts with slogans such as "Camp Auschwitz" and "Civil War: January 6, 2021."[71] Violence and the threat of violence were omnipresent during the event. Particularly notable were the erection of a gallows intended for then–vice president Mike Pence, who wouldn't side with Trump by impeding the certification of votes, and the presence of looters—including organized squads of Proud Boys and Oath Keepers, as well as individual insurrectionists—wielding weapons such as knives, sharpened poles, and toxic chemical sprays. Indicating that they saw this event as part of a long-anticipated racial civil war, some rioters chanted the white power slogan from *The Turner Diaries*—"Day of the Rope! Day of the Rope!"—and an online post declared, "It's time for the DAY OF THE ROPE! WHITE REVOLUTION IS THE ONLY SOLUTION!"[72] In the end, five people died as a result of the coup attempt (and four police officers have taken their own lives, reportedly because of trauma related to that day), including one protester who was trampled to death, ironically while holding the "Don't tread on me" Gadsden flag.[73]

What we hope this roll call of brutality makes clear is that racial violence is a consistent part of American life, and the stakes require that we all better understand how it expresses itself and develops today. We point to white power–related expressions of this violence that we think scholars and activists need to become more aware of, and we maintain that despite seeming contradictions between white power and neoliberal culture, the two social formations are inextricably intertwined and magnify each other's power, as we discuss in the following chapters.

TWO

Immiseration Culture, or How the Family Became a Trope and a Truncheon

AS WE SHOWED IN CHAPTER 1, emboldened white power has been on violent display, especially in recent years, and in the United States the data unequivocally show that political violence is almost exclusively the property of the far right.[1] In the case of mass shooters who left white power manifestos or social media posts, they showed considerable anxiety about what they perceive as a central issue: that white people are being overwhelmed by racialized ethnic "others" due to immigration and low reproduction rates. Whether considering Patrick Crusius's butchery in an El Paso Walmart, or Robert Bowers's attack on the Tree of Life synagogue in Pittsburgh, or, globally, Brenton Tarrant's mass shooting at two mosques in Christchurch, New Zealand, these shooters' words represent the anxieties and fears of white people who perceive themselves being engulfed by "others." For example, Tarrant's manifesto articulates this paranoia:

> Invited by the state and corporate entities to replace the White people who have failed to reproduce, failed to create the cheap labour, new consumers and tax base that the corporations and states need to thrive. This crisis of mass immigration and subreplacement fertility is an assault on the European people that, if not combated, will ultimately result in the complete racial and cultural replacement of the European people.[2]

But for the white power adherent too busy to read Tarrant's seventy-four pages, white power fighter/writer David Lane summarized this white obsession in just fourteen words ubiquitous in white power ideology: "We must secure the existence of our people and a future for white children."

Clearly, no matter how one puts it, the specious idea of white replacement is an apocalyptic clarion call to white identity and a step toward full-fledged indoctrination into white power ideology. The iconic "14 Words" and allied ideologies position race, reproduction, and family at the center of white power. Violence is justified to promote the "future of white children," a context that hinges on white reproduction and pushes women into the role of mainspring of racial identity and keeper of the racial hearth. White power adherents put women's reproductive capability in aggressively possessive terms. One example is Andrew Anglin, the founder of the notorious neo-Nazi website The Daily Stormer: "It's OUR WOMB—that's right, it doesn't belong to her [the white woman], it belongs to the males in her society."[3] The foundation and goal of white power activism has been to use the family as the means to build a white utopian future, usually in terms of white ethnonationalism.[4] And this "focus on the family" (to borrow the term from Christian fundamentalists) actually ties white power ideology together with neoliberalism. As we shall see, it is precisely the immiseration culture produced by neoliberalism that destroys the social safety net and promotes economic policies that redirect wealth to the top, normalizing a destitute underclass and a ballooning wealth gap, while it simultaneously pushes the traditional patriarchal family to the forefront as the sole provisioner of subsistence and explicitly undermines the government's role in caring for the family. And, where neoliberals implicitly presume this family to be white, white power ideologues specifically racialize this family structure as white.

NEOLIBERAL (WHITE-GUY) ANXIETY ABOUT THE FAMILY

The ideologies grounding neoliberalism as an intellectual project were built on a foundation of so-called traditional morality that relies inescapably on the patriarchal family's social reproduction function. Here it is important to remember there are different strains of American neoliberalism. In the United States, in very rough terms, there has tended to be a free market–oriented libertarian wing and a neoconservative moralistically minded wing. The market fundamentalists, associated famously with the University of Chicago, where they all spent at least some part of their lives, include those we often think of when we consider neoliberal theory like the anti-Keynesian free-market branches associated with the economists Friedrich Hayek, Milton Friedman, Gary Becker, and James Buchanan. The moral direction has been more obvious in connection to the neoconservative branch of neoliberalism associated with figures like Irving Kristol, Daniel Patrick Moynihan, and Daniel Bell.[5] But these two branches of neoliberalism unite in an instrumental view of the family.[6] That is, neoliberal thinkers represent the family as the best institution to care for its own members. And they use this family structure to justify the erosion of the social service state, which they will in turn replace with barely there government and an unencumbered market.

So in Gary Becker's account, for instance, the family serves as a kind of natural insurance function that is disturbed when the welfare state socializes insurance; he and other neoliberals maintain that the state gets in the way of the family.[7] But, as we will see, these neoliberal figures make a further leap and insist that if the family is not required to care for its members, the proper family values will not develop. Here, they situate the family in the place of broad public social safety nets that free citizens from impoverishment, homelessness, and hunger. Without being compelled to care for children, the elderly, the sick, and the disadvantaged, the institution of the family would ostensibly disintegrate since it would no longer be needed to sustain its members.[8] For them, family is the keystone of "traditional" social welfare and supports their radical view of the capitalist private sphere. As Wendy Brown helpfully summarizes it, the priorities of neoliberal thinkers revolve around "markets and morals."[9]

Now, it is not our intention to suggest that all neoliberalism is consciously tied to white power, but in fact the Venn diagram of many elements of neoliberal ideology and white power ideology overlap in relation to the paternalistic obsession with family in a way that is not coincidental but fundamental, present at a foundational level as racial patriarchal capitalism. Certainly, this obsession with family may have occurred in pre-neoliberal formations of capitalism just as there certainly were analogous characteristics in the expression of white supremacist ideology during both Reconstruction and now. In both eras, this overlap reflects the distrust of state agendas when applied across racial grounds and outside the patriarchal family unit. But we maintain that what we are seeing is novel in its historical moment: a backlash against the rise of multiculturalism and nonwhites in positions of power (the ultimate being Obama in the White House) in an age when white supremacist rhetoric is not considered socially acceptable, even if white supremacy is built into the institutional framework of the United States.

There certainly were analogous characteristics in the expression of white supremacist ideology in the wake of the 1960s social justice movements. The distrust arises in a starkly dramatic way that makes long-term social and political impacts in the lives of almost every oppressed and minoritized group in the United States, and in the next chapter we will see these impacts play out by looking at the Southern Strategy as a neoliberal maneuver. In this chapter, we will examine the opposition to the 1960s-era social justice struggles in relation to the family and how that opposition ties into the radical capitalist restructuring of work. Here it is worth noting that many of the early American neoliberals had been involved in some version of leftist/liberal politics previous to its realignments in the 1960s. From figures like Daniel Patrick Moynihan and Ronald Reagan to the so-called godfather of neoconservatism, Irving Kristol, their opposition to the Keynesian service state arrangements was not rooted in libertarian distrust of government associated with neoliberalism.[10] These neoliberals did not always oppose "big government" as such. Their opposition was rooted in something much closer to home: the creation of a new cultural moment built on reinstating a family-based, masculinist law-and-morality tradition. Thus, if Lane's "14 Words" articulate a worldview that puts women and child-rearing at the center of a racial fight for survival, Kristol also saw countercultural liberation to be a battleground in his culture war: "liberation from husbands, liberation from children, liberation from family. Indeed, the real object of these various sexual heterodoxies is to disestablish the family as the central institution of human society, the citadel of orthodoxy."[11] And in "My Cold War," an essay written after the collapse of the Soviet Union, Kristol announces that since the 1960s his true existential battle has been with "left-wing political romanticism" because he long ago realized that people were so obviously not equal that socialism was not worth fighting against. He concludes, "There is no 'after the Cold War' for me. So far from having ended, my cold war has increased in intensity, as sector after sector of American life has been ruthlessly corrupted by the liberal ethos . . . that aims simultaneously at political and social collectivism on the one hand, and moral anarchy on the other."[12]

For sociologist and cultural theorist Melinda Cooper, the neoliberal moment emerges out of the conservatives' fears for the patriarchal family resulting from the great social upheavals of the 1960s. As a result, "It would not be an exaggeration to say that the enormous political activism of American neoliberals in the 1970s was inspired by the fact of changing family structures."[13] The Fordist wage that had served as the hegemonic post–World War II American middle-class ideal was set up to enable the family to be supported on the income of the male breadwinner. From this perspective the wage "functioned as a mechanism for the normalization of gender and sexual relationships."[14] And powerful institutions such as mortgage lenders and unions, to name just two, made sure the Fordist family was, generally speaking, a white one.[15] But through the 1970s and '80s this Fordist family dominant was becoming a thing of the past. In the wake of the well-known wage declines of the neoliberal era combined with the gains of civil rights and the rising gender and sexual liberation movements, families would look very different from those pictured previously in hegemonic culture.[16]

This comparison is not suggesting that a white power extremist like Lane and a Jewish New York intellectual like Kristol did or would have associated with each other. However, the centrality of the family within both neoliberal culture and white power align in their shared belief in a patriarchal family ideal associated with whiteness and rooted in an explicit rejection of the 1960s counterculture and the ideals of racial and sexual equality.[17] In the words of notorious white supremacist David Duke, "Wherever the globalist media reaches on this planet, there is an ongoing sexual revolution. It should be called sexual dehumanization. In traditional Western culture, sex is idealized and embedded with the idea of family and children and the deep and sacred respect for the love between a man and a woman, and marriage as a beautiful, even holy, institution."[18] Those 1960s- and 1970s-era social movements led to the direct growth of access to the social welfare state for populations long denied the benefits of American citizenship. From Black Power to the rise of gay rights, from women's liberation to the struggle to gain public support for single and unmarried parents, these social movements fought for expanded citizenship rights for groups explicitly left out and left back. The movements grew up alongside, in response to, and fully connected with the immense capital growth of those years. And with the end of that cultural moment in the wake of economic crisis, social retrenchment, and massive exhaustion, the forces of neoliberalism emerged ready to pass through the breach with their fully formed ideas about the proper role of everything from the social state to democracy to the governance of the family.

Indeed, the 1960s-era changes are also deeply meaningful to white power. For example, the manifesto by the Norwegian white power terrorist Anders Breivik claimed the need to restore traditional patriarchal family structures, including actions against out-of-wedlock childbearing and guaranteed paternal child custody in divorce settlements.[19] In Breivik's words, "Ladies should be wives and homemakers, not cops or soldiers, and men should still hold doors open for ladies." While women should stay home and concentrate on making babies to ensure the white race doesn't disappear, "warrior" men should fight against the creation of Eurabia and other nonwhite bogeymen while simultaneously remaining the heads of household. As he further explains, "I do not approve of the super-liberal, matriarchal upbringing . . . as it completely lacked discipline and has contributed to feminize me to a certain degree."

What is important to realize is what theorists of ideology have long warned about: people's ideological fantasies minimize and justify the truly frightening logical conclusions of oppressive belief structures. Fantasies of family wholeness, whether originating from the white power sphere or run-of-the-mill supporters of family values, all promote profoundly powerful ideologies establishing the supremacy of whiteness and the naturalness of the patriarchal family.[20] These family fantasies isomorphically follow the desire for a white dominant culture that American law and tradition have historically offered as compensation for vast economic inequalities.[21] For example, in her studies of the anti-immigrant Minuteman militia, ethnic studies scholar Paula Ioanide shows how these ideological fantasies join the desire for white monoracial culture and result in an unattainable ideal that is both reassuring and threatening: "The Minuteman constructs his sense of self and purpose through this ideological fantasy and through the constant desire it reproduces because the ideal is always out of reach; [but] acknowledging that the fantasy is unattainable . . . would result in the death of the desire that defines his self-identity."[22] This contradictory state results in an inherently unstable society vulnerable to being overtaken by fringe elements who would push the center very far to the right as they react to and against the dreary realities of everyday life in neoliberal culture—in other words, one version of the Trump supporter.

Even if violent white power extremists represent a political fringe, we argue that their current visibility is the result of neoliberalism's ideological priorities set forth in its earliest history. And the emotional energies as well as fundamental moral positions they tap into are interrelated with those appealing to white conservative Americans from mainstream Republicans to the far right. From the early uses of the Southern Strategy in the 1960s through to Donald Trump and those he inspires in the 2020s, these energies are centered around the white patriarchal heteronormative family restored to what is ostensibly its rightful place as the center of social and political life.

These elements enforce "family values"–based morality; family members are to be positioned as the appropriate safety net instead of the service state. So, returning to our example of Trump's presidency, his reliance on his dangerously dim children to serve in his White House and his efforts to identify them as the future of the Republican Party can be seen not as a symptom of his authoritarian disrespect for expertise and bureaucracies but as a sign of his family values. So too his daughter and son-in-law's willingness to forgo a taxpayer-funded salary could be seen as their filial duty (rather than as a convenient way to avoid taxpayer scrutiny of their corrupt monetizing of their positions).[23]

This traditional patriarchal arrangement is predicated on a division between women's and men's labor, with women's traditional labor at home remaining unpaid and outside the realm of remuneration (ostensibly pay would only demean the value of the labor that women perform).[24] However, an exception is made in the case of paid work done by minoritized populations, who have always been dramatically underpaid and were explicitly left out of the New Deal Fordist compromise and remain left out of most discussions of equal pay today. Moreover, as feminist scholar Laura Briggs puts it in her aptly titled book, *How All Politics Became Reproductive Politics* (2017), "our conversations about reproductive politics are deeply about race, just as they are about sexuality," and are shaped by the forces of neoliberalism.[25] As we will see, these racialized reproductive politics are very much in play when it comes to the neoliberal–white power nexus of the family.

Fairly compensating people for the countless hours of unpaid and underpaid care work that enables capitalist economies to function would radically transform the U.S. economy; according to labor researchers, unpaid care work alone has a monetary value of 10 to 39 percent of GDP, depending on the prevailing wages for domestic work![26] Today, in our era of neoliberal feminism, the movement that was once a liberation struggle for women (with all due caveats for the many categories of women left out of the feminist imaginary) became structured as a deeply individualized effort where each woman is told that if she is underpaid it is her own fault for not "leaning in" to achieve her individual success at work while keeping her babies in tow and somehow managing her "second shift" at home.[27] In the 1970s, "wages for housework" arose as a feminist movement goal that would have radically altered the world's economies.[28] Instead, the rise of neoliberalism transformed those economies and women's and men's lives in a very different way.

POST-FORDISM AND OTHER EXPLOITATIVE RELATIONSHIPS

If labor force participation is generally seen as a precondition for individual autonomy in the positive sense, neoliberal jobs provide a different kind of autonomy that can be frightening since these jobs are known for being deeply contingent and insecure since they are untethered to employers with some responsibility for their workers' well-being.[29] Replacing the Fordist economy's prototypical job—boring but predictable assembly-line work with union wages and job security—neoliberal labor in its prototypical form requires hustling and working around the clock for oneself in various jobs in the gig economy.

Gig labor is that contingent or alternative employment for which workers do not have "an implicit or explicit contract for long-term employment." Counting gig workers is notoriously difficult because of the informality and temporariness of the arrangements, but studies show that the percentage of American workers in the gig economy is around 36 percent, and likely higher, as of 2018.[30] And for many workers, whether it is a side hustle or a full-time job, gig work requires a level of endeavor and self-promotion that so easily becomes a grind, much like the work of the homemaker historically was, demanding a ceaseless day of often undervalued work expected to be completed with cheer and enthusiasm.

The "structural violence of precarity, unemployment, and the fear of being dismissed" means that, among other things, neoliberal labor involves "a high degree of (unpaid) 'relational work.'"[31] In this environment, workers are often forced to become professional nice people who have to be accommodating and conversational, traits not associated with stereotypical masculinity.[32] As a result, managing feelings shows itself to be another key skill that "becomes incorporated into the male habitus and thereby generates a new image of affective masculinity" and also a central worry for conservative patriarchs (and would-be patriarchs) within the neoliberal family.[33] The Fordist archetypes of the paternalistic breadwinning man and the joyfully maternal caregiving woman remain at the center of the family structure ideologically, but they have been eroded structurally by neoliberal capitalism, which undermined the power of unions, automated jobs, and moved production overseas.[34] The American neoliberal culture of angst around the patriarchally rooted family arises as a result of neoliberal capitalism's own erosion of the Fordist New Deal wage regime, thus creating immiseration culture. Fordism as a social compact was built around a compromise that had affirmed a white patriarchal social structure and enabled significant numbers of families to survive comfortably on one generally male, generally white earner's paycheck—as long as the family care work remained unpaid and women who were in the workforce were vastly underpaid. Instead of addressing these inequalities by paying fairly for care work and raising the salaries of women and people of color, neoliberal capitalism addressed those inequities by erod-ing pay for men too, ushering in an era of wage stagnation and highly contin-gent employment for many segments of the U.S. workforce.[35]

In a feedback loop, neoliberalism's attack on the welfare state arose as a means to "protect" the family from supposed overreach by the state and social justice forces. But in real bread-and-butter terms, that family was actually imperiled by the very capitalist policies that to some extent had been reined in by the New Deal Keynesian state. After all, the federal government was able to initiate and protect a minimum wage regime, the rights of organized labor, food stamp programs, and the rest of the welfare state apparatuses. The goal was not altruistic. It arose largely to protect the so-called traditional family and thereby win its support for capitalism in the wake of the alternatives pre-sented by actually existing socialism in the wake of the Great Depression.

Decades later, neoliberalism arose in the United States when dominant cultural and economic forces that were aligned with patriarchal white supremacy no longer feared the demise of capitalism. They were now embold-ened to abandon the New Deal Fordist compromise and refocus politics away from creating and strengthening the social welfare state and toward "protect-ing" the family from the threats ostensibly posed to the existing social order by social justice struggles against white supremacy and patriarchy. Neoliberalism's development was thus spurred on by fear of social justice movements and the economic precarity that emerged as capital abandoned the Fordist family consensus. The family had become, in Cooper's words, "the locus of crisis . . . [as] the grand macroeconomic issues of the time from inflation to budget deficits to ballooning welfare budgets reflected an omi-nous shift in the sexual and racial foundations of the Fordist family."[36]

Thus, neoliberalism became the cultural dominant when families largely moved away from the previous hegemonic standards—whether by choice or by circumstance. It rose to its dominant position by presenting its own neocon-servative narrative to address the hand-wringing resulting from the very eco-nomic changes it initiated. Taking Cooper's perspective, we see neoliberalism arising as a way to express and institutionalize the anxiety shared by a new coali-tion of American economic and cultural conservatives. With great rhetorical success, neoliberal politics prescribed a solution that claimed to save the imper-iled white patriarchal family by destroying the social safety net set up to protect that very family. Under this neoliberal approach, welfare laws were redesigned to make welfare ineffective at ending poverty or promoting personal dignity. The governing assumption was that the traditional family structure would be restored if family members were forced to turn to each other when they could no longer rely on the state to adequately help individuals in need.

Finally, in 1996 the neoliberal Clinton administration worked with congressional Republicans to craft an end to the New Deal–initiated Aid to Families with Dependent Children (AFDC) program by promising "to end welfare as we know it." The replacement, called Temporary Assistance to Needy Families (TANF), would distribute aid predicated on the assumption of a very particular paternalistic set of social norms formalized centuries earlier in England as the Elizabethan Poor Laws. In that tradition families bore legal responsibility for taking care of their relatives.[37] Poor children who could not be cared for by their parents were forced into apprenticeships, and able-bodied nonworkers were fined or imprisoned.[38] Returning to that tradition, which had been in place in the United States through the late nineteenth and into the early twentieth century, the neoliberal welfare laws were sold as part of a family values agenda where family values would be not merely encouraged but required.[39] Marriage would be explicitly endorsed in welfare law; family poverty would be blamed on "deadbeat dads"; and mothers under eighteen would be required to live with their parents in order to collect cash benefits.[40] All the laws were represented as encouraging "personal moral responsibility" and as promoting true humanitarianism.[41]

It is important to remember, however, that this emphasis on personal responsibility became a popular sentiment only when people of color finally gained access to public assistance in the 1960s. In the earlier decades of the twentieth century, assistance was available almost exclusively to white people in the form of widowed mothers' pensions as a way to keep them home with their children and free from the world of paid work. As the ranks of recipients diversified to include people of color, unwed mothers, and divorcées, we see the wider emergence of the family crisis rhetoric. Operating under the belief that the family is in crisis actually set up the punitive regulations for welfare. Just as importantly, it turbocharged the idea of family: family became a trope and a truncheon.

THE NEOLIBERAL WHITE POWER FAMILY AND GENDER IDEOLOGIES

These changes in welfare law align the state with a program that unmistakably targets families existing outside a very particular set of narrow, gendered assumptions. For white power crusaders, family life is an obligation and the silver bullet for propagating the white race, so these changes were in keeping with their ideology. Central to and emblematic of allegiance to this notion of the family is, of course, the role of women expressed, sometimes contradictorily, in white power rhetoric. Although the violent actions of white men are the most visible, white women play a key role in promoting and performing other duties in white power as well. Ultimately, however, there's no doubt that the crucial role played by white women is as a reproductive mechanism for the white race. Part of that role is to be sexually attractive to white men. "Axis Sally," once a commentator on white power ideologue Harold Covington's Radio Free Northwest podcast platform, decreed that "there is no excuse for a white woman to look like ass. Women of our race should, on average, be more attractive than women of other races. . . . If you don't love what you see in the mirror every day, you're doing something wrong and it's your own fault. So fix it."[42]

We see this possessive investment in white beauty with David Lane's lesser-known, alternate fourteen-word slogan, "Because the beauty of the White Aryan woman must not perish from the earth." This "beauty" is at least twofold. It certainly elevates a vain white self-image, but it also rejects white women's individual reproductive agency—they must reproduce Aryans—and implicitly plugs into a larger sexist discourse, popular in white power circles, that contrasts reproductive women with feminists. After all, in conservative discourse feminism is commonly portrayed as "a hideous thing."[43] But in its announcement of a reproductive goal, such statements also offer a uniquely potent if particularly frightening vision of monoracial wholeness that stokes white fears of becoming irrelevant in a zero-sum game.[44]

In her ethnographic studies of women in "organized racism,"[45] sociologist Kathleen M. Blee shows that women comprise nearly 50 percent of new members in some organizations.[46] She describes four major ways that women are represented in white racist groups: "as ethereal Nordic goddesses and racial victims, as potential 'race traitors,' as wifely supporters of male racial warriors and bearers of the next generation of Aryans, or as racist activists in their own right."[47] A theme reiterated by the women she studies is the notion that being in any form of organized racism feels like being part of "a big family"—a feeling that is actively encouraged by at least some of these groups. Again, the nuclear family easily slides into the larger tribal family of whiteness. Blee explains that organized racism emphasizes the notion of the traditional heteropatriarchal family structure along with using family-style relationships to connect people within the groups.[48] The family, very much an ideological structure and mechanism, could be used as a metaphor but is also integral to the perpetuation of the race in literal terms. Taking the example of Breivik as a stand-in for white power generally, one scholar notes Breivik's "abhorrence of contemporary sexual freedoms, with their threat, as he saw it, to the sovereignty of the patriarchal male, and his unmanageable hatred of the liberal state that he believes promotes these freedoms."[49] White power advocates, just like the neoliberals, see the state as the source of threatening ideas about equality and the dismantling of the traditional patriarchal family.

For the white power zealot operating from an assumption of people's inherent inequality (not unlike Kristol's neoliberal outlook, discussed above), gender equity in law or social practice is self-evidently an impossibility. In these environments it is not surprising that, as Blee observes, to some degree work in organized racism follows a "gendered division of labor. [Women cooking and serving meals at events] is common among racist groups."[50] While female racists are not always or simply subservient handmaidens to the "Aryan warrior," they do enact and symbolize the traditional motherly role within the collectivity of whiteness. Indeed, Blee concludes that the overriding function of women in groups that would fall under our rubric of white power is simply producing white babies.[51] This masculine/feminine dialectic is a key adhesive suturing together not only individual families, but the white racial family as well.[52] In this context we can see that the "You will not replace us" chant that became so notorious at the Charlottesville Unite the Right event is more than a proclamation of anti-Semitism and more than a proclamation against immigrants. It also serves as a proclamation against women who operate outside the so-called traditional family. Indeed, the hyperpatriarchy that goes back to older forms of white power (as well as white supremacy) remains current in newer formations for both men and women. Historian Alexandra Minna Stern quotes one red-pilled alt-right activist who posted a viral YouTube video in 2017: "Wife with a Purpose, who asserts that 'her primary duty is having children and supporting her husband,' issued a 'white baby challenge,' throwing down the breeding gauntlet: 'As a mother of 6, I challenge families to have as many white babies as I have contributed.'"[53] Indeed, the far white celebrated the Supreme Court's overturning of *Roe v. Wade* on June 24, 2022; one U.S. congresswoman actually called it a "historic victory for white life" (though she later claimed she misspoke).[54]

Inevitably, "the paternalistic and patriarchal image of the people results in an anti-democratic move."[55] Fueled by what we might see as a toxic blend of testosterone and insecurity on display in everything from the online manosphere to the novels we discuss in chapter 4, the result is an excess of affect that gets channeled into creating a right to be furious, an emotional state that "can be seen as a relief, as a way of de-responsibilizing men and re-sovereignizing masculinity by re-establishing dominance through anger and aggression."[56] For both women and men, white power ideology is lived through the body and thus can unleash powerful emotions, as seen in the 2021 siege of the Capitol. From this perspective, neoliberalism reinforces this vast crisis of masculinity as men deal with the confusing incongruities of achieving hegemonic masculinity within a service-based, communications-oriented economy that values the supposedly nonmasculine emotions of *homo affectus* over the supposedly masculine calculating logic of *homo economicus*. At the level of the state's functions, American neoliberal culture prioritizes a general "masculinizing," emphasizing the military, police, prison, and other capacities for violence. At the level of the community, anxieties are stoked by stimulating the stereotypical "masculine" affects—anger, rage, resentment—and then reassured through the promise of family and a sense of (patriarchally oriented) community.

This general insecurity around masculinity expresses itself in a variety of life experiences. Take the work world as a particular site. The neoliberal service and information economy is well known for its focus on communication and emotion. Sometimes these jobs wield lucrative returns, but as is more typical of anything that is "feminized," they are generally underpaid, underrespected, and highly insecure.[57] As political scientists Otto Penz and Birgit Sauer conclude, the affective regime affiliated with this work world is "based on fear, where security (with regard to the future, oneself, and others) tends to vanish, a regime which transforms security into insecurity.... Never before in history has work been so intellectually and affectively demanding while providing ever less the basis for social security and sustainable life planning."[58]

In this context we can reimagine *homo affectus* from the point of view of besieged and aggrieved white manhood. *Homo affectus* is a product of the emotional economy of neoliberalism and emerges from historically feminized realms of the occupational and cultural landscape.[59] He becomes more salient in the hysterically sexist manifestations of white power. In such right-wing manifestations, the energies surrounding *homo affectus* are dominated by an "obsession with gender" relating to a fear of emasculation that is evident in white power ideology, especially in its motif of hypermasculinity.[60]

From neoconservative visions of society all the way to white power fantasies, narrow perspectives on the qualities that are considered virtuous and moral are promoted as a way to erase the legal and social gains made in dominant American culture by women, people of color, people with disabilities, and LGBTQ+ folx. Throughout the neoliberal era, these groups have been fighting for equality and justice, and in turn neoliberal economics and politics continue to be shaped as a massive reaction formation against them, with white cultural politics becoming one way to wage class warfare. Racial and gender identities become the central political and sociocultural questions. Within the neoliberal worldview's erosion of class and rejection of explanations related to structural inequality, poverty can only be seen as a cultural identity issue. As sociologists Neil Davidson and Richard Saull put it, "Culture is left as the only explanatory residue for apparent behavioural traits that do not conform to a 'meritocratic' neoliberal subjectivity."[61] The political outcome of this meritocratic assumption is an ethnonationalist populism that explodes in outbursts of white (mostly masculine) rage.

UNDERMINING DEMOCRACY

From here it is a short step to further the historic American project of undermining the very democracy that the nation has come to see itself as embodying. After all, democracy as popular sovereignty seems a fantasy to groups who take it as axiomatic that people are inherently unequal and in need of hierarchy; that white women are particularly menaced by Black men; that gay and trans people are a threat to heteropatriarchal families; and that people of color are naturally inferior to whites. Here, the election of the first Black president seemed to be an obvious catastrophe for the far white, and so it responded quickly with a call to arms for the forces of anti-Blackness on the ground, embodied politically first in the Tea Party after 2008 and then as Trump's base in 2016, but invested less in the democratic process than in the desire to restore the hegemony of their vision of American identity as embodied in straight, white male dominance. Indeed, within neoliberalism's larger asocial, apolitical imaginary, whiteness remains as a default category, the "explanatory variable determining membership of, participation in, and contribution to society."[62]

The particular contours of the twenty-first-century version of anti-Blackness are perhaps a crasser version of what had been dubbed decades earlier, in 1975, as an "excess of democracy" in an infamous report by the Trilateral Commission, an early neoliberal organization.[63] For Fredric Jameson, the Trilateral Commission embodied "the recovery of momentum by what must be called 'the ruling classes'" as they responded to the gains made across the globe by revolutionary forces of all kinds in the 1960s.[64] For Wendy Brown, the Trilateral Commission's recommendations synthesize what it means to bring neoliberal theoretical perspectives to life: "Organically evolved rules of conduct, based on inherited and shared principles, are not only to be left untouched, but also made supervenient. Respect for private property, gender norms, and other traditional beliefs—these are the true foundations of a free, moral, and orderly society."[65]

If many neoliberals would not understand themselves to be endorsing fascism, racism, or gender oppression as such, they did and do see democracy as a problem, especially in the face of the global market's demands for order and regularity, which require comfort with fascists, authoritarians, apartheid regimes, and antidemocratic forces of all kinds.[66] If the classic example of this politics has been the neoliberal partnership with Augusto Pinochet, in the 2010s that far-right fascination shifted to Vladimir Putin, Russia's authoritarian leader and (probably) the world's wealthiest man (his net worth cannot be confirmed).[67] In a 2017 article archconservative writer and think tanker Christopher Caldwell calls him an ideological litmus test, "a hero to populist conservatives around the world and anathema to progressives":

> Vladimir Vladimirovich is not the president of a feminist NGO. He is not a transgender-rights activist. He is not an ombudsman appointed by the United Nations to make and deliver slide shows about green energy. He is the elected leader of Russia. . . . His job has been to protect his country's prerogatives and its sovereignty in an international system that seeks to erode sovereignty.[68]

This presentation of Putin's views is certainly articulated with the hobbyhorses of conservatives in mind, but the move to defend him by introducing his social conservative bona fides and to describe him as an "elected leader" speaks to the priorities of today's conservative class, which, just as in the past, have little to do with democracy and nothing to do with social justice. And although Putin's globally condemned invasion of Ukraine would occur a few years after Caldwell's writing, the truth remains that conservatives were very late to condemn his naked aggression. Twenty-first-century neoliberals—like early generation figures such as Hayek, Friedman, Kristol,

Moynihan, and the members of the Trilateral Commission—presented their quasi support of democracy within the context of preserving a system of order that benefited people like them. Their version of personal freedom was decidedly not a robust, socially just democracy but a regime where all compete in a capitalist marketplace stacked decidedly against subaltern populations and with limited protections for the people who lose in the competition. What has arisen, especially since 2008, is what William Davies calls a "punitive" phase of neoliberalism in which, in contrast to earlier phases, the targeted enemies are now internal to the system, including those crushed "by poverty, debt, and collapsing social-safety nets, [who] have already been largely destroyed as an autonomous political force. Yet somehow this increases the urge to punish them further."[69]

The American regime of business regulation and social safety nets that were installed in the wake of the Great Depression (such as they were) not only helped ameliorate capitalism's excesses but also enabled *liberal* capitalism to thrive by both forestalling socialist opposition and offloading the costs of social reproduction. As *neoliberal* priorities became more entrenched and these regulations and safety-net investments meant to temper capitalism's extremes eroded, there emerged a precariat populated disproportionately by unmarried women and people of color—all while the rhetoric of white male oppression was given a new visibility in public discourse and the top economic tier of society thrived. Thus, during the 2020 coronavirus economic collapse, when Wall Street and the nation's wealthiest individuals saw their fortunes rise as the real economy crumbled below, the federal bailouts and economic stimulus meant to mitigate the extraordinary fallout on small businesses ended up disproportionately in the hands of larger corporations.[70] As monetary policy favored equity-based capital, the wealthy increased their share of global capital not despite the economic collapse, but because of it.[71]

Taken together, the lives of the majority of people of all races have become increasingly insecure in American neoliberal culture, the product of a regime in which the rich are free to accumulate with abandon because that is the cost of market stability. As a result, the American neoliberal economy oscillates wildly, creating immiseration culture. We know that in racial capitalism it is people of color who are particularly vulnerable to these oscillations because they are uniquely targeted for exploitation in a relationship that for more than four hundred years has benefited white wealth. This basic exploitative relationship manifests in the United States today in American neoliberal racial capitalism's vast income inequality, which is unmatched in the industrialized world but is matched by the inequality and misery found in the world's poorest nations.[72]

If the neoliberal ideal in the United States has centered on unleashing the purportedly free market and its requirement for self-entrepreneurship linked to incessant hustling, this modern approach to work life has been accompanied by the rise of "traditional" (read: deeply antiquated) moral rules whose mandate hearkens back centuries. To bring such pitiless policies to life, whether in centuries past or in the contemporary era, requires savage rule. In the traditional system with its Elizabethan roots, the so-called idle poor would be incarcerated in workhouses and flogged. Since the Clinton-era reforms, would-be welfare recipients have run a gauntlet meant "partly to punish or shame those who pass through it . . . and partly to weed out those who are not strong enough to withstand its demands."[73]

Those neoliberals who saw themselves embracing the so-called third way of center-left multicultural pluralism—for example, notable heads of state in the 1990s and early 2000s such as U.S. president Bill Clinton and British prime minister Tony Blair—could pretend they were threading some needle between antisocial capitalism and prosocial liberalism. But with policies that hollowed out any sincere notion of social responsibility by eroding public assistance, refusing to meaningfully raise the minimum wage, and removing key financial regulations to even out the economic playing field, capitalism's vast wealth inequalities were accentuated and the profound insecurity that resulted only inflamed social antagonisms. The resulting neglect of social infrastructure has led to widespread misery, profound skepticism, and increasing distrust of democracy, and it has created what we have been calling an immiseration culture, conditions that worsened during the 2008 global economic collapse and in the 2020s under Joe Biden, who presided as Trump's replacement over a collapsing coronavirus-beset economy. The result of this immiseration culture has been a rise in support for authoritarians.

The particular historical trajectories may differ around the world, but oppressive right-wing regimes connected through a new populism have arisen seemingly everywhere. Historian Marco Revelli describes this new populism as "a mood. It is the formless form that social malaise and impulses to protest take on in societies that have been pulverized and reworked by globalisation and total finance."[74] Feeling unrepresented by traditional politics and party establishments, people around the world have turned to strong leaders and would-be dictators who have tapped into this populist mood, often with an ethnonationalist flavor, and to greater or lesser degrees have created states of exception to rid themselves of meddlesome laws and norms in the name of maintaining the "right" people's way of life.

For Hayek and other early neoliberals, it was clear that achieving the desired market economies and traditional social arrangements may well require dictators, strongmen, coups, wars, lies, big lies (*the* "Big Lie"), and violence. Neoliberal luminaries have also accepted these as part of the formula for success. What we have seen in recent years is a turn to despotic figures who have been able to generate fervent, if not fanatical, ethnopopulist support for the ideals and fantasies they embody, which are easily racialized. Davidson and Saull argue that the "contradictory embrace" of neoliberalism and the far right creates a situation where, "for some workers, appeals to 'blood and nation' appear as the only viable form of collectivity still available."[75]

These developments along with the Southern Strategy, which we discuss in chapter 3, created a formula for a kind of *disaster whiteness* as a strategy enabling neoliberals' anti–welfare state agenda. Neoliberals and the Republican Party took advantage of the perceived white patriarchal crisis in the face of civil rights struggles not only to shift voters' political allegiances but also to erode the gains that had raised the working people's economic prospects, including those of the very whites who now were willing to tear it all down and damage not only their own bottom line but also the very democratic process that had expanded the franchise for poor whites who also benefited from movements to end literacy tests and poll taxes.

This neoliberal turn toward authoritarianism propped up by ethnonationalism is mirrored by white power activists and authors who consistently rail against democracy. For example and discussed in more detail in chapter 4, in *The Turner Diaries,* Pierce (writing as Macdonald) maintains that Americans have already blown their chance with democracy, which he identifies as part of a Jewish cabal.[76] After giving up on liberal democracy, the only alternative for white people is a political system based on racial homogeneity. For Pierce, such uniformity automatically leads to a utopia for white people. Because whiteness underpins it, this utopia becomes for him the magic solution to all political, social, economic, and cultural problems. We can think of this magic solution as immersed in religion for figures such as Kenneth Molyneaux, whose belief in the racist religion of Creativity substitutes theocracy for democracy and places racial loyalty above all other allegiances.[77] The founder of the religion, Ben Klassen, held that white people should not fixate on a particular form of ideal government but should instead focus on the cohesion of the white race to provide the foundation and operational structure of a white nation.[78] And, for their part, white power figures like Harold Covington and David Lane reject democracy, respectively, as "a sickness that leads inevitably to chaos, corruption, and the collapse of society" and "the most dangerous and deadly form of government."[79] Both prefer authoritarian figures to democracy. As Lane maintains, democracy's end will "always be followed by a strongman . . . some of them call him dictator. It is the only way to restore order out of the chaos caused by a democracy. Pick your strongman wisely!"[80] Literalizing the excess-of-democracy argument, which is also part of the anti–social justice stance of both white power and neoliberalism, Lane's *88 Precepts* further claims, "The concept of 'equality' is declared a lie by every evidence of Nature. It is a search for the lowest common denominator, and its pursuit will destroy every superior race, nation, or culture"—thus, his embrace of authoritarianism.

This anti-democracy screed also frequently recurs in the manifestos of the violent white extremists we discuss in chapter 1. Anders Breivik wrote at length about the problems of democracy in his manifesto, which includes an entire chapter titled "Democracy not working." As we see with Lane and Covington, Breivik seems to call for a kind of authoritarianism—one that could at least secure a national territory for "a people with a shared identity"—but that also allowed for individual liberties.[81] American mass shooters connected to white power such as John Earnest and Patrick Crusius also lament the hopelessness of American democracy, such as it is. Both of these men were influenced by Christchurch, New Zealand, anti-Muslim mass shooter Brenton Tarrant, who urges in his manifesto, "Do not suffer under the delusion of an effortless, riskless democratic victory. Prepare for war, prepare for violence and prepare for risk, loss, struggle, death. Force is the only path to power and the only path to true victory." And the January 6 Capitol insurrectionists sought to undermine the legitimate democratic victory of Joe Biden over Donald Trump. As expressed in accelerationism, only armed revolt, not political, democratic processes, can realize the "ideal" society: the white ethnonational state.

THREE

Far White Family Values

STRATEGIES FOR NEOLIBERAL TAKEOVER

GOVERNMENTS AND ECONOMIES ARE TOOLS, and these can be wielded to oppress or to serve a population depending on who is handling them. Income gains, though distributed unequally along fissures of race and gender, were made by most American groups in the twentieth century precisely due to the New Deal and Great Society interventions. These income gains were predicated on the maintenance of the Fordist family as part of a grand social compromise that would preserve white patriarchy as long as women bore the burdens of social reproduction without a paycheck for their efforts, leaving men free to earn. To support a family on one wage of course required that wage to be relatively substantial, which meant U.S. employers were shelling out more in salary than they might otherwise. Neoliberalism arose in part to erode the gains won by workers within the Fordist economy, but this erosion obviously presents a key problem for neoliberal thinkers and policymakers: they wanted so-called traditional families led and supported by the paterfamilias, but they also advocated for the erosion of unions and the destruction of welfare supports that were key elements in the high wages that supported the Fordist family.

In this chapter we will explore the way that American neoliberalism mobilizes racism and sexism and uses them to undermine the idea of society that had previously created support for the social welfare and Fordist family state. As Lisa Duggan argues, "The construction of neoliberal politics and policy in the U.S. has relied on identity and cultural politics. The politics of race, both overt and covert, have been particularly central to the entire project. But the politics of gender and sexuality have intersected with race and class politics at each stage as well."[1] In this chapter we focus on these elements as we try to understand how they come together in the workings of

American society. However, we also need to trace their connections to extremist white power ideology, which manifests itself in spectacles and fantasies of violence, in order to understand the current historical moment. Thus, we end the chapter by showing how racism and sexism lead to support for neoliberalism even within the ranks of ultraviolent white power proponents who sometimes claim to oppose capitalism—a discussion that leads us to the white power utopias we analyze in chapter 4. First, however, we need to delve into the misty origins of neoliberalism, into political strategies that helped focus economic priorities in terms of race, gender, and sexuality—in short, we need to understand the intersections of neoliberalism and the white heteronormative family.

THE NEOLIBERAL SOUTHERN STRATEGY, PART I

As mentioned in chapter 2, neoliberalism operates as a feedback loop, creating in circular fashion some of the very conditions that led to disruptions of the family that instigated neoliberal culture's paranoia about the family in the first place.[2] These changing family structures arose as a response to millions of individual circumstances as they interacted with at least two immense structural and cultural forces arising largely in the 1970s and '80s. One was the erosion of the Fordist and Keynesian economic compromise in the wake of globalization, technologization, and financialization that enable "time-space compression," which metaphorically shrinks the planet while literally expanding the profit taken in by global capitalists; these are famously described by David Harvey's field-defining works *The Condition of Postmodernity* (1989) and *A Brief History of Neoliberalism* (2005). The other was the social movement activism of the 1960s and early 1970s in the United States, embodied in the great liberation movements from the Black Panthers to the anti-war movement, from women's rights to Stonewall. From this perspective, we can think back to Jameson's summary statement about the end of the great 1960s-era struggles as "an immense and inflationary issuing of superstructural credit," a metaphorical debt that had to be paid in the form of neoliberalism in the 1980s.[3] Emerging from these forces was a new conservatism built by mobilizing the white patriarchal fear of the ascendant power of women and minoritized populations; stoking this fear was the noted rise of divorce rates in the 1970s and '80s to more than 45 percent.[4] Now it is not just neoliberal white power that represents the bill coming due, as we saw in the previous chapter, but it is also the rise of the totality of American neoliberalism itself.

Mainstream neoliberals, whether aligned with left or right electoral politics, found a hammer in big government's toolbox to impose family values of a very narrow patriarchal kind. But what needs to be understood to conceptualize what that idealized family looks like in the United States is the deep imbrication of whiteness within dominant ideological American family structures. The benefits of whiteness are literalized in the politics associated with what political scientists Angie Maxwell and Todd Shields call "the Long Southern Strategy," which they see as a series of decisions on race, women, and religion starting with the 1964 presidential election.[5] The Southern Strategy operationalizes the political will of the majority of southern voters and enabled the changes in the American social service state at the electoral level. Historically, for this voter, the big government of the New Deal was not really anything to object to—as long as it focused on helping white people.[6] When it worked primarily for whites, and especially when it was officially unfair to Black folks, southerners tended to vote for it. In everything from New Deal programs such as the Federal Housing Administration's loan programs, which required redlining and neighborhood segregation, to minimum wage protections exempting farm and domestic work—two employment sectors overrepresented by nonwhite people—the federal government maintained or exacerbated racial segregation and discrimination.[7] It was decades later, especially after the Johnson-era Great Society moment when the federal government began recognizing nonwhite and single-mother families as eligible for its services and protections, that big government somehow became part of the problem rather than part of the solution to economic inequality for most southerners.[8]

The Southern Strategy was created to reroute American politics by turning the formerly Democratic stronghold of the U.S. "Solid South" to the Republican Party by mobilizing racial, gender, and religious antagonism. We have explored the way 1960s-era social justice changes to the political economy created a crisis that was critical for the rise of neoliberalism, and American whiteness had confronted a somewhat comparable crisis in its position after the Civil War. But in the late 1960s to early 1970s, as geographer Joshua Inwood reminds us, "the broader ideologies of racism were being challenged and at the very moment economic crises surplussed large amounts of US productive capacity."[9] So at the same time as the United States was undergoing massive economic crises from seemingly every direction—developments well discussed by David Harvey—racist and patriarchal governmentalities also transformed under pressure from broad political and social rebellions throughout the racial state and mobilized antagonisms that could be redirected against the social welfare state, now seen to have abandoned white people and taken the side of racial and gender minorities in a zero-sum calculus that enables the disaster whiteness discussed in chapter 2.

We should note here that the racialized political subjects of the Southern Strategy were not necessarily located only in the U.S. South, but that is their traditional base and seat of power. One political calculation by a young Pat Buchanan working for Richard Nixon optimistically envisioned more than half the country would side with the Republicans based on the issue of race: by cutting "the country in half, my view is that we would have the far larger half."[10] As Maxwell and Shields argue,

> The coded campaign rhetoric attracted Americans well outside of the South sometimes because they did not understand the code and sometimes even when they did. Privilege and patriarchy and fundamentalism, of course, have no geographical limitations.... Fear and rage and resentment, the bread and butter of the Long Southern Strategy, often drive more people to the polls than optimism or likability or hope, no matter where they live.[11]

The Southern Strategy comes to fruition largely as a reaction to the same leftist social movement activism that the neocons reacted against. Both the neoconservative neoliberals and the Southern Democrats had been part of the New Deal coalition, but after the successes of the 1960s movements (limited as they may have been), both groups willingly sacrificed their previous politics and the advantages they received from the social service state, reversing those gains, which they perceived as threats to the white heteronormative patriarchal family.[12] And a development they found particularly bothersome was the expansion of welfare eligibility.

A BRIEF TREK THROUGH THE "BREAKDOWN OF THE NEGRO FAMILY"

There has been a long history in the United States of demonizing the racial "other" in the consolidation of the ideal family as specifically white. On the West Coast in the mid-nineteenth century, "the racialized category of coolie labor enabled the working-class movement to articulate its goals not around the issue of proletarianization but around the demand for the restoration of craft privileges and the family wage."[13] Regarding the "Mexican problem" in the 1920s, the discourse assumed that "maladapted parents reproduced Mexico's cultural pathologies within the family setting."[14] As 1920s University of Southern California sociologist Emory Bogardus maintained, "It is necessary to first of all to consider the Mexican immigrant in light of the family culture traits of the peon classes of Mexico."[15] In both cases, the white family was situated as the norm and ideal in comparison to these racial "others."

But, not surprisingly, special attention has been paid to the role of the family in the "Negro problem." Even E. Franklin Frazier, the first African American person to serve as president of the American Sociological Association, in 1948, and a thinker with a complex understanding of the Black family, reflected his times by contributing to the discourse of the dysfunctional "Negro family":

> However [unlike the stability with rural families], the urbanization of the Negro population since 1900 has brought the most momentous change in the family life of the Negro since emancipation. This movement, which has carried a million Negroes to southern cities alone, has torn the Negro loose from his cultural moorings. Thousands of these migrants have been solitary men and women who have led a more or less lawless sex life during their wanderings. But many more illiterate or semi-illiterate and impoverished Negro families, broken or held together only by the fragile bonds of sympathy and habit, have sought a dwelling in the slums of southern cities. Because of the dissolution of the rural folkways and mores, the children in these families have helped to swell the ranks of juvenile delinquents.[16]

This "problematic" family continued as African Americans migrated to other cities around the country as part of the Great Migration. And although Frazier ends his book with optimism about African Americans adjusting to modern American society, it is clear that the "Negro family" had at the time become a social problem, destined for social services. However, what is important to note for our purposes here is that although the white family has been historically fetishized directly over the nonwhite family, the difference at the end of the twentieth century, with the rise of neoliberal values and strategies, is that the white family now needed this reification of its status because it was facing market fundamentalism *and* changing demographics *and* ideologies regarding racial equality.

To be clear, over the course of the twentieth century welfare had unfairly become associated with Blackness and single mothers. Critiques of the impoverished family that turned to social services became racialized hetero-patriarchal screeds against Black families themselves and their "startling increase in welfare dependency," to quote the infamous, if clichéd, 1965 Moynihan Report. Authored under the direction of early neoliberal Daniel Patrick Moynihan, *The Negro Family: The Case for National Action,* as the report is officially titled, has remained in the public memory for decades as a historic relic. With the exception of the word *Negro,* the report speaks the language of the current conservative perspective on the problems within African American communities, and perhaps more to the point, both the report and today's conservatives seem to see many of the problems plaguing the United States as the fault of African American communities.

Certainly, W. E. B. Du Bois had, at the beginning of the century, assessed the "Negro problems" of his time, which he saw as the "problems of poverty, ignorance, and social degradation" caused fundamentally by "widespread conviction among Americans that no persons of Negro descent should become constituent members of the social body." He warned that future generations will "curse the nation, unless we grapple with [these problems] manfully and intelligently."[17] In his attempt to grapple with these issues "manfully and intelligently," Swedish economist and sociologist Gunnar Myrdal along with a broad team working beside him produced the massive 1944 study *An American Dilemma: The Negro Problem and Modern Democracy,* which offered the sunny assessment that the foundational "American Creed" of fairness and equality was too compelling to Americans for them not to address the naked problem of racial inequality. But even this optimistic, World War II–inflected pro-Americanism did not stop him from accurately assessing that the "Negro problem" was actually, as he put it, a "white man's problem" caused by a vast racist inequality that is "an integral part of . . . the whole complex of problems in the larger American civilization."[18]

For his part, Moynihan produced a kind of model for a neoliberal rhetoric of care that would be very useful to white supremacy, despite his own protests that he was trying to solve the problem of racism. And, just as importantly, this rhetoric enabled liberals like Moynihan himself to bypass the very painful political and intellectual work required to actually promote social justice in U.S. society by diagnosing the problems of inequality as the fault of the Black family. The report illustrates a common tendency to see poverty, crime, and dependency less as results of racial and economic oppressions than as evidence of the "breakdown of the Negro family," which is decayed precisely because it is insufficiently dominated by men.

Today the same concerns operate as Kamala Harris, the first woman and the first Black / South Asian vice president, has been vocally and publicly labeled by prominent religious leaders as a "Jezebel"—a reference to the biblical story of the queen who insisted she was equal to her husband, Elijah, but that later in common retelling morphed into a trope for Black women as hypersexual and without decency.[19] It is this kind of damning dismissal that resonates with the Moynihan Report's stigmatizing of high-achieving Black women in a chapter characteristically titled "The Tangle of Pathology," where we are told that "a fundamental fact of Negro American family life is the often reversed roles of husband and wife. . . . 'Negro husbands have unusually low power.'"[20] The report reserves particular criticism for Black mothers, since they apparently emasculate their boys and raise families without relying on a strong father. The report expresses hope that things could improve, but only if the "distortions" of matriarchal families and their disproportionately high-achieving daughters come to reflect the white world more—that is, if women become less capable in comparison to men. So too readers learn that "white children without fathers at least perceive all about them the pattern of men working. [But] Negro children without fathers flounder—and fail."[21]

The report is one of the key early documents of American neoliberalism as its diagnosis of the Black family's "tangle of pathologies" subjects that family to the kind of biopolitical solutions that became characteristic of neoliberal culture. Indeed, theorist Grace Kyungwon Hong shows how Moynihan links the civil rights struggles in the United States to the decolonial revolutions across the world, but in the report's framing, this discourse marks people of color *globally* as deviant and punishable, thus justifying "the regulation of working-class women of color within a new global division of labor" rooted in the postcolonial, post–civil rights "political economies based increasingly on a feminized proletariat and on domestic and service labor."[22]

Characteristically, when the report expresses shock at the unemployment statistics among Black teens, by which it seems to mean among Black male teens, it enables dominant power to blame Black people, by which it seems to mean Black women, with the reasoning that the statistics "reflect lack of training and opportunity in the greatest measure, but it may not be doubted that they also reflect a certain failure of nerve."[23] The evidence for this failure-of-nerve diagnosis? The next line offers this anecdote: "'Are you looking for a job?' Secretary of Labor Wirtz asked a young man on a Harlem street corner. 'Why?' was the reply."[24] Indeed, for Moynihan these problems are more than economic since "it is probable that at present, a majority of the crimes against the person, such as rape, murder, and aggravated assault are committed by Negroes." However, the report quickly adds a caveat, claiming, "There is, of course, no absolute evidence; inference can only be made from arrest and prison population statistics."[25]

Ultimately, the strength of the evidence is irrelevant. It is clear in these and many other passages that Black people are presumed not merely to have problems but to be a problem. They are a problem for which Black families are to blame. As Moynihan concludes, "A national effort towards the problems of Negro Americans must be directed towards the question of family structure," and welfare was seen as that deviant family's enabler. For the many social conservatives riding this idea train, to fix Black people's problems required "fixing" the Black family by affixing the place of men so that each home had a strong paternal presence. Welfare was ostensibly the expression and the enabler of the "pathology" at the root of Black families and thus had to be cut.[26]

By the 1980s and '90s, the ascendant neoconservative figures within American neoliberalism "focused their energies on reviving the punitive and pedagogical function of welfare,"[27] and to do that required the "end of welfare as we know it," to use a phrase popularized by Bill Clinton in his 1992 presidential campaign.[28] The creation of the new welfare regime in the Clinton years tore a massive hole in the U.S. safety net in the name of reform. Abandoning the welfare state, with its promise of redistribution and security, was key to the rising preeminence of neoliberalism as an affective regime as much as a governmentality and an ideology. By the time Clinton had come along, the drive to erode the welfare state was a crucial item on American neoliberal culture's list of priorities, and the success of his presidential bids shows that the Southern Strategy could be as useful for Democrats as it was for Republicans.

THE NEOLIBERAL SOUTHERN STRATEGY, PART 2

From the other side of the New Deal coalition, white southerners looked in anger and fear at radicalized Black folks and women of all races claiming a right to have rights in the wake of the social justice movements of the 1960s.[29] The deployment of the "long Southern Strategy" entered as a way to imbricate neoliberal and neoconservative priorities with white patriarchal Christian identity politics. And to the extent that Republicans embraced these values—which most did with little public reservation—the Southern

Strategy paved the way for the neoliberal Republican Party to come to power by the 1980s by breaking up the Solid South and eroding the many social service state programs and worker protections introduced by New Deal Democrats and promoted by social forces such as unions throughout the twentieth century, programs that had successfully helped redistribute a great deal of wealth in the United States from the rich to the non-elite.[30]

At the end of the twentieth century, Southern Democrat Bill Clinton, having jumped on the neoliberal train headed toward welfare reform–cum–destruction, endorsed myths of the (implicitly) Black superpredator criminal, who needed to be locked away forever in prison, and was able to profit politically from the Southern Strategy. Taking advantage of existing hostilities, the strategy opened the way for a vast restructuring of political conditions across the United States rooted in and capitalizing on the racial antipathy of white people "by appealing to a kind of universal white supremacy . . . [that] provided cultural cover for the restoration of class power."[31] It is important to note that the Southern Strategy does not mark a moment of radical departure in U.S. history but is rather the neoliberal emanation of the more generalized assertion of white supremacy and heteropatriarchal privilege. In more recent times, the Southern Strategy certainly shaped the Obama administration's response to the 2014 Black Lives Matter uprising in Ferguson, Missouri, when it refused to abandon the federal role in militarizing local police.[32] And certainly the strategy either formed or enabled Trump's political agenda and public persona, marked as it is by racism (he launched his presidential bid by calling Mexican immigrants rapists), vulgarity-laced sexism ("when you're a star . . . [women let you] grab 'em by the pussy!"), and his embrace of Christianity (although not personally pious, he was unabashedly willing to use churches and Bibles as props during the 2020 Black Lives Matter protests). We can see Trump's political life as the fever dream of George Wallace, a characterization he solidified by renouncing his geographic history as a lifelong New Yorker in 2019 and declaring Florida—a Civil War secessionist state—to be his home.

Trump understood there is widespread but deeply vague support in the United States for the working people and the poor against a moneyed elite—as evidenced in the rhetoric from both the left and the right, especially visible in archetypes such as Joe Sixpack and the like. But within many segments of the population, more potent than the desire for dignity for working people is a deep well of enmity toward the poor who accept support from the taxpayer through government programs—*as long as it is assumed that those who accept support are people of color.*[33] This is the right-wing logic of populism. Drawing on Ernesto Laclau, journalist John Judis explains this logic as one that places "the people" in the middle fighting against both the elites at the top, which for them includes the left, and the "takers" at the bottom. It is this "triadic" structure that allows race and other forms of social difference to be transcoded by the middle to the bottom.[34]

In earlier decades of the neoliberal era in the United States, this transcoding relied on old standby characters such as "welfare queens" and "illegal aliens," figures that could be passed off as undesirables taking advantage of the selfless generosity of hardworking Americans presumed to be white. Being tied to some notion of unfairness, typical complaints—such as welfare is supposed to help people but not to make them rich, or immigrants are welcome here except that so many are criminals and take our social services—operated as a coded language for racism. But after the panic created by the election of the first Black president came the unabashed and outspoken backlash that resulted in the election of "the first white President," to borrow a phrase from Ta-Nehisi Coates.[35] Political representation became particularly stark and outspokenly racist. For example, after Barack Obama's signature achievement of a greatly expanded health insurance system he was widely depicted in the media as an African witch doctor. So too Donald Trump unabashedly declared that too many immigrants come from "shithole countries," that Muslim immigrants should be banned, and that undocumented children should be unceremoniously taken from their parents and imprisoned.

The Southern Strategy as anti-Keynesian class-race warfare works only as long as it is assumed that the fight for welfare-state fairness is also a fight for racial and gender uplift; in that case, impassioned opposition arises to government efforts to fight poverty and improve living conditions—especially because everyone benefits, not just white people.[36] Which is to say, neoliberal ideology imagined outside of racial capitalism obscures the question of who the social state should serve so that the population in general could imagine itself as opposed in principle to the welfare state because it enables problematic people. But viewing the economic system as centered around racism opens the way to a different set of conclusions, not necessarily that citizens want the welfare state to be dismantled, but that many of them want it only to serve white people—a view rooted in racial resentment and fear of status loss. This status is anchored in what George Lipsitz called "the possessive investment in whiteness," which works metaphorically but also in real economic terms as wealth creation in the United States has historically favored white people in myriad ways.[37]

The emotional and logical conclusion to this position was that the true enemies are the nonwhite or insufficiently white poor, who accept help from the bureaucrats and the "bleeding heart liberals" who offer that help (now viewed dismissively as "social justice warriors"). Anger at a lost social status motivates the era's increasing political turmoil and desperate desire "to achieve status via dominance," and eventually through violence.[38]

NEOLIBERALISM OF THE FAR WHITE

If it became unacceptable to openly express racism in mainstream political discourse during earlier decades of the American neoliberal era, when racism was hidden in dog whistles, after the election of the nation's first Black president in 2008 racist rhetoric became unabashedly more explicit and pro-white chauvinism more brazen, thus creating the conditions for "far whiteness." If the Black Lives Matter movement that began in 2013 captured the imagination and political energy of coalitions across the country, its rise only made the issues starker for retrograde forces operating within a kind of Schmittian friend-enemy politics in which political decisions are made from a zero-sum calculus by which there can only be winners or losers.

So if true libertarians actually want to shrink the government, almost everyone else wants the state to use its vast apparatuses to work for them. Indeed, Trump performed a key role after Obama's presidency: he enabled white men to assert their place in a friend-enemy world, re-envisioned beyond the established opposition between takers and makers as the dualism between deserving and undeserving *within a perceived crisis of white extinction anxiety.* In sociologist Arlie Hochschild's interviews of MAGA supporters, she finds that Trump "masculinizes government benefits in their eyes—as long as the benefits are for white people and especially white men." The "King of Shame" has mocked most other groups—"women, people of color, the disabled, immigrants, refugees"—as people manipulating the system to unfairly take advantage, but for so-called real Americans there is no stigma in seeking help, as long as the help comes from a white-oriented government program.[39] This move takes us away from the logic of neoliberalism rooted in a definition of freedom embodied in the individual as entrepreneur (especially as Michel Foucault's famous formulation of the entrepreneur of the self) but brings us closer to the logic of neoliberalism as rooted in affective economies and conjunctural crisis in the way Stuart Hall understood it.[40]

In this way Trump is like nationalist and populist political figures around the world who have risen in opposition to austerity politics and global capitalist productivity demands—in the name of particular preferred ethnic groups. Indeed, as political theorist Verónica Gago shows, populism "rehabilitates the logic of friend versus enemy . . . [and] the idea of society with conflict as its nature."[41] In contrast to much of the American political experience in the neoliberal era, global politics show very well that social conservatism and economic austerity are often disconnected politically.[42] In Europe, for instance, Rassemblement National (formerly Front Nationale), Lega, and Brexiteers are notable populist or ethnonationalist anti-immigrant groups that support a strong social service state and prioritize social welfare spending. The key is that this spending be reserved for people who look or worship like the majority.

When it comes to the achievements of the United States' first Black president, the same logic applies. Thus, if the Obamacare insurance program was unacceptable, a vague Trumpcare would be an exciting improvement, even if his administration never announced a specific plan—in fact, especially *because* it never announced a specific plan. After all, what was really on offer was an imagined white alternative to the Black president, with his Black healthcare and his Black government. Indeed, shrouding the benefits of the welfare state in the cloak of xenophobia and racism is a common feature of today's ethnonationalist politics. We would argue that this move to support welfare for only a select group brings contemporary conservative politics in the United States full circle from its days before the political changes of the 1960s. Historian Alexandra Minna Stern identifies 1965 as "year zero" and the 1960s as "the demographic sweet spot" for the alt-righters and white nationalists she studies because they could still think of the United States as a white ethnostate before 1965.[43]

Today, American neoliberal forces exploit a common lack of knowledge of political processes[44] and exploit the rhetorics of white supremacy and the emotional privileges of "white fragility" and white rage.[45] These forces promote a more generalized erosion of the category of the social—that is to say, of society as such and of the social welfare state as a particular social vision. Using xenophobia, racism, sexual oppression, and, increasingly, political party affiliation to erode the notion of society, neoliberal ideology presents people as monads competing in a freewheeling economy, while neoliberal governmentality sets up conditions that insist people see themselves in competition.[46] Indeed, we may well ask if neoliberal politicians are afraid of making policy promises that their actual economic policies match because, by and large, it seems they have no intention of governing in alignment with their promises concerning big government and are only biding time until they can destroy all democratic institutions so that they will no longer have to make those promises at all.

At the heart of neoliberal culture is an isolation marked by ressentiment and distrust in the idea of the social. Neoliberal icon Margaret Thatcher made the archetypal proclamation in this regard, asserting, "Who is society? There is no such thing! There are individual men and women and there are families."[47] Interestingly, she argued later that her statement was actually not opposing the idea of society but asserting that society is a "living structure of individuals, families, neighbors, and voluntary associations."[48] She claimed she was merely positioning people at the center of society rather than seeing society as an abstraction. However, to take the state away and center the "voluntary" character of commitments utterly erodes the idea of society that has been economically beneficial to those outside the dominant group; instead, the social service state positions access to a safety net, healthcare, and food as a *right*. Indeed, rights-based models of citizenship do require a higher level of resource redistribution (that is, taxing the rich) than neoliberals' affective model of citizenship, which centers on "strategies to interpellate 'active and affective citizens' in times of rising unemployment, cuts in welfare provisions, and a less protective and redistributive state." These "affective citizens, however, have only limited opportunities for political participation."[49] Their good citizenship involves having the "right" kind of family values, the "right" targets of anger, and the "right" orientation toward the social.

Since the late nineteenth to early twentieth centuries, "the social" has referred to a kind of obligation to members of a particular territory connected to the nation. With unprecedentedly globalized economies and the state's traditional monopoly on violence aligning apart from the nation (sometimes beyond it and sometimes within it), the challenges to the seeming obviousness of the national social state and the nation—itself figured as a society—became impossible to ignore.[50] Wendy Brown argues that "the existence of society and the idea of the social—its intelligibility, its harboring of stratifying powers, and above all, its appropriateness as a site of justice and the commonweal—is precisely what neoliberalism set out to destroy conceptually, normatively, and practically."[51]

Gago's conception of neoliberalism "from below" shows the results of those neoliberal efforts. Today, the idea of society stretches outside the national frame in the context of the "feminized" subaltern subjects that she studies—women, migrants, children, the unemployed—who operate in the unofficial spaces of informal economies. In the wake of vast economic crisis, the social continues to exist, even if it is not being instated from above, "as a space of survival." Thus for her, the social as seen from above has become "primarily nostalgic," replaced by a version of society as mutual cooperation and solidarity at the level of the street "as an everyday public space and as a domestic space."[52] Society as a feminized space of survival enables a very different life than society rooted in a robust system of public services that guarantee food, healthcare, education, and housing.

For *homo economicus*—the rational, self-interested economic agent who serves as one kind of embodiment of neoliberalism—the neoliberal state operates as an alternative to the ostensible tyranny of the Keynesian state with its conception of society-from-above and its emphasis on regulation and redistribution.[53] These are the entrepreneurialized subjects in a de-democratized state in a depoliticized economy who are governed through their freedom to select from among a very narrow array of choices—framed as a choice to be entrepreneurs of themselves or to be poor, unsuccessful freeloaders.

For *homo affectus,* the emotion-oriented neoliberal subject, subjectivization emphasizes different energies when part of a right-wing discourse. This affective governmentality trades in insecurity and fear while opening up the possibility of unleashing violent passions against the deprived and those said to be unsuccessful.[54] Ultimately, neoliberalism removes the obligations that individuals have to each other as fellow citizens and sometimes even as human beings; it "liberates" citizens from the ostensible tyranny of big government; and it enables the anti-government ideology articulated by Ronald Reagan in his notorious slogan, "The most terrifying words in the English language are: I'm from the government and I'm here to help."[55] In the neoliberal ideology of the time, the populist rhetoric combines with the classic bootstrap mythology and anti-government ideology. Reagan summarized these in his first inaugural address, which is sometimes called his "Government is the problem" speech: "From time to time we've been tempted to believe that society has become too complex to be managed by self-rule, that government by an elite group is superior to government for, by, and of the people. Well, if no one among us is capable of governing himself, then who among us has the capacity to govern someone else?" He punctuates this argument by dipping into the rhetoric of discrimination, adding, "The solutions we seek must be equitable, with no one group singled out to pay a higher price," an admonition that could reference the United States' history of racism but in context is a dog whistle eliciting a sense of victimhood that comes with aggrieved whiteness.

Neoliberalism thus married the family-as-safety-net ideology to the conservative lament that the institution of the family is threatened by the very existence of other families living in dignity without the guidance of mom and dad in place and with dad firmly ensconced as the head of the household. Starting with the Thatcherite assumption that there is no such thing as society leads to different solutions than social justice approaches for dealing with the problems of racism, sexism, and economic exploitation; it usually leads to the clichéd conclusion that people should pull themselves up by their own bootstraps. But in the wake of Trump, it leads to another conclusion that has become more salient with the increasing prevalence of white power rhetoric. We have known for some time that neoliberal rhetoric includes the family within the realm of the individual, as perfectly encapsulated by Thatcher's "no society" sentiment; what has become clear is that *white people as a whole are increasingly figured as family* in American neoliberal culture's current right-wing manifestation, especially in combination with white power ideology.

This family subject position plays out in multiple ways. Combining Gago's perspective of a society of the subaltern with the understanding of right-wing populism as demanding a third position between the state and the subaltern conception of the social, we argue that white ethnocentrists are trying to position themselves as representing a squeezed middle way, the natural choice in a zero-sum game in which the rich have closed off admittance to their ranks at the top, and the poor occupy the feminized ground level. By extension, the white middle way becomes the space for the patriarchal family and the subject position for white men and for "their" women. Even if their jobs position them as part of that feminized space of service-oriented labor, their embrace of far-right whiteness positions them outside subalternity in that space assumed by far-right populism. This, however, is not neoliberalism from below, nor is it a middle way, but it is neoliberalism from the far right and for the far white.

In its earliest days American racial capitalism was made possible because race was presented as a meaningful category that bolstered the interests of wealthy European-Americans by recruiting non-elite European-Americans as a control stratum against Indigenous Americans and enslaved Africans. Racialization discouraged non-elites from building a class-based, cross-race alliance since hegemonic forces offered race as a detour to route poor whites' antagonisms against the inequalities of the system. Flashing forward, the Southern Strategy was a version of this approach for a post–civil rights era. In more recent times, we have seen the addition of a far-right, far white populism that does not necessarily oppose the social service–oriented, trade-protectionist state.

Of course, in the United States the social state is not a comprehensive institution woven into daily life to the extent that it is in most other industrialized nations. Americans certainly rely upon its benefits, but again, historic racism and racial exploitation created a massive barrier to a full and robust implementation of a social welfare regime. Thus, during the New Deal years in the 1930s, when many of the most valued social services were institutionalized, the powerful block of Southern Democrats made sure millions were excluded by default, as, for instance, when minimum wage laws largely excluded farm labor and other care work in which Black people were disproportionately employed at the time. When this exclusion strategy was no longer effective in light of historic developments, including the Cold War and the civil rights struggles that compelled the United States to align its domestic politics with its global pro-democracy/pro-equality rhetoric, the Southern Strategy helped maintain racial inequality by opening the way for a broad-based neoliberalism. The Southern Strategy served the goals of the neoliberal coalition of conservatives and free marketeers by opening new ways for the rich to retain or increase their wealth and for white supremacists to oppress minoritized people in an era when the law no longer allowed open segregation and race-based access to the benefits of the state and social life.

But as neoliberal policies squeezed the middle and working classes, the conditions were ripe for exactly the kind of anti-austerity, pro-racist politics offered by Trump. By bringing race explicitly into his political appeals, Trump was able to square the circle of neoliberal economics in the way racial capitalism had always done. The possibility of accommodation for the poor was tantalizingly offered (though his administration was too inept or uncaring to ever push those policies through), it being clear that these accommodations were accompanied by anti-BIPOC politics (for example, the forced separation of migrant children from their parents, the demonization of Black Lives Matter, and a trade war with China) and by massive reductions in regulation and taxation (such as opening up protected lands for mining and drilling, allowing oil pipeline expansions, and massively reducing taxes for the wealthy). We may well imagine that had he followed through on the possibilities opened by his big-government rhetoric, particularly of healthcare for all (especially valuable during the COVID-19 pandemic) and a robust program of infrastructure improvements (especially valuable in a time of economic dislocation due to the pandemic), he could have won the 2020 election.

Historically, government programs made changes that enabled a systemic preservation of the status quo. Even the monumental changes of the New Deal had been put forward to preserve the foundations of American capitalism in the wake of the threats posed by the 1930s Great Depression, and it had been popular with white socially conservative voters (an essential New Deal constituency), in contrast to what we might expect by listening to the rhetoric of small government that has dominated conservative politics in the wake of the 1960s Southern Strategy. Maxwell and Shields argue that as access to the benefits of the social grew outside the hegemonic group, "any government expenditure deemed as providing a leg up for African Americans was [now] understood only as an attack on whites in this zero-sum game." And, more tellingly, the "fixation of the South with small government and the accompanying rallying cry of state's rights developed only when the region seemingly lost power over the federal government."[56]

The Southern Strategy of mobilizing white ressentiment moved millions into the camp of Republican voters who actively worked to undermine the Keynesian interventionist state they formerly supported. The insincerity of their opposition to big government was obvious to anyone who considered the rise of the U.S. national debt and annual deficits under every Republican administration since the 1980s. Their hostility to big government, which was key to American neoliberalism's gains, was in reality aimed at the expansion of the social service state to people of color, women, and LGBTQ+ folx and thus at political equality. Supporting social exclusions and distancing themselves from rights claims made by people of color, women, and sexually minoritized populations opened the South not only to the Republican Party but also to neoliberalism. Decades later, Donald Trump, a nonreligious New

York Yankee whose closest family members are Jewish, was nevertheless able to develop a cultlike following even among the most reactionary southerners largely on the same kind of promises that populist politicians in Europe offer: to use the state's powers to resist globalization and to commit to not shrinking the state but to reserving and expanding its benefits for the right kind of white people.

Of course the category of whiteness is itself a deeply unstable classification, even if conservative politics are often built around protecting it. After the legal designation of slavery was eliminated in the nineteenth century and when the legal separations between the races were struck down in the twentieth, the only way to protect the system was through culture war fighting for white patriarchy and squashing its opposition (that is, anyone who does not support white male privilege).[57] So, if support for the U.S. social service state eroded as it began serving nonwhite people, we conclude that this erosion of support is not for the service state or for social welfare as such. It is an erosion of support for a service state that helps Black and Brown people. Today's racism builds on this base but takes shape through the circumstances surrounding the current dominant cultural and economic logics, which are the products of a deeply entrenched neoliberalism.

In this way we can understand that race, racism, and U.S. capital—always interrelated—work within the particular historic conditions of their present. In the neoliberal era, the erosion of the Keynesian economic state combined with the backlash by the "silent majority" against the successes of social justice movements (limited though they were) enabled an environment of resentment to flourish.[58] This resentment coalesced into a more generalized opposition to the idea of society as a whole and especially the idea of social obligation through laws and service. And this oppositional ideology and the accompanying governmentality have played no small role in neoliberal accumulation strategies redounding upward to the wealthiest people, also called "the 1 percent." This economic erosion of the 99 percent was exacerbated by the interchangeability of political parties through so-called third-way politics that were particularly popular in the 1990s and early 2000s and left the 99 percent with few alternative political directions. After all, the neoliberals' "*depoliticizing of economics* leads to the politicizing of everything else."[59] And because the 99 percent is a cross-gender, cross-race construction it has little traction among white people long used to their specific gender and race serving as key segments of their families' total "wages," especially those for whom race and gender are the only valuable elements of those wages.

According to anthropologist Dána-Ain Davis, neoliberalism hides racial inequality behind a more general capitalist inequality and then "reassign[s] identity-based biases to the private and personal spheres.'"[60] This elaborate construct shelters white grievance identity through what geographer Joshua Inwood calls the "neoliberal racial fix."[61] This contemporary racial fix builds from neoliberal politics and culture through to the economic conditions and racism that shape U.S. life. This is a neoliberal cultural logic that Wendy Brown argues "assaults" the very foundations of U.S. democracy and society: "White working-class and middle-class economic suffering and racialized rancor, far from distinct from these assaults, acquire voice and shape from them."[62] Thus, in their patriarchal form, these are the "angry white men" Michael Kimmel describes all around us, certainly in the white power circles we've referred to, but also on the roadways, the suburban soccer fields, and corporate offices.[63]

IMAGINING WHITE NEOLIBERAL COMMUNITY

Out of the social vacuum created by the neoliberal racial fix, one version of an imagined community seems to have gotten new life, and that is white racial identity. This form of imagined community expands the neoliberal family structure to a tribal level of kinship, albeit one based on a very loose and fungible notion of what can be whiteness. For Brenton Tarrant, the white power shooter in New Zealand, white consciousness—recognition of oneself as part of the tribal family of whiteness—is essential, no matter how ambiguous and arbitrary that designation might be. Tarrant sees the corrosiveness of individualism as destroying not just the racial family but also one's own immediate family: "There are myriad reasons behind the decline in fertility rates and the destruction of the traditional family unit. We must inevitably correct the disaster of hedonistic, nihilistic individualism." Later he returns to this theme of a "society of rampant nihilism, consumerism and individualism, where every individual is a competitor and the rights of the individual override all notions of responsibility. In this hell the individual is all and the race is worthless, something to rail against and use whenever possible, a power structure to climb, or topple." (As we will see in chapter 4, this echoes sentiments by white power novelists.) Though his rhetoric seems to contradict neoliberalism's traditional ideal of individualism, more importantly his solution reinforces the fetishized family on the levels of both nuclear and tribal racialism. Like others indoctrinated into the white power ideology, Tarrant sees "globalism" (which at times functions as code for "Jewish" conspirators), corporate capitalism (also labeled as Jewish), and democracy as antithetical to racial unity and even to survival: "Globalized capitalist markets are the enemy of racial autonomists. If an ethnocentric European future is to be achieved[,] global free markets and the trade of goods is to be discouraged at all costs." According to anti-fascist journalist and blogger Matthew N. Lyons, "Like most current-day white nationalists, Tarrant opposes neoliberal policies and globalized markets as a threat to European racial autonomy."[64]

Contrary to such assessments, we would argue that this white power worldview is actually congruent with neoliberal ideology, and that its apparent opposition to neoliberalism is easily reinscribed by neoliberals foregrounding ideology and policy that elevates the white patriarchal family. Political sociologist Christian Joppke similarly notes that what he calls the "new nationalism"—one oriented around (racialized) ethnic identity that is part of what we are calling white power ideology—"is on the one hand *reactive* and *oppositional* to neoliberalism, but, particularly in its statist incarnation, it has also *complemented* and even *incorporated* elements of neoliberalism, most importantly its rhetoric of 'responsibilizing' the individual."[65] Thus, El Paso Walmart shooter Patrick Crusius's manifesto specifically identifies corporate capitalism as the primary problem for creating what he sees as "America . . . rotting from the inside out." However, he is not against corporations outright: "Corporate America doesn't need to be destroyed, but just shown that they are on the wrong side of history. That if they don't bend, they will break."[66]

We find again that white power and neoliberalism are conjoined in the current historical moment despite their at times contradictory impulses. Their enshrining of the family—including the racial family—acts as something like a prime directive. Beyond that, as Tad Tietze, scholar of Anders Breivik's white nationalist violence, notes, apparent differences between neoliberalism and unabashedly authoritarian right-wing ideologies actually obscure much more fundamental commonalities. "In particular, both projects are comfortable with the exercise of coercive state power. . . . So while Breivik is critical of 'laissez-faire' ideologies, he is not opposed to free markets under the purview of a strong state."[67]

In the context of Breivik's convoluted thinking in his manifesto, Tietze emphasizes the openness of iconic neoliberal thinkers like Friedrich Hayek and Milton Friedman to strong states and authoritarian leaders—from neo-fascist dictators to constitutionalist authoritarians arising around the world throughout the neoliberal era—at least so they can initially create the conditions for a free market or maintain it in the face of market failures such as in 2008's global recession.[68] In fact, it is easy to forget that even Hayek himself was ambivalent about laissez-faire approaches since, as he put it, "The question whether the state should or should not 'act' or 'interfere' poses an altogether false alternative, and the term 'laissez faire' is a highly ambiguous and misleading description of the principles on which a liberal policy is based."[69] Indeed, Tietze maintains that the idea that economic liberalism is hostile to fascism arises because of the presumed "socialism" of national socialism. More accurate is a "lack of clear boundaries between economic liberalism and neoliberalism on one side, and far Right and fascist politics on the other."[70]

The story of neoliberalism has never quite been linear or straightforward. Against the backdrop of U.S. electoral politics, the story of American neoliberalism is not one of clear supporters and opponents.[71] In the United States these figures are most notably associated with white supremacy in a complex series of developments that are rooted in the very inception of the United States and the institutionalization of racial capitalism. White ethnonationalist populists—just like neoliberal economic fundamentalists and moral conservatives—are happy to accommodate a strong and wide-ranging government as long as its benefits accrue to whites. So perhaps it is more appropriate to think of *nationalism* or even *populism* in their racialized forms not as nationalism or populism per se, but rather as racial tribalism—in other words, a racialized ethnonationalism. Those who are embraced by such a structure are those who possess the racially "correct" identity.

Thus we return to the notion of family, taken here in its widening form to encompass those who identify as white. It's no surprise that one of the primary mantras of white power is expressed in Lane's "14 Words," which echoes ideas from William Pierce's *The Turner Diaries* that are then thematized in Harold Covington's Northwest novels. In Covington's *Freedom's Sons* (2011), which narrates the birth of the Northwest as a white utopia, one character proclaims, "We *want* to encourage teenaged marriage and pregnancy, since the overriding national imperative has to be that *there must be more of us*. Right now, White people under the age of 60 are only eight per cent of the planet's population, and White women of child-bearing age are less than three percent. We *have* to get those numbers up!"[72] Moreover, this reproduction of the white race requires conscious action to counteract the cultural programming by the sinister cabal: "The Jews literally stole the babies from our people's cradles, through abortion and feminism and a capitalist economy that forced women to work all their lives just to survive alongside men. We are going to fill those cradles up again."[73] From this perspective, the Jewish cabal (often figured as the banking interests of neoliberalism) orchestrated a conspiracy to lower white reproduction, stringing together capitalism with feminism. Moreover, in a white power utopia such as Covington's, the government actually plays the role of the welfare state by providing support and incentives to encourage the reproduction of the white race.[74]

The "we" referred to in Covington's proclamations is not just individual white people but the white community as a whole. In his landmark novel William Pierce, using the pen name Andrew Macdonald, previewed this call for racial survival in the face of racial apocalypse: "Our struggle is to secure the future of our race." "No race which neglects to insure its own survival, when the means for that survival are at hand, can be judged 'innocent,' nor can the penalty exacted against it be considered unjust, no matter how severe."[75] For white power figures like Pierce, Molyneaux, Lane, and Covington, whose work we will discuss in the next chapter, there is a vital need for white people to think of themselves as part of the white racial family, not simply to maintain hegemony as the majority of the population and the benefits of white privilege that accrue to that, but for survival from the "impending" racial apocalypse.

FOUR

The "Family" at the Core of
White Power Utopia

TO UNDERSTAND HOW THE CONTEMPORARY rise of white power col-
ludes with American neoliberal culture through the social technology of the
family (both nuclear and tribal), we turn to a selection of white power utopian novels that emphasize white ethnonationalism: *The Turner Diaries*
(1978) by William Luther Pierce (using the pseudonym Andrew Macdonald),
the neo-Nazi who formed the National Alliance; *White Empire* (2000) by
Kenneth Molyneaux, a devotee of the racist "religion" Creativity; *KD Rebel*
(2002) by David Lane, the widely influential white power ideologue most
noted for the "14 Words"; and *The Hill of the Ravens* (2003) by H. A. (Harold
Armstead) Covington, the neo-Nazi who, before his death in 2018, tirelessly
promoted white nationalism through his organization the Northwest Front.[1]
These four novels serve as tutor texts exemplifying the white power vision of
the revolution necessary to "free" white people from domination by multicultural ideology, racial diversity, sexual liberation, and all its other bogeymen, as well as its vision of the white ideal.

The most influential white power novel, *The Turner Diaries,* is predominantly concerned with white insurrection against the U.S. government leading to the creation of a partially glimpsed white power utopia, while *White
Empire*—the least well known of these texts—shows us what a full-fledged
white power utopia would look like under the auspices of the World Church
of the Creator and its self-proclaimed religion of whiteness. *The Hill of the
Ravens* also figures the accomplishment of a white utopia in considerable
detail, while *KD Rebel* offers a glimpse at the origins of white separatism
fighting for a white future. Through these texts, we can better understand
neoliberalism in relation to the United States' very long history of racial

capitalism and the white ethnonational utopian fantasies expressed by at least some proponents of white power.[2]

As part of the larger framework of racial capitalism, white power and neoliberalism are inextricably tied, anchored by the fetishization of the white heteropatriarchal family, which plays a dual role as both the traditional nuclear family and the tribal family of whiteness. As we will continue to argue in this chapter, neoliberalism is the most recent version of racial capitalism disenfranchising a large majority of Americans—of all races—and producing the conditions that enable white power to move toward the mainstream through the support of alienated white people suffering from economic hardships, thus making a new form of fascist white power attuned to the neoliberal era attractive. (It is no surprise that the four authors under consideration here all had or have ties to, or at least sympathy for, neo-Nazi fascism.) Indeed, the economic austerity manufactured by neoliberal policies enables white power ideologies to gain credibility by providing a scapegoat in the form of a racial "other"—a process that also occurred in earlier historical periods when race and racism were used to consolidate whiteness across economic gaps.

The more recent historical and economic conditions become clear when reading these and other white power utopian works, as they enact the affectivity that promotes white racial consciousness and the white backlash against racial justice and leftist notions of social progress. The neoliberal persona of *homo affectus* embodies that consciousness and backlash, operationalizing the rage that white power aims against the acceptable norms of multiracial and multicultural pluralism in play since at least the civil rights movement. Thus, utopia acts as a mechanism through which white consciousness can activate the ideal of whiteness as a racial tribalism, leading to the fantasy of a white ethnostate centered around the family—a construct whose affective power is not just imaginary but deeply ideological and rooted in white power ideologies.[3]

WILLIAM PIERCE'S INFLUENTIAL CALL TO ARMS

Described by the Southern Poverty Law Center (SPLC) as the United States' most important neo-Nazi during his lifetime, William Luther Pierce (1933–2002) had a long career as a National Socialist, joining various white power groups such as George Lincoln Rockwell's American Nazi Party and eventually founding his own group, National Alliance, which was one of the more influential and even commercially successful organizations of its kind, capitalizing as it did on white power music ("hatecore"). He established his own compound in West Virginia, which acted as a base for his various activities. As a former physics professor with a doctorate, Pierce was somewhat of the intellectual stalwart of white power, and he went out of his way to distance himself from "rednecks" and "good ol' boys" in his writing.[4] He also disparaged other white power groups and tried to portray his own version of white supremacy that has become part of what we refer to as white power.[5]

His novel *The Turner Diaries* is uniquely influential among American white power adherents. It inspired the likes of Robert Matthews and his group The Order, which included David Lane, to mimic some of its strategies to start a race war in the 1980s (for example, the group drew its name and strategies from the novel and committed robberies to finance its white power activities). Later, Timothy McVeigh and his cohort drew on Pierce's novel in detail for the Oklahoma City bombing in 1995. One estimate of the lasting influence of *The Turner Diaries* concludes that white terrorist readers of the novel committed more than two hundred murders.[6] Meditating on the book's widespread embrace in white power circles, extremism expert J. M. Berger argues that because the novel does not promote a singular ideology, many white people of different persuasions are able to draw inspiration from the text, from hardcore activists to run-of-the-mill white chauvinists.[7] McVeigh was one case of someone intimate with the novel and who saw white power members as his "brothers in arms," even if he lacked clear ties to a specific group.[8]

There is no doubt that the book has been and remains an important touchstone for white power advocates and strikes a particular chord with those who fear anything from the loss of Second Amendment rights to the waning of white dominance in nations with an influx of nonwhite immigration, high nonwhite fertility rates, and the rise of progressive social equality—in short, those who ascribe to the "great replacement" theory. Pierce's racial views, put into narrative form in *The Turner Diaries,* can be summed up in a proclamation from a National Alliance web page:

> After the sickness of "multiculturalism," which is destroying America, Britain, and every other Aryan nation in which it is being promoted, has been swept away, we must again have a racially clean area of the earth for the further development of our people. . . . We will not be deterred by the difficulty or temporary unpleasantness involved, because we realize that it is absolutely necessary for our racial survival.[9]

What is significant in *The Turner Diaries* is the bemoaning of the loss of a "pure" nation (as if any nation ever was or could be) and its call for violence to ensure the survival of the white race (as if it actually were threatened with extinction). These white ethnonational fears are projected in all the novels we discuss here, not to mention in real-life calls for some kind of nationalized racial purity (of which Covington's Northwest Front organization, dedicated to actualizing the white ethnonational fantasy, is only one example). As discussed previously, this fantasy does not, on the surface, fit well with neoliberal ideology in its globalist orientation toward promoting open borders for markets and free-floating entrepreneurial individuals whose race is irrelevant. And yet, apart from the globalization of capital, white power aspires to its own form of globalism in a worldwide community of whiteness exemplified in white mass shooters in various countries name-checking each other (as discussed earlier), William Pierce's penchant for Eastern European wives, the Creativity Alliance website's availability in several European languages, David Lane's homage to Russia in *KD Rebel* ("the salvation of the White race would come from Russia"), and the wide transnational distribution of texts and ideas like French author Jean Raspail's *Le Camp des Saints* (1973), pushed in the United States by Trump advisors like Steve Bannon and Stephen Miller.[10]

Moreover, with its ability to suture conflicting strands of ideology, neoliberalism can be and has been articulated in ethnonational terms; while promoting neoliberalism for itself and the world, "America" still maintains and asserts its national specificity (which can, has been, and continues to be racialized as white—most recently with Trumpism), even as national borders become increasingly eroded in the world of global trade. Although Pierce's form of white power intentionally avoids participation in politics—and, as we've discussed previously, disparages capitalism (similar to Molyneaux, Lane, and Covington)—its primarily affective appeal speaks persuasively to neoliberal subjects as they confront neoliberal capitalism's attack on working-class jobs.

As the title suggests, *The Turner Diaries* takes the form of diary entries written by one of the white guerrillas on the front lines of the revolution and, similar to Margaret Atwood's *The Handmaid's Tale* (1985), it looks back at the events from a hundred years later.[11] Although the characters often rail against the U.S. government (called "the System") for disenfranchising whites, it is the state's pro-racial policies under the influence of a Jewish cabal based in Israel rather than its intrusion into citizens' lives that cannot be tolerated. The revolutionary group in the novel—known as the Organization, with an internal elite cadre named the Order—has neither time nor patience for either the progressive left or the conservative right (or even libertarians) in its race war: "Of all the segments of the population from which we had hoped to draw new members, the 'conservatives' and 'right wingers' have been the biggest disappointment. They are the world's worst conspiracy-mongers—and also the world's greatest cowards. In fact, their cowardice is exceeded only by their stupidity"—how prescient of the beginning of the 2020s. Referring to one character, the novel disparagingly describes how his "were the motivations of a libertarian, the sort of self-centered individual who sees the basic evil in government as a limitation on free enterprise."[12] The bottom line for Pierce's philosophy in the novel is that whites must band together and recognize their identity *as white* rather than as discrete individuals defending their own individual liberties, and this white consciousness crosses borders, dovetailing with neoliberalism's global aspirations.

Pierce saw himself as following the philosophy of historian Brooks Adams, who belonged to the famous family that produced historically important figures, including two presidents and a world-renowned author. Using Brooks Adams's dichotomy of "spiritual man" and "economic man," Pierce eschews the notion of the individual as an essentially economic figure (a version of which neoliberalism valorizes), turning instead to the spiritual man who has pride and fundamental concern for "his" race (a version of what we have described as the neoliberal *homo affectus*).[13] While the autonomous individual is often projected as the key social unit in neoliberalism, we have shown how the social unit can simultaneously be converted by neoliberals into the family, in which the lone patriarch rules: the family becomes merely an extension of the individual's privatized interests. Moreover, this emphasis on the family as the fundamental human resource gets expanded in white power ideologies to a more tribal notion of family, that is, the white racial family.

The necessity of raising white racial consciousness is the primary emphasis in this novel as well as for real-world white extremists and forms the basis for their white utopianism. As the Marxist literary and cultural critic Fredric Jameson argues in *The Political Unconscious* (1981), a primary form of utopia is class consciousness, an expression of collectivity that applies to any ideology and any type of class consciousness, whether dominant or subaltern.[14] *The Turner Diaries* operates with precisely this generic sense of utopia as collective consciousness, in this case racial: "We are forging the nucleus of a new society, a whole new civilization, which will rise from the ashes of the old."[15] As Pierce turns toward what he sees as the collapse of American society, race war (both physical and statistical) and the creation of a white ethnonational utopia are the solution:

> This whole evacuation amounts to a new form of warfare: demographic war. Not only are we getting the non-Whites out of our area, but we're doing two additional things which should pay off for us later by getting them into the enemy's area: we're overloading the System's already strained economy, and we're making life next to intolerable for the Whites in the border areas.[16]

The racial and ethnic cleansing includes the ominous "Day of the Rope," during which white people allied with nonwhite or Jewish people are lynched and left out in public wearing signs announcing, "I betrayed my race." While this allows Pierce to take revenge on academics from whom he presumably became alienated because of his racist views, it is women who engage in miscegenation that the novel holds up for particular shame:[17]

> There are many thousands of hanging female corpses like that in this city tonight, all wearing identical placards around their necks. They are the White women who were married to or living with Blacks, with Jews, or with other non-White males.
> There are also a number of men wearing the I-defiled-my-race placard, but the women easily outnumber them seven or eight to one.[18]

Pierce's efforts at raising white consciousness apply directly to white women, who play an important role in constructing whiteness as a collective in both the diegetic and the real world.

We know that white power groups emphasize women's roles in several essential ways. Reproduction is obviously central. As discussed in chapter 2, sociologist Kathleen Blee learned in her interviews of women in hate groups that the role of wife and mother as producer of white children is crucial for what we call white power groups; they thus become powerful symbols of whiteness, its future, and even its vulnerability.[19] Indeed, the role of white women as victims has historically been central to the narrative of white supremacy in the form of white male warriors defending white women against Black male aggression, characterizations reiterated in white power. Sometimes white women can also play the role of race warrior if necessary. But whichever role they play, race consciousness is key. In Pierce's novel the protagonist's girlfriend "began acquiring a sense of racial identity, overcoming a lifetime of brainwashing aimed at reducing her to an isolated human atom in a cosmopolitan chaos," after discovering her female roommate raped and murdered by a Black man.[20] This standard trope of white supremacy in which Black men rape white women has consistently authorized acts of white terror throughout U.S. history and is littered throughout this novel, occurring at least eighteen times. *The Turner Diaries* essentially updated this and other themes and strategies of white supremacy for the era of white power.

There can be no question that Pierce's vision of the ideal is patriarchal. After all, he viewed liberalism as "an essentially feminine, submissive world-view" (as mentioned previously, a view echoed by Breivik), and in the novel he claimed that "'women's lib' was a form of mass psychosis which broke out during the last three decades of the Old Era. Women affected by it denied their femininity and insisted that they were 'people,' not 'women.' This aberration was promoted and encouraged by the System as a means of dividing our race against itself."[21] Underscoring a sentiment that comes up later in Molyneaux, Lane, and Covington's texts, Pierce claims that the ethno-future envisioned by white power advocates requires women to focus on their sacred duty of reproducing the race. Indeed, he claims that this focus actually ensures a better treatment of women: "Although unmarried female members are theoretically 'equal' to male members, in that they are subject to the same discipline, our women are actually cherished and protected to a much larger degree than women in the general society are."[22]

Thus, by eschewing individualism, capitalism, and democracy (the latter of which the novel disparages as "liberal-Jewish"), the text actually works its way back to an emphasis on the white tribal family.[23] And after expansive and violent acts of ethnic cleansing, this and other white power utopias invoke powerful affective ties binding the white "class" together. Racial consciousness overrides all other political, economic, and social concerns. Given that Pierce was more interested in how whites could revolt and that he remained unconcerned with the details of how a white utopia would work in both *The Turner Diaries* and his other novel, *Hunter* (1989), we can only conclude that for him utopia is precisely the idealization of whiteness as collectivity and consciousness rather than a social or economic blueprint for a noncapitalist system of social reproduction. At the heart of his utopian vision is the white heteropatriarchal family—and its expansion into the global white tribal family—that ensures biological reproduction of the white race and serves as a countersymbol to social justice movements. The idealization of this family in neoliberalism reinforces this rhetoric and ideology, thus supercharging the confluence of race and capitalism.

Information on (the "Reverend") Kenneth Molyneaux is difficult to find apart from his allegiance to the Creativity Movement, formerly known as the World Church of the Creator (WCOTC) (led by Matt Hale from 1996) and, before that, as the Church of the Creator (founded in 1973 by Ben Klassen).[24] The SPLC describes the group as a "self-styled religious organization" whose only theological tenets are "the inherent superiority and 'creativity' of the white race."[25] They identify the WCOTC's ideology as neo-Nazi and add that it has broken down into scattered groups that still promote Creativity, the religion itself, but in a less organized and unified way. Not satisfied with Lane's "14 Words," Creators (as they refer to themselves) display their own "23 Words" motto on their website: "What is good for the White Race is of the Highest Virtue; / What is bad for the White Race is the Ultimate Sin."[26]

Despite the lack of available information about Molyneaux, we can grasp his ideological commitments through his deep identification with the beliefs and activities of the WCOTC. Officially, the group has distanced itself from neo-Nazism, but it still promotes "a pan-White racialism, or 'racial socialism.'"[27] Molyneaux's official biography describes his transformation into a racist:

> During my high school days, I became racially aware as I noticed the vast differences between Whites and [n-----s]. I realized that I preferred my own Race while abhorring the obnoxious behavior and stupidity of the inferior blacks. My high school was mostly White but there was a large population of blacks so that I could see first hand that the notion of equality was simply a fairy tale. Being in honor and AP classes, I saw first hand the superiority of the White Race as my classes were overwhelmingly White.[28]

Although this anecdotal passage disregards the structural and institutional racism that affects educational demographics, the sentiment can easily be reified in the experience of other, and even less extreme, white people. Molyneaux goes on to describe his embrace of neo-Nazism along with acceptance of the belief in a Jewish conspiracy and his indoctrination into the WCOTC.

In his history of the WCOTC, political scientist George Michael explains that Klassen led far-right and white racist organizations away from Christianity toward a self-described "theology" according to which the white race is destined to take over the entire world and eliminate all Jewish people and "mud people" (i.e., nonwhites).[29] In *The White Man's Bible*, originally published in 1981, Ben Klassen lays out four dimensions of Creativity in its practice of "Salubrious Living" encapsulated in the saying "a Sound Mind in a Sound Body in a Sound Society in a Sound Environment." This program includes what is essentially a vegan diet, regular exercise, interaction with "our White Racial Comrades," "healthy expression of our sexual instincts," rejection of medicinal drugs, and fasting.[30] This salubrious lifestyle becomes a refrain in Molyneaux's book.

For Creators, the racial identity of whiteness supersedes national identities, and the WCOTC provides the only means to unify the white race against its enemies. The group's "Sixteen Commandments" requires whites to "assure and secure for all time the existence of the White Race upon the face of this planet" (echoing Lane's "14 Words"), "populate the lands of this earth with White people exclusively," treat "the inferior colored races [as] our deadly enemies" (especially Jewish people), and, central to our argument here, "honor, protect and venerate the sanctity of the family unit."[31] Once again, hegemonic neoliberalism's fundamental social unit, which coincides with white power advocates' emphasis on reproducing the white race, and tribal loyalty are key to the ideology. Klassen was no stranger to others espousing similar white power ideologies, including Pierce and Covington, both of whom he communicated with despite antagonism with each.[32] Several acts of deadly violence have been attributed to terrorists (or would-be terrorists) influenced by the WCOTC, including various murder sprees and plans to assassinate high-profile Black leaders including Al Sharpton, Louis Farrakhan, and even Public Enemy's Chuck D and N.W.A.'s Eazy-E[33]—all in the name of "accelerating" the race war, as we see with other white power ideologues and terrorists. And although the WCOTC was and remains a fairly small-scale fringe movement and is currently fragmented, "it has had a disproportionate influence on the broader racialist movement,"[34] perhaps most famously with the term *RaHoWa*.

Molyneaux eventually produced a white power utopian novel entitled *White Empire*. The affective center of this novel, which is based around a masculinist power fantasy of the white race as all-powerful and all-intelligent, aligns with Lane's *KD Rebel* and similar projects with what we can only describe as the emotional depth of a fourteen-year-old boy. The beginning of the novel bears this out: "A sleek F-35 fighter aircraft glided silently through the summer air somewhere over the jungles of Africa."[35] The pilot of the plane is characterized as having "a strong jaw and powerful cheek bones to match his powerful frame. John loved the outdoors and being in shape and his tanned, muscular body showed that he was in excellent physical condition"—evidence of his salubrious living.[36] The titular White Empire has already emerged in the near-future setting, encompassing the "Creator States of America," Canada, England, Europe, and the conquered lands of Mexico, South America, the Middle East, and North Africa.[37] The empire is at war with what remains of the rest of the world, propelled by the superiority of the white race—and especially white men—in science and technology, as well as physical activity and moral competence; as the narrator tells us in the first paragraph, "Everything in the White Empire was supreme."[38] The White Empire steamrolls over anything that might "dare to defy" it, as mentioned repeatedly throughout the novel. Any form of resistance by Jewish or "mud people" is quickly squashed by the White Empire's military, its victories always attributed to its natural superiority. Incorporating another Creativity catchphrase, one character refers to "our holy mission to make this a Whiter, Brighter World."[39]

Of course, this fantasy is structurally supported by demonizing the enemies of the white empire: "The [n-----s] were scantily clad, wearing what looked like grass skirts that clearly showed the backward nature of these people. The natives were violently gyrating and contorting their bodies in a grotesque fashion and John wondered if they actually considered what they were doing to be dancing."[40] The book describes Jewish people as "hideous," cowardly, parasitic, and having "whiny voices" (presumably in contrast to the deep, strong voices of the white male characters).[41] Although the author characterizes Asians as being a stronger opponent than Africans and South Americans in the White Empire's conquest of the world, he also describes them as "mainly a hedonistic lot which didn't even tend to take care of their wounded despite their bloodied bodies laying close nearby" and having a "bizarre and animalistic nature."[42]

In contrast to the rest of the world, the White Empire constitutes a racist utopia. The white utopia originates in the United States around the year 2030 (or 47 AC in the novel's diegesis), led by the WCOTC and the magnetic power of Creativity.[43] The time before the establishment of the White Empire is termed "the Doom Age," when things like multiculturalism, equality (racial, gender, and sexual), democracy, and Christianity prevented the white race from gaining racial consciousness and realizing their superiority. Moreover, those qualities created a miserable life for everyone, especially white people: "People living in the Doom Age dreamt of happiness but here it was commonplace. The majority of the citizens of the White Empire never knew of despair, sadness, or misfortune in their own lives. The only way they even knew the meaning of such words was by reading the history of such horrible times such as the Doom Age."[44] Belying Creativity's racial socialist ideology, everyone is provided with enough food as long as they work to contribute to the empire.[45] Also, "There was no work considered menial as everything needed to be done. Therefore, there was no class warfare between people but there was healthy competition that encouraged everyone to do the best possible job they could and promote the interests of the White Race in everything they did."[46] As one character explains to her lover, recalling Klassen's creed, "Now, we are in a golden age of prosperity and the four dimensions of a sound mind, sound body, sound society, and a sound environment are spread across our great White Empire."[47]

On a quotidian level, this utopia (similar to Covington's) has some characteristics associated with other utopias, especially those that are left/progressive: the banning of cars with combustion engines, organic farming, reverence for nature, temperance, a robust cultural life, and salubrious living.[48] Even with the restrictions and directives of a strong state governing daily life, "this wasn't to say that no one had any fun or any hobbies as indeed they did, but it was rightfully regarded that [white] society as a whole was far more important than one single individual."[49] Nevertheless, it is clear that the society operates in a fairly regimented fashion, based on the authoritarian, centralizing force of the religion itself and especially its charismatic leader, Ben Klassen. As in other white power utopias, the inhabitants are able to live happy, fulfilling lives while also putting the race above individual concerns. This, of course, is facilitated by the affective power of class (or, in this case, racial) consciousness as described by Jameson.

And it is precisely this racial consciousness, embedded in the teachings of Creativity, that enables the utopia. Somewhat similar to Pierce, Creators imbue the fetish object of a pure white race with magical qualities that will bring a smoothly functioning society into being. The novel does everything it can to enshrine Klassen and the WCOTC's principles discussed above. In one instance this takes the form of a traditional recitation of "the five fundamental beliefs of Creativity":

We believe that our Race is our Religion. We believe that the White Race is Nature's Finest. We believe that racial loyalty is the highest of all honors, and racial treason is the worst of all crimes. We believe that what is good for the White Race is the highest virtue, and what is bad for the White Race is the ultimate sin. We believe the one and only, true and revolutionary White Racial Religion—Creativity—is the only salvation for the White Race. RAHOWA![50]

As Michael makes clear in his study of the group, Klassen and other key figures in the WCOTC took the politics-based principles of other white supremacist ideologies like Nazism and invested them with an even higher level of emotional power by structuring them as a religion, which was later propagated through cultural forms like white power music. Fusing the irrational exuberance of politics (witness any political rally) with the deep and transcendent commitment offered by religion is one way to provide the glue necessary to create the racial unity necessary for Creativity to thrive. Indeed, in Molyneaux's utopia all politicians were required to be ministers of the church. This effectively combines the state and church so that only the best interests of the white race are promoted.[51]

Creativity shares the prime directive embedded in Lane's "14 Words." Racial reproduction is key to the survival of the white race, which is at risk from the threats typically feared in white power ideologies: an imbalance of low fertility rates for whites and high fertility rates for nonwhites; nonwhite immigration to lands where whites predominate; miscegenation; the Jewish conspiracy to diminish the supremacy of the white race through politics, mass media, and other means; and so on. As the novel states, "Being fruitful and multiplying was a basic premise in the religion of Creativity and immortality was possible, in a metaphoric way, by having a family and continuing the long golden chain of the White Race. Having children was a major and lasting contribution to the White Race."[52] While a kind of voluntary eugenics ensures that the best and brightest are produced, the citizens dream of having as many children as possible and divorce has become a thing of the past.[53] And, as with all the other white power utopias we look at, and as with white power in general, consolidation of "traditional family" structures and the heteropatriarchy is fundamental to the purification and perpetuation of whiteness. Not surprisingly, it is the women who care for the children at home (as exemplified by the main character's wife) while the men go off to fight in the wars and conquer the world.[54]

These stereotypical gender roles are rife throughout the text. The casual performance of gender takes us back to an "ideal" rooted in an era that passed long ago: "John gazed longingly at the beautiful woman that walked femininely towards him with the gracefulness of a ballerina dancer"; "Marie, unlike John, did not struggle against her tears."[55] These roles are further solidified in mass media like film, as in this case in which a female character speaks with her male lover: "I found a movie that we both should like. It is an adventurous romance. It has the gallivanting spirit of the hero that you will no doubt enjoy combined with the emotional aspects of love that will satiate myself."[56] Even when little girls are shown to participate in activities typified as masculine (like sports), they are safe in their traditional gender identities.[57] These performances and the structure of the family emerge from an almost biological essentialism that is very familiar:

> Bickering and fighting between married couples was quite infrequent as the Empire promoted good marriages through education. This education pointed out the obvious facts that men and women are different and have different needs so cooperation between the two parties was essential with the individual with the most talent in an area working in that area. Usually, women were more able in raising the children and men were more suited to providing for the family and, as such, that was the norm in the White Empire.[58]

With the family social unit safely ensconced in the White Empire, the biological reproduction of the white race is ensured.

The novel illustrates what cultural critic Henry Giroux has argued is true of neoliberalism: it eschews democracy and the good of the people as a whole, and it makes fascism, misogyny, and xenophobia part of a militaristic national identity serving the white race.[59] Moreover, neoliberalism creates the conditions for the populist turn toward a strong state through what political scientist David Lebow calls "inverted fascism" in the rise of Trumpism: neoliberalism produces a populace susceptible to the market rationalization of society and the destruction of social support; this makes an authoritarian demagogue attractive or even desirable, one who sows social confusion and suspicion (even conspiracy theories) rather than using the force of the state to make people act in the desired way. The immigrant ("illegal" or otherwise) becomes the particular racialized other and becomes the scapegoat against which white people constitute themselves as the legitimate citizens of the state under an authoritarian figure.[60] In fact, neoliberalism needs a strong leader or state to ensure the continuation of the market economy, especially in the midst of social chaos. Thus, we see a special affinity in neoliberalism for the type of fascism pictured in some of these white power utopias.

In *White Empire* the authoritarian figure is represented by both the religion of Creativity and Klassen. "Mud people" become the scapegoats. It is no surprise that when one of the main characters is asked what past political regime he would choose to live under, he responds, "While I admire the intelligent and creative Greeks and respect the practical bringers of law, order, and grand architecture of Rome, I think I would choose to be a citizen of National Socialist Germany."[61] Thus, as we have argued previously, a strong state and a full-fledged authoritarian leader can optimize neoliberal priorities, such as those advocated in Molyneaux's racialist socialism (as well as in Covington's Northwest Republic, discussed below). In other words, the national/racial socialism we find in many white power utopias is not antithetical to neoliberalism. A fascist political state can be complementary with economic neoliberalism, which also created the historical conditions for the rise of white power.[62]

DAVID LANE'S FANTASY OF THE PROTO-UTOPIA OF WHITENESS

David Lane (1938–2007) was not only known as an author but was himself a white power activist and leader. An ethno-terrorist with ties to both the KKK and neo-Nazism, he belonged to the white power group The Order. As we have discussed previously, he is best known today for coining the white power slogan the "14 Words": "We must secure the existence of our people and a future for white children." Lane left behind a great deal of other writing, which he produced while incarcerated for a string of crimes, including participating in the assassination of Jewish radio personality Alan Berg in 1984 and a $3.6 million heist of an armored car, both as a member of The Order.[63] Lane became a martyr for the cause when he was sent to prison in 1985 for what would effectively be a life sentence. While in prison he continued to develop his white power thinking and writing, and the SPLC has dubbed him "one of the most important ideologues of white supremacy."[64] He and his wife, whom he met and married while behind bars, started their own publishing organization called 14 Word Press to release his work until his death in 2007. Notably, Lane published *88 Precepts,* his statement of what he dubbed "natural law," which included such decrees as "No race of people can indefinitely continue their existence without territorial imperatives in which to propagate, protect and promote their own kind."[65]

He became an avowed Wotanist (or Odinist), and he developed his own version of the Nordic religion called Wotansvolk because he said Norse mythologies were the most appropriate for white people, who need a Viking warrior mentality for their struggle. He presented this Viking mentality in action in *KD Rebel,* a near-future novella about a white separatist revolutionary group living in western U.S. states in a territory they call Kinsland. From their white power homeland they stage raids on the System, which, in a nod to *The Turner Diaries,* is their name for the United States, now a mostly mixed-race nation due to open borders, miscegenation, and official antiwhite legislation.

KD Rebel details a few weeks in the lives of two Kinslanders as they raid the Denver metro area, kill a grotesque Jewish strip bar owner and a hedonistic white couple who support miscegenation, and abduct three young and of course beautiful white women who, after they are tested and found to be free of incurable STDs, undergo a "reeducation" process. They read Nietzsche and Spengler and learn that "a White man named Edison invented electric lighting, another White man named Alexander Bell invented the telephone system, and Cleopatra was a White woman."[66]

Because their abductors are so handsome and do not rape them even though they constantly remind the women that it is their right as warriors to do so, the women come to understand the necessity of the white power struggle and the superiority of these strong, handsome men. As the lead character, Trebor (an honorific anadrome for his fellow Order member, Robert Jay Matthews), says to himself when he looks at a couple of beautiful white strippers he is about to kidnap, "He would have to be harsh and ruthless with re-education and discipline, which wasn't his nature with women. Yet he could not bear the thought of their genetic beauty not being passed on."[67] In keeping with his "14 Words," Lane is obsessed with white procreation, and thus family units become the fundamental building block of Kinslander society. Importantly, however, the Kinslanders are tied by Aryan blood to the larger kin of the white race that supposedly hasn't been despoiled by miscegenation. So, while *The Turner Diaries* presents itself as the blueprint to the "racial holy war" called for by the WCOTC and others, *KD Rebel* shows the shift in focus to the family as the machine that will ensure the future of the white race in an early form of the white ethnonational state (an idea that is fleshed out in Molyneaux's and especially in Covington's novels).

The Kinslanders live in communities where much activity is done in common. People have their own possessions and live in their own homes, but these are built by everyone together and furnished by visiting a bombed-out village and stealing the furniture of the previous residents. Without exchange of money, the community comes together to help the injured. Children are educated in common. The women often live polygamously as sister-wives, supposedly so that the white race can reproduce more quickly; they are taught not to be jealous of the other women but to see themselves as united in a common cause. Men are the paterfamilias and women and children their property, while women are entrusted with the responsibilities of social reproduction—childcare, schooling, health care. The model that arises, then, is of a homophobically patriarchal family united by the desire to promote the white race. So ultimately, and unsurprisingly, theirs is a deeply conservative family model that fits well with the neoconservatism of figures such as Irving Kristol. Even though this model of the family is presented in what might be considered a leftist communitarian form, it also aligns with the fascistic strain that runs throughout all these white power novels because, even in its embryonic form, the white ethnostate still provides centralized social services and engages in quasi-military activity (the armed raids outside Kinsland). This strict order and narcissistic moral structure contrast with the everyday world in the System, which is a multicultural morass in which people are lacking in relevant purpose and morals.

Perhaps what is most compelling about this text for those who embrace white power is precisely the alternative that Lane provides—as do Pierce, Molyneaux, and Covington—in the fantasy of a pure racial whiteness that can be collectivized and given a clear purpose: the biological and social reproduction of the white race. Again, we see the fundamentally neoliberalized affective work that these white power utopias engage in through *homo affectus*. It is no surprise that feminist scholar Sara Ahmed begins her essay "Affective Economies" with an epigraph from the website of Aryan Nations, the white power organization widely influential until the early 2000s, that extols love as the primary motivation of white nationalists—the love, that is, to hate the racial other: "*Together we hate, and hate is what makes us together.*"[68] Here, and in the other white power novels we discuss, racial affect performs the work of utopia, providing a seemingly stable identity and the social glue to suture together subjects that might otherwise be alienated or disaffected.

Although, in real life, neoliberalism has evolved to provide the economic structure in the United States since the 1970s, it—and capitalism generally— does *not* provide social stability for whites or anyone else. White power does promise to stabilize identity and life for those whites who are angry about their economic dispossession and, moreover, provides clear enemies with which to engage, whereas neoliberalism does not. Nevertheless, the shared emphasis on the traditional heteropatriarchal family shows the convergence between neoliberalism and white power.

THE NORTHWEST TERRITORIAL IMPERATIVE
AND THE WHITENESS OF UTOPIA

Harold Armstead Covington (1953–2018) was also a neo-Nazi, styling himself a mercenary in Rhodesia—itself a place of mythical significance within white power circles, where referencing it has come to be an insider stand-in for swastikas or rebel flags.[69] He was connected to the Greensboro massacre in 1979, during which members of the Communist Workers' Party and Black protestors were killed or injured by the Klan and the American Nazi Party. He eventually designated himself the voice of what had become known as the Northwest Territorial Imperative: a utopian plan—"eutopian" only for white racists—to found a separate nation for whites somewhere in the northwestern part of the United States. Covington rebranded this "the Northwest Front," complete with a fully developed website designed to recruit "Aryans" through various media (podcasts and pictures of white people smiling and embracing each other against what can only be called "Mayberry, USA" backgrounds) and even traditional, if satirical, clichés ("as American as apple pie").[70]

In all of Covington's activities, there is reason to believe that his roles were mostly nonphysical and on the sidelines, even as he presented himself as an active soldier and leader.[71] His most recent claim to fame was being referenced in the manifesto accompanying Dylann Roof's 2015 mass shooting at the Emanuel AME Church in Charleston, about which Covington said it was "a preview of coming attractions" even as he denounced the lone shooter.[72] But Roof's own words explaining his actions summarize the beliefs embedded in all white power rhetoric addressing people of color while reflecting a belief in white patriarchal solidarity: "*Y'all* are raping *our* white women. *Y'all* are taking over the world."[73] As mentioned above, these fears about the rape of white women by nonwhites, or even consensual romantic relationships between the two, are a constant refrain in all these white power utopias and in white power ideologies in general, with obvious antecedents going back to the various incarnations of the KKK but also to the origins of slavery in the United States.

Covington's particular vision of the Northwest Territorial Imperative and how it might come into being is laid out in his Northwest series of five novels. *The Hill of the Ravens* narrates the white utopian enclave called the Northwest American Republic (NAR), which spans Idaho, Oregon, Washington, Wyoming, Northern California, western Montana, Alberta, British Columbia, and Alaska.[74] Below the NAR lies "Aztlan [*sic*]," which includes Southern California, sections of Colorado, Utah, Arizona, New Mexico, and southern and western Texas. (The region is named for the symbolic and mythical homeland for Chicanx activists especially in the late 1960s, but also sensationalized by the media as an example of the immigrant reconquest of the U.S. Southwest.)[75] The novel presents a number of utopian characteristics to appeal to heteropatriarchal advocates of white power ethnonationalism:

- returning to racial restrictions on immigration
- allowing only male jurors
- instituting English as the only legal and acceptable language
- reinstating arranged marriages and "the traditional household with the breadwinning husband and father as the head of the family and the wife and mother as the heart"[76]
- expunging Jewish people and nonwhites
- installing a "ruling élite, for such is the nature of human society"[77]
- making citizenship hierarchical through military/political service and marriage and childbirth for women
- reviving lynching[78]
- ensuring the existence of and purifying the white race
- abolishing capitalism

The Hill of the Ravens is a clear response to the perceived vulnerability of whites who face the threat of nonwhite minorities in the United States and the "flood" of nonwhite immigrants. Thus, the utopian desire expressed in the novel reveals a sense of frustration and disenfranchisement of all white people as a revolutionary social class, especially those who are economically disenfranchised by neoliberalism. While the antipathy toward capitalism—also expressed by Pierce—seems to contradict the essence of neoliberalism as a capitalist formation, what we have tried to outline in this book as a whole is that neoliberalism won't hesitate to capitalize on the affectivity of white power to consolidate a political base (as seen with Trumpism). At the same time, neoliberalism has also played a role in manufacturing a class of dispossessed white people who can redirect their anger at that dispossession toward figures like nonwhite immigrants and others who supposedly take advantage of social welfare in the United States.

Notable in the above list is the emphasis on the "traditional" heteropatriarchal family as the primary unit of "the *volk*," a unit that "had once more become reality in the Northwest."[79] In addition to the "14 Words" appearing in the text, there is also government intervention into family planning:

> In the hall just outside the principal's office, Don glanced over the bulletin board and saw a large pink pastel flyer posted from the school's guidance counselor. "SENIOR GIRLS—Is The Marriage Track Right For You?" it read. "Under the new Family Enhancement Act passed by Parliament in January, you can now earn C-1 citizenship on marriage and a promotion to two-vote B category on the birth of your first child!"[80]

Women become baby machines and are rewarded for their contribution to the social reproduction of the white race with more political power in the form of doubling the value of their votes, and the individual family unit functions not in isolation but as inextricable from the larger family of whiteness. In fact, one of the "Ten Principles of National Socialist Thought" is "LOVE YOUR BROTHERS AND SISTERS. You owe your existence to your racial family; let your love of them be your overriding passion in life."[81]

In the Northwest novels, of which *The Hill of the Ravens* represents the utopia most fully fleshed out, survival is understood as the survival of the white race (loosely described as "Aryans") against its many "others," including anyone considered to be nonwhite, but especially Jewish people (in the figure of the Zionist Occupied Government [ZOG]) and, most often, Black people. Likely based on Covington's roots as a neo-Nazi, the state in this novel is quite intrusive and actively intervenes in people's lives. Covington's utopia does not share the fetishization of small government and reduction of social services that neoliberal ideology theoretically champions (see chapter 2). In fact, the government is decidedly large, though with touches of libertarianism (no income tax, religious freedom), and provides utilities (featuring a "broadcast rotational power grid that allows Northwesters to pluck their heat and light and sound out of the very air"), fashion trends (nostalgically drawn from the 1930s and even the 1890s: "reintroducing leg-of-mutton sleeves and long lace-up boots for women as well as bowler hats, sweeping moustaches, sideburns and high winged collars with cravats instead of ties for men"), public schooling, "Life Grants from the state," and extensive public transportation.[82] Covington's antipathy to democracy makes room for his predilection for the fascism of national socialism to inform his vision of the white utopia. In a description of *The Hill of the Ravens,* he presents his preferred political form for that vision: "a realistic form of authoritarian but participatory government."[83] Like Lane and Molyneaux, Covington was not averse to the need for a strongman to lead in the transition to white utopia from "politically correct" multicultural democracy—with all of what Pierce, Molyneaux, Lane, and Covington would consider its supposed social chaos resulting from race mixing. Unlike Pierce, Covington wasn't satisfied with the simple ideal of racial homogeneity and strove to describe how that society should operate. As he put it, he was trying to provide the "cover of the puzzle box" that would allow white people in real life to formulate a white nation.[84]

Part of Covington's skepticism of unvarnished capitalism emerges in the contempt he shows for the neoliberal development of the corporate sector as well as an unacceptable form of big government. As one character declares,

> When that country [the NAR] doesn't have to pay for massive drug addiction, Third World diseases, rampant crime, billions in foreign aid to puppet governments around the world, and maintaining armies of occupation over sullen Third World conquered nations, then there's money for little extras like a space program. When that country doesn't have gargantuan multinational corporations gorging themselves on the national treasury, then it's astounding what a chunk of change becomes available for other things. Forty million people all working in synch in a land of peace and freedom from materialism can perform miracles they never dreamed of in the last century when big business ruled. . . . When you don't have to maintain millions of people in prisons and forced labor camps, when you have stability and unity in a racially homogenous society, when you've got real free enterprise as opposed to monopoly finance capitalism, when the government is only as big as it needs to be to maintain the state, and above all when you have no goddamned lawyers to suck everything dry, you'd be damned amazed what a small country like ours can accomplish.[85]

And yet even with a supposedly minimal state, the government in this utopia still controls essentially all aspects of life in the spirit of national socialism. Indeed, all NAR citizens have a direct role in the state as each person is required to do national service for a period of their life and receives "Life Grant" subsidies from the government.[86] Like Pierce (whom Covington criticizes in the novel), Covington also expresses disdain for the neoliberal ideal of "economic man." In the words of one character, "If you are a National Socialist, you would hold that Man is a part of Nature, while the American way teaches that he exists apart from it and above it and therefore is immune to Nature's laws. Materialism, ladies and gentleman [*sic*]. The world view of man as an economic animal rather than as a spiritual being with a soul."[87]

Thus, if neoliberalism initially valorized economic man, what is left in this and the other white power utopias we've discussed is the neoliberal man of affect, and there's no question that emotional power—usually expressed in racial terms—is crucial to holding together the unity of the white utopia. For Covington, similar to Molyneaux, fascism and strong states can travel the same ground as neoliberalism. Some of the white power authors we've discussed here have professed antipathy for capitalism, but this opposition is shallow and contradictory. For instance, in Covington's case the novel expresses a stereotypically neoliberal openness to a free-market system, but one that necessitates the strong state to ensure its existence. Again, white power ideologies are conflicted and not internally consistent; the crucial connections to neoliberalism are the promotion of the family (individual and tribal), the appeal to a racialized affectivity, and the socioeconomic conditions created by neoliberalism to push disenfranchised white people to various forms of white power ideology.

CONCLUSION: MAKING AMERICA WHITE SUPREMACIST AGAIN

While there are contradictions and antithetical notions between white power and neoliberalism (such as the former's disdain for the latter), the two ideologies are, like race and capitalism more generally, intimately intertwined. The importance and resurrection of the traditional white heteropatriarchal family is the major area of overlap. At the same time, the neoliberal version of *homo affectus* is also important in binding white power to neoliberalism. Moreover, as we have argued in previous chapters, neoliberalism can and does coincide with a violent authoritarian state as shown in Molyneaux and Covington's utopias and, in the real world, with Pinochet in Chile as an ur-case—a connection contemporary white supremacists play up by wearing pro-authoritarian merchandise with casual quips like "Pinochet did nothing wrong" and "Free helicopter rides," inspired by the neoliberal dictator's notorious murders of his political opponents by throwing them out of helicopters.[88]

As we have seen in U.S. politics throughout its history, racial emotions can provide a strong affective lure and cover over the economic class differences between poor and more affluent whites across the spectrum. As we have argued from the beginning of this book, neoliberalism, as a form of racial capitalism, does not hesitate to draw on seemingly contradictory ideologies such as white power in order to perpetuate itself, and white power ideologies (especially their fascistic dimension) can indeed coexist with and feed into neoliberal economics, especially as both are anchored in the fetishization of the white heteropatriarchal family. As sociologist Randolph Hohle argues, "Only a construct as powerful as race can stabilize the internal tensions of neoliberalism,"[89] and, as we have seen in these novels and in the manifestos discussed throughout the book, white power ideologies provide an especially powerful racial construct. Neoliberal policies even created the economic disenfranchisement susceptible to a new kind of neoliberal ethnonational authoritarianism. There is a further collaboration by what we have termed the "far white" (some of which overlaps with white power) pushing a neoconservative Republican agenda that fits squarely with neoliberalism and was eventually co-opted by Trump. As such, the confluence between neoliberalism and white power continues the legacy of racial capitalism in the United States.

Certainly, those in the dominant position can also utilize utopia against those who are oppressed to build a form of class consciousness. As historian Alexandra Minna Stern writes, "The potential emotional appeal of the white ethnostate should not be underestimated. It taps into longings for group solidarity, self-determination, and sustainable communities. As a construct soaked in ultranationalism, the ethnostate arouses romanticism, sentimentality, and the promise of comfort and fellowship."[90] But white power advocates can also appropriate the literary form of utopia, which has traditionally been the territory of socially progressive groups and individuals, to envision their own anti-progressive ideal futures. This is what we see in these white power utopias. What becomes clear by examining them is the centrality of race as the form of consciousness to be deployed in calling for "revolutionary" social change. However, there needs to be a glue to unify the collectivity that racial consciousness invents. In neoliberal terms, the affectivity is built around the dismantling of the Fordist economy and the consequential sense of loss, especially for white heteropatriarchal men, of stable jobs and wages.

Amplifying that loss are the success of racial minorities in claiming their share of the welfare state (perceived as a zero-sum loss to white people) and social justice victories for those other than the white heteropatriarchal subject. From a racial angle, the loss is multiplied by the trauma of the Vietnam War.[91] All these perceived losses produce the fragility and aggrievement of the white male subject, who can then be enabled by white power ideologies to scream out and "fight back" against the shift toward multicultural pluralism replacing open racism as the cultural ideal and norm. Even though in reality white identity politics is trying to consolidate existing white privilege and dominance—what George Lipsitz has definitively shown as "the possessive investment in whiteness"—the shift is experienced and articulated as attacks on white people as a supposedly disenfranchised group.[92] And certainly large segments of the white working class have experienced some form of disenfranchisement, especially in relation to their rights as laborers. Extreme reactions to the shift emerge in the form of white power and violence, which are exemplified by the string of mass shooters and would-be shooters we discuss in chapter 1, not to mention other less spectacular acts of white racism that occur on a daily basis.

The white power utopias we have discussed here express this affective fragility of the white male subject, and, at least in the case of *The Turner Diaries,* influence real-world action. We also see this sense of embattled whiteness in events like the Charlottesville Unite the Right rally in August 2017 and the Capitol insurrection in January 2021. As Cynthia A. Young and Min Hyoung Song noted in a 2014 forum in *American Quarterly,*

> If the civil rights movement made it harder to express explicit racial antipathy, it also provided a language and a set of strategies through which whites could hold on to their racial privilege by paradoxically claiming their own marginalized status. That is, a perception of lost prestige—and it is only that, a perception—has lent itself to the framing of whiteness as an identity characterized by vulnerability and victimhood.[93]

This perception of lost prestige has been building since at least the 1960s, with deeper roots in the Civil War, and has helped to drive the formation of white identity politics and white power as a stage for a demagogue like Trump.

Yet even with this sense of lost prestige, which sometimes does result in economic loss, whiteness still maintains its power and privilege in American society. We should acknowledge that white power ideologues are in fact reacting to social and political changes like predictions for a "white minority" by midcentury or the appointment of the first Black female Supreme Court justice who doesn't represent reactionary conservative interests—in other words, the types of changes that do indeed endanger the sense of white privilege and dominance that whiteness, especially for males, has always provided in the United States. However, even in the case of the demographic changes, we should note that the hysteria and panic these changes inspire in white power and far white circles downplays the fact that whites will still be the dominant racial/ethnic group and will only be a "minority" in the sense that all other racial/ethnic groups will have to be combined to confer a minoritized status on whites. Nevertheless, these and other fears are then used in a demagogic way from the fringe all the way to the mainstream with figures like Trump and his fellow travelers. Thus, there *is* actually something for white extremists to "fight back" against, symbolically marked in the 2010s by the presidency of Obama, which exacerbated the sense of loss, and in the Trump era became shaped by fears about what the United States will inevitably become.

The fact that many Americans, including many white people, consider hard-fought gains in social justice (such as they are) as progress puts the racial war in stark relief and belies the racist ideals this country was founded on. The United States was created as a country divided by wealth, gender, and race, even though its founding documents can in fact be used to enable racial, gender, and class equality. Historian Roxanne Dunbar-Ortiz provides a critical insight: "When extreme white nationalists make themselves visible . . . they are dismissed as marginal, rather than being understood as the spiritual descendants of the settlers. White supremacists are not wrong when they claim that they understand something about the American Dream that the rest of us do not."[94] White power activists and adherents do actually have something to cry over in those instances in which the United States makes stuttering steps toward ideals of inclusion and away from unquestioned white supremacy.

What makes the anger and resentment seen in the examples of extreme white identity politics most terrifying is the ground that they have gained as they have encroached into moderate or middle-of-the-road right-wing conservatism. One of Richard Spencer's objectives with the alt-right movement was to make media spectacles of racist statements and positions that could then make more moderate backlashes against racial justice gains seem legitimate to the center of the electorate. At the same time, he and others have promoted a more "acceptable" image of white racism and white identity politics that eschews the traditional image of racism as hooded Klansmen or goose-stepping neo-Nazis.[95] This rebranded image of white racism was on full display at the Charlottesville Unite the Right rally, which, as we've discussed, presented racist white identity in fashions more associated with the Gap than with the Klan. So the problem is not just that white terrorist violence was and has been on the rise in the 2010s and 2020s; it is also that voting rights can be attacked in a racialized way, and that Black Lives Matter, not to mention Antifa, can be (incorrectly) claimed by right-wing conservative politicians and media as equivalent to the Proud Boys and the Oath Keepers.[96]

The contemporary jumble of racial chaos has been produced by the convergence of neoliberalism and white power, which feed off each other in promoting a racial divide that also covers over the widening and deepening social and economic problems we now face in the United States. In the process, neoliberalism and white power each help shore up the internal contradictions of the other. Racism provides a rationale for dismantling the welfare state in order to deprive social services to nonwhites. Neoliberalism sanctifies the white heteropatriarchal family already fetishized in white power ideologies, and the right-wing manifestation of these latter in figures like Trump provides a life preserver to non-elite whites in the chaotic sea of demographic change and immiseration that neoliberalism itself created. The white ethnonational state imagined in these white power utopias provides a political fantasy that fetishizes the ideal of the white heteropatriarchal family central to American neoliberal culture.

Conclusions in Strange Times, or Life within the Conjuncture of Neoliberalism and White Power

WHAT THE PREVIOUS CHAPTERS tell us is that white power and neoliberalism supercharge each other, especially around the idealized white heteropatriarchal family. In a bubble of extreme affect, the family is often and easily converted into an extension of white racial tribalism presented as the solution to America's problems. Teamed up with generalized xenophobia and "America first" opposition to immigration, the family has played a key role in maintaining white supremacy in general. However, this racism is inextricable from the workings of heteropatriarchal capitalism and its gendered economic disparity. The patriarchal family becomes a fetish object, held up in white power circles as the most important tool in the maintenance of the white race. For neoliberals, this family fetish is simply the easiest way to shunt the costs of social reproduction to the private family—with increased wealth disparity as a result. Sifting this mix, we see the commonality between white power and neoliberalism is that they use the family as a vehicle to propel their opposition to equality. Neoliberalism and white power are at the center of contemporary American inequality and have led to the horror and violence that we have been discussing in this book. In this conclusion, we offer final thoughts on the causes of this horror while we gesture toward the approaches needed to combat white power's influence on American neoliberal culture, especially during a time when many are proclaiming the end of the neoliberal model.[1]

. . .

The twenty-first century has seen a steady stream of violent white extremist brutality in the United States. Indeed, white power fuels itself on conspiracy theories and feeds the racist violence that goes back to the foundations of the country. White power activists are a fringe of American society; however, their reach consumes not only those who would commit violence but also those who willingly buy into the fake news that the neoliberals and far right have to sell. But we want to make clear we are not making an argument here that white racists have been naively duped by these forces to oppose their own best interests—though this caveat does not rule out self-deceptions. Whiteness developed as a valuable reward for loyalty to the U.S. elite, expanding through the years to include many Europeans, such as Italians and Jews, who the established white Americans had originally left out.

The value of attaining this status can be difficult to quantify. It certainly opened access to an array of public spending programs, particularly what we might call white lifestyle investment projects—including affordable home loans, restricted neighborhoods that provide the basis for wealth building, access to comprehensive education, and the other accessories of wholesale suburbanization. When white power and the far white voice their concerns about "white replacement," they are protecting an idea of freedom that is defined through exclusion that can be traced back to the origins of the country. When Americans of any race endorse racist ideas, they are protecting a way of life, but this way of life is founded on what political economist Heather McGhee calls a "zero sum hierarchy," which she defines as a mythology that "white people should see the well-being of people of color as a threat to their own. [It is] one of the most powerful subterranean stories in America."[2] This zero-sum assumption was developed at the nation's founding and entrenched in the idea of freedom that became dominant in the world's oldest modern democracy. Built through the theft of Native land and the enslavement of African people, freedom was ultimately defined as *not* being *non*white. These negations remain as an existential imperative for those jealously guarding the perks associated with being white. They are key to public goods, the economy, and the role of government: if nonwhite people benefit from it or support it, so the logic goes, white people must oppose it.

Research shows a more nuanced view. Historically, the labor and property of people of color has been expropriated/stolen to benefit white wealth. The very scale of this theft and the steadfast refusal to seriously entertain (or even to bring up) reparations—indeed, the intensity of the opposition to as modest a measure as affirmative action—resound in philosopher Charles W. Mills's memorable formulation, "If there is such a backlash against affirmative action, what would the response be to the demand for the interest on the unpaid forty acres and a mule?"[3]

But it is also clear that racism fiscally damages almost all people. According to a 2020 Citigroup study examining the impact of anti-Black racism, if the United States had closed gaps between white and Black people in significant social and economic indicators such as unemployment, net worth, debt, wages, spending on education, and imprisonment, the U.S. GDP would have benefitted by an estimated $16 trillion. The report estimates that 6.1 million jobs were lost due to discriminatory lending practices.[4] Clearly racism is more than an ethical problem that can be solved if individuals would just stop being individually racist. It is, among other things, also an economic problem even for the very white people who racism elevates ideologically. In the neoliberal era white workers have largely not been the beneficiaries of the changes brought on by neoliberalism, even though many have been willing accomplices to them, so desperate is the "possessive investment in whiteness," as George Lipsitz puts it. Certainly, communities of color have been hit hardest when we look only at measures of economic standing, but when we look at economics combined with feelings of hopelessness, levels of incarceration, poor health outcomes, poverty, drug and alcohol addiction, and rising mortality rates, some studies show that white working class people are less resilient in the face of psychosocial adversities and more susceptible to depression, anger, and substance abuse than other ethnic groups.[5] If previously whiteness acted as a "glass floor below which the white citizen could see but never fall," the rise of neoliberalism spawned profound economic insecurity and poverty across all racial groups such that it threatens even those living the white lifestyle.[6] In short, white working people are seeing "the stagnation of the wages of whiteness."[7]

It is important to understand that the top tenth of the top one percent possess about as much wealth as the bottom ninety percent, and yet both progressives and conservatives cling to the idea that mean wealth data point to a deep but simple economic difference between white people and people of color. However, the data show that when the wealthiest people are taken out of the statistics and the wealth of the median white person is matched against the median wealth of those in other groups, the differences are not so stark.[8] Data that examine mean wealth strictly along racial lines both obscure and incorrectly highlight the facts of racial capitalism. Examining the starkest divide, the mean wealth of white households is $900,600, while the mean wealth of Black households stands at $140,000. But because the very richest segments of the U.S. population are white, they in fact skew *all* data about wealth. When the median wealth of the bottom

50 percent of white people is compared to the median wealth of the bottom 50 percent of Black people, that difference is relatively small—$23,100. That sum may well be enough to encourage the racialized opposition to all attempts to address inequality, but we would argue that the privilege that many white people cling to is wrapped up in something that includes economic inequality but is much larger: the privilege of being presumed to be good and righteous and hardworking, presumed to be worth taking a chance on, presumed to be worthy of what sociologist Randolph Hohle calls "good white-private citizenship."[9]

African American studies scholar Eddie Glaude argues that the United States was founded on a "value gap," which is the idea that "in America, white lives have always mattered more than the lives of others." This gap is bridged by a fundamental deception that "black people are essentially inferior, less human than white people." Glaude refers to this value gap as simply "the lie" and claims it is rooted in "the narrative assumptions that support the everyday order of American life, which means we breathe them like air. We count them as truths."[10]

As we take a broad view of neoliberalism and white power, recognizing this fundamental lie opens up other self-deceptions rooted in capitalism itself. If, as American studies scholar and prison activist Ruth Wilson Gilmore shows, "capitalism requires inequality and racism enshrines it," then racial capitalism is the name for this system.[11] So, from this perspective, white supremacists are right when they see the stakes as zero-sum: the end of racial capitalism would be a catastrophic loss for them as well as for the 1 percent. Generally, however, when democratic and anticolonial forces organize against racial capitalism, global economies and national governments are restructured to counter those very pro-democracy and anticolonial efforts. As part of capital's response, debt crises and austerity have led to the defunding of basic investment in infrastructures. This process, otherwise known as accumulation by dispossession, in which the commons is eroded and privatized, creates tremendous hardships, inequalities, and dire poverty for people across races and backgrounds.[12] The direness of the situation is evidenced in the death tolls of pandemics that are facilitated by massive inequality and daily regimes of austerity combined with widespread disillusionment with the major institutions of civic life, especially government, journalism, education, and science. This mistrust has been accelerated by desperate right-wing populisms that promote a zero-sum attitude to maintain fear among people who have chosen not to see the world outside a friend-enemy perspective.

What the popularity of ethnopopulist demagogues and the growth of white extremism shows is that many people deeply missed the privilege of being able to publicly and unabashedly act on whatever savagery or even mundane racism they wished to. The exponential growth of online hate shows that even people who would not act out with physical violence will act out through other forms of violence—issuing the vilest of threats, publicizing personal information, and harassing and verbally intimidating others—and the circle of violence created by the online world leads to the increase of physical acts of terror in response.

As we write this, we see the United States at a moment of danger: a global pandemic, an obliquely growing authoritarianism, and environmental collapse are just three of the horsemen of this apocalypse. Historically, neoliberal forces propel themselves by taking advantage of each rising crisis (expanding into disaster whiteness). If the history of neoliberal capitalism is a history of intensified control coordinated with intensified consolidation of wealth, the response will have to be an intensified consolidation of opposition with new forms of struggle. As the radically unequal system of this latest iteration of racial capitalism produces new crises, we should not be surprised that the far white and white power's response is not only to challenge the system itself, but to revel in the perquisites it does provide. However, we hope this book has shown that we should also not be surprised by the extent to which the neoliberal establishment chooses to embrace politicians who themselves embrace a reflexive mistrust and cataclysmic worldview rather than to pursue the ideals of democracy that American ideology has touted for hundreds of years. When it is easier to trust the Pizzagate/QAnon conspiracy theories that liberal politicians and celebrities eat babies and shoot California with Jewish space lasers than to trust the Biden administration promising public assistance to combat a pandemic, we have to see that the stakes are absurdly profound.[13]

Because ideology and its contradictions are certainly overdetermined, we should attribute this madness not solely to specific individuals or movements such as QAnon or white supremacists like the Proud Boys, the Oath Keepers, and other January 6 Capitol insurrectionists, but also to the range of social, political, and economic conditions that emanate from racial capitalism in the conjuncture of white power and neoliberalism and to the people unwilling to challenge these conditions. Unwavering support for a washed-up campaign by those willing to vote for Trump and his like showed that a vast appetite exists for at least some white-identified populist politicians whose appeal lies in claiming to be victims of liberal political correctness. These politicos and their followers demonize big government when it helps people of color but embrace it when it helps whites.

The classic neoliberal strategy has been to increase the size of government when it comes to policing and defense and to mobilize those against people of color while reducing social spending, justifying their stinginess by insinuating that only greedy minorities benefit from social programs. But in today's relatively miserable conditions, we find that welfare state assistance focused on social spending is popular. (As a measure of the times, no less than the Ayn Rand Institute asked for a loan using the federal government's Paycheck Protection Program during the heart of the COVID-19 economic crisis!)

So the broad success of the Republican Party's electoral strategy of outspoken racism, starting with the political developments of 2016, seemed to signal an evolution if not the end of the usual "dog whistle politics," as Ian Haney López calls it.[14] Trump's failure in 2020 suggested yet another approach would be needed, however, and as the next generation of conservative activists cues up to fight liberals and progressives, the post-2020 attack on critical race theory suggests one direction. Indeed, *The Federalist* proclaims that the movement against critical race theory is the "new cultural Tea Party" against the "woketopian agenda that redefines the United States as a racist empire rooted in white supremacy."[15]

For all its obvious racism, the Tea Party was also a political movement for small government. A cultural Tea Party announces a whole other set of priorities, without the Southern Strategy's cover of reducing taxes and promoting small government. Indeed, we see violent groups trying to normalize themselves while mainstream Republicans radicalize themselves by joining in common cause, as when the Proud Boys have shown up in uniform at civic events like local school board meetings discussing critical race theory or at other Republican-identified social causes such as events opposing mandates for COVID vaccinations or masking. These appearances are intended to normalize white extremists' presence throughout American life and to assert their legitimacy as part of the body politic.[16] There are new ways to signify race or perhaps new jobs for race to do, and a cultural Tea Party may well be used as a smokescreen within disaster whiteness to redirect those significations to further erode the social service state and let the racial and class politics in through a different door. The U.S. conservative love affair with Hungarian authoritarian prime minister Viktor Orbán suggests another mode for the deployment of race, what is often dubbed the rise of "illiberal democracy," in which pluralism is utterly eroded and personal freedom is hollowed out: voters continue to vote but they have few options, few civil liberties, and almost no access to alternative information. Moreover, the Orbán regime seems to suggest yet another example of the intermixing of authoritarianism, neoliberalism, and an ethnopopulist racialization of the other.[17]

The zero-sum attitude has promoted the notion that if big government helps nonwhite groups or causes they have associated with nonwhiteness, then white people will necessarily be damaged, and so white people have to oppose racial equality because majority gains can only be built on minority losses. The evidence suggests something very different. At mid-twentieth century following World War II's global war on fascism, the benefits of big government investment in jobs, education, and social programs that we have generally classed in this book as the New Deal were shared broadly across class lines. These programs enjoyed wide support, and indeed they vastly expanded wealth. It was only when the excluded, especially people of color, demanded their share of the resources that had been largely reserved for white people that support for government social spending eroded. We have pointed to the neoliberal attack on big government spending and taxation that colluded with white racial patriarchal politics, each using the other as a cover. What these efforts obscured is a fairly obvious fact: when rich people keep more of their wealth for themselves, there is less of it for everyone else. Race becomes part of the justification for economic inequality.[18]

For those not in the higher echelons of the neoliberal regime, the world of waged labor is shaped by the dictates of neoliberal capitalism. Indeed, the 2010s marks the first time in human history in which the majority of the world's population (54 percent, to be precise) was engaged in wage labor— defined as "formally free and substantially unprotected labor, disembedded from family subsistence and constantly at risk from polluting conditions, from accidents, sickness, unemployment, and from old age frailty."[19] Neoliberal capitalism is well known for how it has shaped the state's abdication of Keynesian social welfare and social reproduction roles so that at the same time as more people are engaged in wage labor, more care work must be undertaken by family members and charitable volunteers who do not get paid for their efforts. So while the requirements of our paid work expand to fill more hours, the demands for the unpaid work of caregiving for the family and society have to find a way to be accommodated, leading to the "second shift" of work taken on after the first shift of waged work. Indeed, the formal economy depends on this informal labor, feeding off of it but also drawing on the creativity and energy of those who find innovative ways to meet their own and others' needs.

Too often politics and movements invoke the rhetoric of the family—as we have shown white power and neoliberalism do—as a way to prop up politics that should have been abandoned long ago. In response, our politics must keep a vision of utopia but root it in the quotidian and on the streets through conscious organizing.[20] The term "quotidian" originates, of course, from the Latin word for "everyday," and few things are as everyday in capitalism as the requirement to find and maintain paid labor at all costs and to somehow balance that with the needs of daily existence for ourselves and our families and friends. Central to resistance work in the streets is a politics in alliance with the workers who creatively survive in the face of dispossession and informal work arrangements—too often taken in addition to waged labor.[21] This alliance then must be rooted in an unambiguous non-heteronormative feminist anti-racism as the politics that resists austerity and prioritizes the needs associated with social reproduction—that is, a politics that organizes around people at the level of their day-to-day lives with its demands that can make life a struggle, tasks that are mundane and monumental depending on one's particular circumstances and luck: getting to work, caring for elderly parents, finding nutritious food, negotiating immigration laws, arranging child care, finding a home, paying off student loans, paying onerous fines and fees at the risk of legal jeopardy, sleeping restfully, taking time off to recuperate, and any number of other quotidian tasks that dog daily life in a system that cares very little for actual people.

In the United States, a left politics must emerge that is unequivocal in calling out the zero-sum attitude and that insists on a collective vision of a new politics rooted in meeting the demands of social justice at the level of the institutions that support daily life. The process of what most consider positive social change must be wide-ranging. Today, the grand projects of utopia such as the traditional Marxist vision of capitalism becoming socialism and eventually communism have largely been abandoned for micro-utopias (small-scale communes like the long-running B. F. Skinner–oriented Twin Oaks Community in Virginia). Though these small communities play out a form of micro-collectivity based in racial, gender, and individual equality, they are necessarily limited in scope, creating enclaves rather than addressing wider social structures. But instead of utopia as social design, what has become more immediately realizable is utopia as collective praxis, and what's important about the praxis is that we engage in it collectively on the progressive side seeking social justice.

As utopian scholar Tom Moylan writes, the individual eutopian[22] subject must become part of collective utopian desiring and action—in Moylan's economical phrase, "becoming utopian."[23] What we are seeing now are eruptions of collective consciousness around the world. We have spent most of our attention in this book on the consciousness-raising efforts of white power; however, formations of collective consciousness are also occurring against neoliberal capitalism (the 99 percent of the "Occupy" movement in the United States in 2011–12), against racism (Black Lives Matter since 2013), against gendered oppression and violence (global women's strikes and marches starting in 2017), and against authoritarianism (the ongoing protests for democracy in Hong Kong against the Communist Party of China from 2019, the people of Myanmar's backlash against the political coup by the military in 2021). All these, though unaligned, are examples of socially progressive formations of collectivity. What we need in order to subvert white power and neoliberalism is more and more of these kinds of collective consciousnesses—and, importantly, the alignment of isolated formations of oppositional groups into the networks of political action that political philosophers Michael Hardt and Antonio Negri described as the "multitude": "new circuits of cooperation and collaboration that stretch across nations and continents and allow an unlimited number of encounters."[24]

Of course, as it perhaps always is in struggles like this, the rub is how to connect these disparate groups, and in such a way that does not privilege a single center. What is required is a model of collectivizable subjectivity that could accommodate the social and individual differences of what would be, in essence, a revolutionary subject (what Moylan would term a "utopian" subject). In order to combat white power and neoliberalism (as the current manifestations of white supremacy and racial capitalism), this subject would be anti-racist, anti-capitalist, anti-sexist, and anti-homophobic, at the very least.

The elaboration of a full program of utopian liberation is certainly beyond the scope of this short book; what we have tried to offer in this brief intervention is a diagnostic of what we see happening in the United States as two crucial formations, white power and neoliberalism, converge more explicitly. What we *can* do here is gesture toward what is needed at a moment when white power (in all its various guises) is on the rise and neoliberalism limits the horizons beyond which too many can imagine something beyond racial capitalism. We should especially keep in mind that many of those working for the death of American neoliberalism are doing so from the far right, and part of what they challenge is neoliberal small-government austerity rather than nativist racism. It then becomes incumbent on those of us who want a future based on *true* equality and social justice to imagine a better alternative. Liberal humanism has proven unable to collectivize a subject that can accommodate the various social differences, especially race, and in fact ideologically supports the various stages of capitalism, including neoliberalism.

So is there something like an American model of subjectivity that can accommodate our various social identities and be compelling enough to push for significant and positive social change? How can we bring individuals together to create social justice for all? At the risk of engaging in "woketopianism" we have tried to show here the deep structural inequality and injustice at the heart of American life today that results from neoliberal and white power ideologies, practices, and rationalities. To make the profound, systemic changes needed to move away from the violence and injustice of these requires new practices and logics of social reproduction to be at the heart of any society that is different from that of the present moment. Key to any reimagining of our present is to move past the sequestered territories of "identity politics" on one side and class-based politics on the other. Neoliberal capitalism has always been a racial capitalism and a sexist/heteronormative capitalism that has been propped up by defining work in very circumscribed ways that rely on an untenable separation between people of differently raced groups, between public and private, between the gendered work of the private home and the public world of work—as if the home was ever not a workplace and the public was ever not many people's home.

At the same time, the forces of hate have been sparked in recent years by a combination of economic insecurity, the erosion of the Fordist compromise, and the easy radicalization tools provided by social media. Moreover, the rise of women, LGBTQ+ folx, and people of color into positions of institutional power are all visible signs, from the perspective of white identity politics, of the need for unequivocal white power. Indeed, white power has found its revolutionary subject. It urges the forces against social justice to call for white supremacy more loudly and more proudly—and with more vulgarity and violence. To stand up to these forces requires a politics that does not depend on enemies for its coherence and for its passion. In contrast to the strong current in the realm of contemporary politics that is inseparably bound up in the fascistic friend-enemy opposition, we call for a politics that refuses the false choices of prioritizing issues of class or race or gender or any other social difference, as if racial capitalism would ever allow for the disaggregation of these issues. Opposition today requires a comprehensive perspective on the institutions of neoliberalism and white power.

To produce a new, socially just vision for the United States requires the broad lens provided by understanding oppression as rooted in racial capitalism and relying on unpaid labor in the work of social reproduction. It requires resisting austerity and calling for a redistribution of wealth. It requires a reorganization of the classic oppositions that have enabled racial heteropatriarchal capitalism—an unquestioned vision of the private in opposition to the public and of a vast erosion of the commons. It thus opposes the theft of public goods and defends community, but it is a global vision of community, even if it has to think locally and nationally to achieve specific goals. It is about recognizing that nothing essential stands between people. The distances have enabled a history of violence, and they will not be bridged through forgetting that history or through investing all hope in future generations who will somehow see the world differently. We have to start the journey across the divides today, trying to build bridges through the awareness that there are many struggles and that they will be taken on differently by the people most wounded by them.

We take heart from the incredible energies and global impact of Black Lives Matter and #MeToo, which are particularly important as social and political responses to Trump's presidency. There also seems to be a pivot to the left in several major Latin America countries with the leftist electoral wins in 2021 in Chile and Honduras and in 2022 in Colombia, which also elected its first Black woman as vice president. Although it is certainly too soon for any type of celebration—there's plenty to despair about—we should not discount the cracks in white supremacy, neoliberalism, and patriarchy represented by the emergence of these movements. In order to build toward a new, socially just future, Americans must reach out and create interconnections across populations and divides, as Ta-Nehisi Coates does in *Between the World and Me* when he meditates on life as an African American man and develops the following advice for his son:

> Remember that you and I are brothers, are the children of trans-Atlantic rape. Remember the broader consciousness that comes with that. Remember that this consciousness can never ultimately be racial; it must be cosmic. Remember the Roma you saw begging with their children in the street [in France], and the venom with which they were addressed.[25]

We would call what Coates points to a politics of utopia. As a properly progressive and equalizing project, it starts with rejecting a fundamental element of white supremacist society that Mills identifies as an "epistemology of ignorance" in *The Racial Contract:* "an agreement to *mis*interpret the world . . . *producing the ironic outcome that whites will in general be unable to understand the world they themselves made.*"[26] Honestly discussing injustice opens the possibility for moving cosmically to connect with people across borders and histories and allows us to come together in a relentless and collective quest for justice.

NOTES

INTRODUCTION

1. Julian Borger, "Donald Trump Denounces 'Globalism' in Nationalist Address to UN," *Guardian,* September 24, 2019, www.theguardian.com/us-news/2019/sep /24/donald-trump-un-address-denounces-globalism.

2. Carol Anderson, *White Rage: The Unspoken Truth of Our Racial Divide* (New York: Bloomsbury, 2016).

3. Stuart Hall, "The Neoliberal Revolution," *Soundings* 48 (2011): 9.

4. Jennifer Lawn and Chris Prentice offer a useful discussion of the disagreements over whether the concept of neoliberalism exists with any coherence in "Introduction: Neoliberal Culture / The Cultures of Neoliberalism," *Sites* 12, no. 1 (2015): 1–29.

5. Hall, "The Neoliberal Revolution," 12.

6. Hall, "The Neoliberal Revolution," 10 (emphasis in original).

7. For an interesting discussion of this phenomenon, see Danzy Senna, "Robin DiAngelo and the Problem with Anti-Racist Self-Help," *The Atlantic,* September 2021, www.theatlantic.com/magazine/archive/2021/09/martin-learning-in-public -diangelo-nice-racism/619497/.

8. Patricia Ventura, *Neoliberal Culture: Living with American Neoliberalism* (New York: Routledge, 2016); Edward K. Chan, "The White Power Utopia and the Reproduction of Victimized Whiteness," in *Race and Utopian Desire in American Literature and Society,* ed. Patricia Ventura and Edward K. Chan (Cham, Switzerland: Palgrave Macmillan, 2019), 139–59.

9. Mitchum Huehls and Rachel Greenwald Smith, "Four Phases of Neoliberalism and Literature: An Introduction," in *Neoliberalism and Contemporary Literary Culture* (Baltimore, MD: Johns Hopkins University Press, 2017).

10. Friedrich Hayek, *The Road to Serfdom* (London: Institute of Economic Affairs, 2005), 35.

11. Angie Maxwell and Todd Shields, *The Long Southern Strategy: How Chasing White Voters in the South Changed American Politics* (New York: Oxford University

Press, 2019), 8; George Lipsitz, *The Possessive Investment in Whiteness: How White People Profit from Identity Politics* (Philadelphia: Temple University Press, 2018), loc. 470–72, Kindle.

12. Maxwell and Shields, *The Long Southern Strategy*, 8.

13. W. E. B Du Bois, *Black Reconstruction: An Essay Toward a History of the Part Which Black Folk Played in the Attempt to Reconstruct Democracy in America, 1869–1880* (New York: Harcourt, Brace, 1935); David R. Roediger, *The Wages of Whiteness: Race and the Making of the American Working Class,* revised ed. (New York: Verso, 2007).

14. Patrik Jonsson, "After Obama's Win, White Backlash Festers in US," *Christian Science Monitor,* November 17, 2008, www.csmonitor.com/USA/Politics/2008/1117/p03s01-uspo.html.

15. "White Supremacists See Hope in Obama Win," CBS News, August 8, 2008, www.cbsnews.com/news/white-supremacists-see-hope-in-obama-win/.

16. Southern Poverty Law Center, "Hate Groups Reach Record High," Southern Poverty Law Center, February 19, 2019,www.splcenter.org/news/2019/02/19/hate-groups-reach-record-high.

17. Quoted in Robin D. G. Kelley, "Births of a Nation, Redux: Surveying Trumpland with Cedric Robinson," *Boston Review,* November 5, 2020, https://bostonreview.net/race-politics/robin-d-g-kelley-births-nation.

18. Jodi Melamed, "Racial Capitalism," *Critical Ethnic Studies* 1, no. 1 (2015): 79.

19. See Jason Read, "A Genealogy of Homo-Economicus: Neoliberalism and the Production of Subjectivity," *Foucault Studies* 6 (2009): 25–36, and Rosalind Gill, "Culture and Subjectivity in Neoliberal and Postfeminist Times," *Subjectivity* 25 (2008): 432–45.

20. Otto Penz and Birgit Sauer, *Governing Affects: Neoliberalism, Neo-Bureaucracies, and Service Work* (London: Routledge, 2019).

21. Birgit Sauer, "Authoritarian Right-Wing Populism as Masculinist Identity Politics. The Role of Affects," in *Right-Wing Populism and Gender: European Perspectives and Beyond,* ed. Gabriele Dietze and Julia Roth (Bielefeld, Germany: transcript Verlag, 2020), 32.

22. Andrew Macdonald [William L. Pierce], *The Turner Diaries,* 2nd ed. (Fort Lee, NJ: Barricade Books, 1996), loc. 2612, Kindle.

23. C. Richard King and David J. Leonard, *Beyond Hate: White Power and Popular Culture* (New York: Routledge, 2016), 9; Kathleen Belew, *Bring the War Home: The White Power Movement and Parliamentary America* (Cambridge, MA: Harvard University Press, 2018), ix. See also Chan, "The White Power Utopia," 141–42, and Alexandra Minna Stern, *Proud Boys and the White Ethnostate: How the Alt-Right Is Warping the American Imagination* (Boston: Beacon Press, 2019), 8–9.

24. See Kathleen Belew, "There Are No Lone Wolves: The White Power Movement at War," in *A Field Guide to White Supremacy,* ed. Kathleen Belew and Ramón A. Gutiérrez (Berkeley: University of California Press, 2021), especially p. 317.

25. Robert Pape, "Why We Cannot Afford to Ignore the American Insurrectionist Movement," Chicago Projects on Security and Threats, August 6, 2021, https://cpost.uchicago.edu/research/domestic_extremism/why_we_cannot_afford_to_ignore_the_american_insurrectionist_movement/. Additionally, one poll finds that 30 percent of Republicans support the statement, "Because things have gotten so far off track, true American patriots may have to resort to violence in order to save our country" ("Competing Visions of America: An Evolving Identity or a Culture Under Attack," Public Religion Research Institute, November 1, 2021, www.prri.org/press-release/competing-visions-of-america-an-evolving-identity-or-a-culture-under-attack/).

26. Pape, "Why We Cannot Afford to Ignore the American Insurrectionist Movement"; "Competing Visions of America."

27. Andy Meek, "Fox News Channel Has Now Spent 20 Years in the #1 Spot on the Cable News Rankings," *Forbes.com,* February 1, 2022, www.forbes.com/sites/andymeek/2022/02/01/fox-news-channel-has-now-spent-20-years-in-the-1-spot-on-the-cable-news-rankings/?sh=1a9de06872f2.

28. Charles W. Mills, *The Racial Contract* (Ithaca, NY: Cornell University Press, 1997).

29. Maxwell and Shields, *The Long Southern Strategy.*

30. Mike King, "Aggrieved Whiteness: White Identity Politics and Modern American Racial Formation," *Abolition Journal,* May 4, 2017, https://abolitionjournal.org/aggrieved-whiteness-white-identity-politics-and-modern-american-racial-formation/.

31. For Reagan as for Trump, these words did not lead to actual cutting of government as much as redirecting big government to benefit the favored cause of their white constituency, which tended to involve an attempt to make the American homeland impenetrable, whether in the air through the Star Wars missile shield or by land through a border wall.

32. Ronald Reagan, "Inaugural Address (2)," January 20, 1981, Ronald Reagan Presidential Foundation & Institute, video, www.reaganfoundation.org/ronald-reagan/reagan-quotes-speeches/inaugural-address-2/.

33. On neoliberalism's antipathy toward democracy, see Christian Joppke, *Neoliberal Nationalism: Immigration and the Rise of the Populist Right* (Cambridge: Cambridge University Press, 2021), loc. 690, Kindle.

34. We refer readers interested in deeply exploring this world to the fantastic journalism and investigations by Bellingcat.com, an independent collective of researchers and citizen journalists. We also recommend Matthew N. Lyons, *Insurgent Supremacists: The U.S. Far Right's Challenge to State and Empire* (Montreal: Kersplebedeb Publishing; Oakland: PM Press, 2018).

35. Robert Evans, "Shitposting, Inspirational Terrorism, and the Christchurch Mosque Massacre," Bellingcat, March 15, 2019, www.bellingcat.com/news/rest-of-world/2019/03/15/shitposting-inspirational-terrorism-and-the-christchurch-mosque-massacre/.

1. Despite efforts by law enforcement, journalists, and others to avoid naming mass shooters or reproducing their manifestos, we have decided that we need to include names to pinpoint specific incidents and to quote from their manifestos and social media postings in order to uncover their ideological frameworks, which are fundamentally tied to white power. For the case not to name, see Adam K. Raymond, "The Push to Not Name Mass Shooters Is Catching On," *New York Intelligencer,* May 9, 2019, https://nymag.com/intelligencer/2019/05/the-push-to-not-name-mass-shooters-is-catching-on.html, as well as Texas State University's Advanced Law Enforcement Rapid Response Training website, dontnamethem.org.

2. The term "red-pilled" refers to the character Neo in *The Matrix* choosing the red pill and therefore "the truth" instead of living in an illusory world.

3. Tad Tietze, "Anders Breivik, Fascism and the Neoliberal Inheritance," in *Hayek: A Collaborative Biography: Part IV, Good Dictators, Sovereign Producers and Hayek's "Ruthless Consistency,"* ed. Robert Leeson (Basingstoke: Palgrave Macmillan, 2015), 287.

4. Sindre Bangstad, *Anders Breivik and the Rise of Islamophobia* (London: Zed Books, 2014), 86.

5. Janet Burns, "Cut Off from Big Fintech, White Nationalists Are Using Bitcoin to Raise Funds," *Forbes,* January 3, 2018, www.forbes.com/sites/janetwburns /2018/01/03/cut-off-from-big-fintech-white-supremacists-are-using-bitcoin-to-raise -funds/?sh=73a4ac6633b3.

6. Stuart Hall "The Neoliberal Revolution," *Soundings* 48 (2011): 18.

7. We discuss racial capitalism in more detail below.

8. Michael Kimmel, *Angry White Men: American Masculinity at the End of an Era* (New York: Nation Books, 2013).

9. Cynthia Miller-Idriss, *Hate in the Homeland: The New Global Far Right* (Princeton, NJ: Princeton University Press, 2020), 7.

10. Naomi Klein, *The Shock Doctrine: The Rise of Disaster Capitalism* (New York: Picador, 2007), especially p. 6 and 580.

11. Rick Perlstein, "Exclusive: Lee Atwater's Infamous 1981 Interview on the Southern Strategy," *The Nation,* November 13, 2012, www.thenation.com/article /archive/exclusive-lee-atwaters-infamous-1981-interview-southern-strategy/.

12. Theda Skocpol, "Resistance in American Politics: Lecture by Political Scientist Theda Skocpol," *Radboud Reflects,* October 16, 2019, www.youtube.com /watch?v=_RMHI5dmsDU. Melissa Deckman, *Tea Party Women: Mama Grizzlies, Grassroots Leaders, and the Changing Face of the American Right* (New York: New York University Press, 2016).

13. Steven Benen, *The Impostors: How Republicans Quit Governing and Seized American Politics* (New York: William Morrow, 2020).

14. Andrew Macdonald [William L. Pierce], *The Turner Diaries,* 2nd ed. (Fort Lee, NJ: Barricade Books, 1996), loc. 918, Kindle.

15. On the history of zero-sum perspectives on race in the United States, see Heather McGhee, *The Sum of Us: What Racism Costs Everyone and How We Can Prosper Together* (New York: One World Press, 2021), especially chapter 1, as well as Michael I. Norton and Samuel R. Sommers, "Whites See Racism as a Zero-Sum Game That They Are Now Losing," *Perspectives on Psychological Science* 6, no. 3 (2011): 215–18.

16. Wajahat Ali, "Deradicalizing White People," *The New York Review*, August 18, 2018, www.nybooks.com/daily/2018/08/16/deradicalizing-white-people/.

17. See Karen Brodkin, *How Jews Became White Folks and What That Says about Race in America* (New Brunswick, NJ: Rutgers University Press, 1998); Noel Ignatiev, *How the Irish Became White* (New York: Routledge, 2009 [1995]); and Matthew Frye Jacobson, *Whiteness of a Different Color: European Immigrants and the Alchemy of Race* (Cambridge, MA: Harvard University Press, 1999 [1998]).

18. Steve Martinot, *The Machinery of Whiteness: Studies in the Structure of Racialization* (Philadelphia: Temple University Press, 2010).

19. Cedric J. Robinson, *Black Marxism: The Making of the Black Radical Tradition,* 2nd ed. (Chapel Hill: University of North Carolina Press, 2000), 28, 66–67.

20. For how revolutionary and crucial Robinson's work was and continues to be, see Robin D. G. Kelley, foreword to *Black Marxism,* by Cedric Robinson (Chapel Hill: University of North Carolina Press, 2000), and "What Did Cedric Robinson Mean by Racial Capitalism," *Boston Review,* January 12, 2017, http://bostonreview .net/race/robin-d-g-kelley-what-did-cedric-robinson-mean-racial-capitalism, as well as Jodi Melamed, "Racial Capitalism," *Critical Ethnic Studies* 1, no. 1 (2015): 76–85.

21. Tyler Stovall, *White Freedom: The Racial History of an Idea* (Princeton, NJ: Princeton University Press, 2021), 4.

22. W. E. B. Du Bois, "The Wealth of the West vs. a Chance for Exploited Mankind," *National Guardian,* November 28, 1955, reprinted in *Newspaper Columns by W. E. B. Du Bois,* vol. 2, ed. Herbert Aptheker (New York: Kraus-Thomson Organization Limited, 1986), 939, quoted in Jodi Melamed, "Spirit of Neoliberalism: From Racial Liberalism to Neoliberal Multiculturalism," *Social Text* 24, no. 4 (89) (2006): 11.

23. There are many resonances but also some discontinuities between our connection of neoliberalism with racial capitalism and Jodi Melamed's very compelling version in *Represent and Destroy: Rationalizing Violence in the New Racial Capitalism* (Minneapolis: University of Minnesota, 2011). For example, as we discuss in chapter 3, we see neoliberalism integrating itself with racial discourse and ideology earlier than she does. However, we certainly agree that a "neoliberal-neoracial capitalism" emerged in the 2010s (see her epilogue). We have also seen the ascendancy of a particularly neoconservative phase of neoliberalism, especially in relation to its rapprochement with white power ideology, that challenges the hegemony of the kind of neoliberal multiculturalism that Melamed convincingly shows characterizes some phases of American neoliberalism, especially that of the George W. Bush years. Today's punitive neoliberalism (see William Davies, "The New Neoliberalism," *New Left Review* 101 [September–October 2016]: 121–34) operating under the influence

of white power ideology's vision of ethnonationalism challenges the hegemony of neoliberalism as unfailingly globalist, even as white power ideology is itself an intensely global formation. Dylan Rodríguez's formulation of "multicultural white supremacy" in *White Reconstruction: Domestic Warfare and the Logics of Genocide* (New York: Fordham University Press, 2021) is also a useful way to understand how white supremacy engages with Melamed's notion of "liberal" and "neoliberal" multiculturalism at a specific historical moment, and we would agree with him that white supremacy "exceeds particular state, economic, and/or social forms" (34, 36–37).

24. David Harvey developed the term "accumulation by dispossession" to name a contemporary form of primitive accumulation in which the commons and public goods become privatized or when individuals are forcibly dispossessed of their private property as part of an accumulation strategy for private capital interests. For information on race and the subprime crisis, see Jacob S. Rugh and Douglas S. Massey, "Racial Segregation and the American Foreclosure Crisis," *American Sociological Review* 75, no. 5 (2010): 629–51.

25. Sheryll Cashin, *White Space, Black Hood: Opportunity Hoarding and Segregation in the Age of Inequality* (Boston: Beacon Press, 2021), 7.

26. Randolph Hohle, *Race and the Origins of American Neoliberalism* (New York: Routledge, 2015), chapter 1, especially 4–14; *Racism in the Neoliberal Era: A Meta History of Elite White Power* (New York: Routledge, 2018), 7.

27. Hohle, *Race and the Origins of American Neoliberalism*, 221.

28. Eduardo Bonilla-Silva, *Racism without Racists: Color-Blind Racism and the Persistence of Racial Inequality in the United States* (2003; Lanham: Rowman & Littlefield, 2018); Patricia Hill Collins, *Black Sexual Politics: African Americans, Gender, and the New Racism* (New York: Routledge, 2004); David Theo Goldberg, *The Threat Race: Reflections on Racial Neoliberalism* (Malden: Blackwell, 2009).

29. Cindy Boren, "Richard Sherman Frustrated by Reaction, Equates 'Thug' with Racial Slur," *Washington Post,* January 23, 2014, www.washingtonpost.com /news/early-lead/wp/2014/01/23/richard-sherman-frustrated-by-reaction-equates -thug-with-racial-slur/.

30. Florida's "anti-woke act" is a typical such law. See Tim Craig, "Florida Legislature Passes Bill That Limits How Schools and Workplaces Teach about Race and Identity," *Washington Post,* March 10, 2022, www.washingtonpost.com/nation /2022/03/10/florida-legislature-passes-anti-woke-bill/.

31. Joe Helm and Lori Rozsa, "African Americans Say the Teaching of Black History Is Under Threat," *Washington Post,* February 23, 2022, www.washingtonpost .com/education/2022/02/23/schools-black-history-month-crt/.

32. The idea of whiteness as a wage is a particularly potent concept for American studies and helped to initiate the field of whiteness studies through works such as David Roediger's book *The Wages of Whiteness: Race and the Making of the American Working Class,* revised ed. (New York: Verso, 2007), which he built on the pathbreaking work of W. E. B. Du Bois's *Black Reconstruction: An Essay Toward a History of the Part Which Black Folk Played in the Attempt to Reconstruct Democracy*

in America, 18601880 (New York: Harcourt, Brace and Company, 1935). Whiteness as property has been extensively analyzed in legal terms by Cheryl I. Harris in "Whiteness as Property," *Harvard Law Review* 106, no. 8 (1993): 1707–91.

33. As Fran Shor argues, "One cannot separate Trumpism from the reign of the neoliberal order." Moreover, "As the hidden injuries and humiliations built into the class cultural system have taken their toll on significant segments of the white working class, the increase of fear, anger, and resentment, all part of the sociopsychological domain, has opened up the political space for demagogues like Trump." Fran Shor, *Weaponized Whiteness: The Constructions and Deconstructions of White Identity Politics* (Chicago: Haymarket Books, 2019), 33, 37.

34. Susan Searls Giroux, "Sade's Revenge: Racial Neoliberalism and the Sovereignty of Negation," *Patterns of Prejudice* 44, no. 1 (2010): 17. Searls Giroux proleptically captures Trump's tweets and worldview describing neoliberal culture as "war, sexual scandals, arson, rape, political corruption, explosions, crashes, crime, corporate-sponsored coups and massacres, mutilation, revolutions, internet pornutopia and torture" (p. 17).

35. As we will discuss in chapter 3, the true expansive power of the Southern Strategy, one of the fundamental political strategies of the American neoliberal culture era, is key to the instrumentalization of southern whiteness as "the gravitational force holding everything in its place." Angie Maxwell and Todd Shields, *The Long Southern Strategy: How Chasing White Voters in the South Changed American Politics* (New York: Oxford University Press, 2019), 8.

36. Wendy Brown, *In the Ruins of Neoliberalism: The Rise of Antidemocratic Politics in the West* (New York: Columbia University Press, 2019), 164.

37. Heidi Beirich, "The Year in Hate: Rage Against Change," Southern Poverty Law Center, February 20, 2019, www.splcenter.org/fighting-hate/intelligence-report/2019/year-hate-rage-against-change.

38. Robert Farley, "The Facts on White Nationalism," FactCheck.org, March 20, 2019, www.factcheck.org/2019/03/the-facts-on-white-nationalism/.

39. Our thanks to an anonymous reviewer who asked us to discuss this sartorial choice.

40. George Lipsitz, *The Possessive Investment in Whiteness: How White People Profit from Identity Politics* (Philadelphia: Temple University Press, 2018), loc. 629, 3918, Kindle.

41. Robert Pape and Chicago Project on Security and Threats, "Understanding American Domestic Terrorism: Mobilization Potential and Risk Factor of a New Threat Trajectory," April 6, 2021, https://d3qi0qp55mx5f5.cloudfront.net/cpost/i/docs/americas_insurrectionists_online_2021_04_06.pdf?mtime=1617807009.

42. For specific examples, see "'The Great Replacement': An Explainer," Anti-Defamation League, April 19, 2021, www.adl.org/resources/backgrounders/great-replacement-explainer.

43. Flora Garamvolgyi, "Viktor Orbán Tells CPAC the Path to Power Is to 'Have Your Own Media,'" *Guardian,* May 20, 2022, www.theguardian.com/us-news/2022/may/20/victor-orban-cpacp-republicans-hungary.

44. "Tucker Carlson Tonight," Fox News, April 12, 2021, https://archive.org /details/FOXNEWSW_20210413_050000_Tucker_Carlson_Tonight.

45. Sheryll Cashin, "How the Buffalo Massacre Proves There's No 'Great Replacement,'" Politico, April 21, 2022, www.politico.com/news/magazine/2022/05 /21/buffalo-massacre-great-replacement-segregation-00034177

46. Achille Mbembe, "Necropolitics," trans. Libby Meintjes, *Public Culture* 15, no. 1 (2003): 17.

47. See Lois Beckett, "A History of Recent Attacks Linked to White Supremacy," *Guardian,* March 15, 2019, www.theguardian.com/world/2019/mar/16/a -history-of-recent-attacks-linked-to-white-supremacism.

48. Jacob Davey and Julia Ebner, *"The Great Replacement": The Violent Consequences of Mainstream Extremism* (London: Institute for Strategic Dialogue, 2019), 13, www.isdglobal.org/wp-content/uploads/2019/07/The-Great-Replacement-The -Violent-Consequences-of-Mainstreamed-Extremism-by-ISD.pdf.

49. For more on these types of acts and plots, and context for the rise of white supremacist/power violence, see the section "The Rise of White Supremacist Killings" in Cassie Miller and Howard Graves, "When the 'Alt-Right' Hit the Streets: Far-Right Political Rallies in the Trump Era," Southern Poverty Law Center, August 10, 2020, www.splcenter.org/20200810/when-alt-right-hit-streets-far-right -political-rallies-trump-era.

50. One idiosyncrasy of Roof's racist worldview is that he believes that East Asians "are by nature very racist and could be great allies of the White race. I am not opposed at all to allies with the Northeast Asian races." Also, as many have noted, one of the two film quotations that Roof cites in his manifesto is from the Japanese film *Himizu* (Sion Sono, 2011).

51. Robert O'Harrow Jr., Andrew Ba Tran, and Derek Hawkins, "The Rise of Domestic Extremism in America," *Washington Post,* April 12, 2021, www .washingtonpost.com/investigations/interactive/2021/domestic-terrorism-data/.

52. Paula McMahon, "Nikolas Cruz Left 180 Rounds of Ammunition," *Sun Sentinel,* March 2, 2018, www.sun-sentinel.com/local/broward/parkland/florida -school-shooting/fl-florida-school-shooting-nikolas-cruz-left-180-rounds-20180302 -story.html.

53. Weiyi Cai et al., "White Extremist Ideology Drives Many Deadly Shootings," *New York Times,* August 14, 2019, www.nytimes.com/interactive/2019/08/04 /us/white-extremist-active-shooter.html.

54. Luke Mullins, "Inside the Mind of the MAGA Bomber," *Washingtonian,* August 13, 2020, www.washingtonian.com/2020/08/13/inside-the-mind-of-the -maga-bomber-the-trump-superfan-who-tried-to-wreak-havoc-on-the-last-national -election/.

55. Emma Green, "The Fight to Make Meaning Out of a Massacre," *The Atlantic,* September 29, 2019, www.theatlantic.com/politics/archive/2019/09/pittsburgh -politics-violence-gun-reform/598885/.

56. Brett Barrouquere and Rachel Janik, "A Gunman Opened Fire on a Synagogue in Pittsburgh, Killing at Least Eleven People and Wounding Others," South-

ern Poverty Law Center, October 27, 2018, www.splcenter.org/hatewatch/2018/10
/27/gunman-opened-fire-synagogue-pittsburgh-killing-least-eleven-people-and
-wounding-others.

57. It's notable that both Breivik and Tarrant expressed considerable fascination
with the Serbian radical nationalism of Slobodan Milošević (Jasmin Mujanović,
"Why Serb Nationalism Still Inspires Europe's Far Right," *Balkan Insight,* March
22, 2019, https://balkaninsight.com/2019/03/22/why-serb-nationalism-still-inspires
-europes-far-right/). Our thanks to Rebecca Hill for pointing this out.

58. Marilyn Elias, "Sikh Temple Killer Wade Michael Page Radicalized in
Army," Southern Poverty Law Center, November 11, 2012, www.splcenter.org
/fighting-hate/intelligence-report/2012/sikh-temple-killer-wade-michael-page
-radicalized-army.

59. Elias, "Sikh Temple Killer."

60. Cai et al., "White Extremist Ideology Drives Many Deadly Shootings."

61. Andrew Theen, "Umpqua Community College Shooting: Killer's Manifesto
Reveals Racist, Satanic Views," *Oregonian,* September 8, 2017, www.oregonlive
.com/pacific-northwest-news/2017/09/umpqua_community_college_shoot_3
.html.

62. Cai et al., "White Extremist Ideology Drives Many Deadly Shootings."

63. Samira Said, Steve Visser, and Catherine E. Shoichet, "Houston Shooting:
Nine Injured, Suspect Dead," CNN.com, September 27, 2016, https://edition.cnn
.com/2016/09/26/us/houston-shooting/index.html.

64. Cai et al., "White Extremist Ideology Drives Many Deadly Shootings."

65. Cai et al., "White Extremist Ideology Drives Many Deadly Shootings."

66. Cai et al., "White Extremist Ideology Drives Many Deadly Shootings."

67. Jason Riley, "Accused Kroger Shooter Has History of Mental Illness and
Racist Comments," WDRB, October 25, 2018, www.wdrb.com/news/crime-reports
/accused-kroger-shooter-has-history-of-mental-illness-and-racist/article_3dfb9159
-6e5c-56db-be12-483897bd42d1.html.

68. Though not all parts of the boogaloo movement and Groypers are necessar-
ily tied to white power, many promote anti-Semitic and racist viewpoints. "The
Boogaloo Movement," Anti-Defamation League, www.adl.org/boogaloo; "Groyper
Army and 'America First,'" Anti-Defamation League, March 17, 2020.

69. Richard Winton, Maura Dolan, and Anita Chabria, "Far-Right 'Boogaloo
Boys' Linked to Killing of California Law Officers and Other Violence," *Los Angeles
Times,* June 17, 2020, www.latimes.com/california/story/2020-06-17/far-right
-boogaloo-boys-linked-to-killing-of-california-lawmen-other-violence.

70. A. C. Thompson, Lila Hassan, and Karim Hajj, "The Boogaloo Bois Have
Guns, Criminal Records and Military Training. Now They Want to Overthrow the
Government," ProPublica, February 1, 2021, www.propublica.org/article/boogaloo
-bois-military-training.

71. See Stephanie K. Baer, "Trump Supporters Flaunt Racist Symbols at US
Capitol Coup Attempt," Buzzfeed News, January 6, 2021, www.buzzfeednews.com
/article/skbaer/trump-supporters-racist-symbols-capitol-assault.

72. "'Will Be Wild!': Trump Tweet Summoned Jan. 6 Mob after Advisers Refused to Back Stolen Election Claim," DemocracyNow!, July 13, 2022, www.democracynow .org/2022/7/13/trump_summoned_mob_after_unhinged_meeting.

73. Evan Hill, Arielle Ray, and Dahlia Kozlowsky, "Videos Show How Rioter Was Trampled in Stampede at Capitol," *New York Times,* May 31, 2021, www .nytimes.com/2021/01/16/us/politics/videos-show-how-a-rioter-was-trampled-in -the-stampede-at-the-capitol.html.

CHAPTER TWO: IMMISERATION CULTURE

1. Cassie Miller, "Accusations in a Mirror: How the Radical Right Blames Rising Political Violence on the Left," Southern Poverty Law Center, June 11, 2019, www.splcenter.org/hatewatch/2019/06/11/accusations-mirror-how-radical-right -blames-rising-political-violence-left.

2. Although here Tarrant indicts corporations (a metonym for neoliberal capitalism) for fueling nonwhite immigration, we will see later in this chapter and in chapter 4 that the relationship between white power and neoliberalism is far from consistent and this type of resentment actually obscures their joint idealization of the family.

3. Andrew Anglin, "What Is the Deal with WMBF Relationships?," Daily Stormer, September 19, 2016, https://archive.is/3TrgB.

4. As utopian studies scholar Gregory Claeys puts it, "The group prototype is the family unit, later the basis for many forms of utopian affective association" (*Dystopia: A Natural History* [Oxford: Oxford University Press, 2017], 38). However, we should note that this statement is actually couched in terms of the negativity of group behavior (especially crowds).

5. In other countries neoliberalism looks different. For instance, in Germany neoliberalism tends to be associated more with using regulation and expertise to force capitalism to operate in what they see as its optimum market form. And the work of Verónica Gago, who studies Latin American neoliberalism, especially in Argentina, identifies what she calls "neoliberalism from below," discussed in chapter 3, where subjects who from one frame can be seen as neoliberalism's victims find ways to reshape and reformulate neoliberal imperatives and thereby reorient neoliberalism itself toward their interests and without the intervention of the state. See her *Neoliberalism from Below: Popular Pragmatics and Baroque Economies* (Durham, NC: Duke University Press, 2017).

6. Melinda Cooper, *Family Values: Between Neoliberalism and the New Social Conservatism* (Cambridge, MA: Zone Books, 2017).

7. Cooper, *Family Values,* 100. Gary S. Becker's *A Treatise on the Family,* enlarged ed. (Cambridge, MA: Harvard University Press, 1991), which Cooper brilliantly analyzes, begins, characteristically, in this way:

The family in the Western world has been radically altered—some claim almost destroyed—by events of the last three decades. The rapid growth in divorce rates has greatly increased the number of households headed by women and the number of children growing up in households with only one parent. The large increase in labor force participation of married women, including mothers with young children, has reduced the contact between children and their mothers and contributed to the conflict between the sexes in employment as well as in marriage. The rapid decline in birth rates has reduced family size and helped cause the increased rates of divorce and labor force participation of married women.

8. Cooper, *Family Values,* 57–61.

9. Wendy Brown, *In the Ruins of Neoliberalism: The Rise of Antidemocratic Politics in the West* (New York: Columbia University Press, 2019).

10. Neoconservatives include neoliberals closely associated with the group known as the New York Intellectuals and with the journal *Partisan Review,* with figures such as Kristol and Norman Podhoretz; their colleagues such as Moynihan; and their adherents and children such as William Kristol. In the Trump era this group has tended to label themselves "Never Trumpers" and oppose his antiglobalist "America Firstism."

11. Irving Kristol, *Neoconservatism: The Autobiography of an Idea* (New York: Simon and Schuster, 1995), 142. For commentary, see Cooper, *Family Values,* 52.

12. Kristol, *Neoconservatism,* 486.

13. Cooper, *Family Values,* 8.

14. Cooper, *Family Values,* 8.

15. See a contemporaneous discussion in Herbert Hill, "Labor Unions and the Negro: The Record of Discrimination," *Commentary,* December 1959, www .commentarymagazine.com/articles/herbert-hill/labor-unions-and-the-negrothe -record-of-discrimination/; see also University of Richmond's Digital Scholarship Lab, "Introduction," *Mapping Inequality: Redlining in New Deal America,* https:// dsl.richmond.edu/panorama/redlining/#loc=11/41.081/-81.702&city=akron -oh&text=intro.

16. Stephen Ruggles, "Patriarchy, Power, and Pay: The Transformation of American Families, 1800–2015," *Demography* 52, no. 6 (2015): 1797–1823.

17. Indeed, this fetishization of the white family in white supremacy has a history that is codified in popular culture in D. W. Griffith's *The Birth of a Nation* (1915), as discussed by George Lipsitz building on Michael Rogin's work: "By representing slave emancipation and the radical reforms of the Reconstruction era as threats to the integrity and purity of the white family, Griffith's film forged a renewed narrative of national unity and obligation based on connections between patriotism and patriarchy—between white patriarchal protection of the purity of the white family and the necessity for whites to forget the things that divide them in order to unite against their nonwhite enemies." George Lipsitz, *The Possessive Investment in Whiteness: How White People Profit from Identity Politics* (Philadelphia: Temple University Press, 2018), loc. 2398, Kindle.

18. Quoted in David Neiwert, "Huffing about Sexual Mores, Calls the Kettle Black," Southern Poverty Law Center, November 18, 2010, www.splcenter.org /hatewatch/2010/11/18/david-duke-huffing-about-sexual-mores-calls-kettle-black.

19. Barry Richards, "What Drove Anders Breivik?," *Contexts* 13, no. 4 (2014): 44–45.

20. Stephanie Coontz, *The Way We Never Were: American Families and the Nostalgia Trap* (New York: Basic Books, 1993).

21. David R. Roediger, *The Wages of Whiteness: Race and the Making of the American Working Class* (New York: Verso, 2007 [1991]), and Steve Martinot, *The Machinery of Whiteness: Studies in the Structure of Racialization* (Philadelphia: Temple University Press, 2010).

22. Paula Ioanide, *The Emotional Politics of Racism: How Feelings Trump Facts in an Era of Colorblindness* (Stanford, CA: Stanford University Press, 2015), 18.

23. Jay Willis, "How Don Jr., Ivanka, and Eric Trump Have Profited Off Their Dad's Presidency," *GQ*, October 14, 2019, www.gq.com/story/trump-kids-profit -presidency.

24. Tellingly, the Trump family honored this arrangement as well, with daughter Ivanka acting as a kind of advisor–cum–first lady while son-in-law Jared was actually tasked with solving the United States' opioid-addiction crisis, helping manage the White House's coronavirus response, and—presumably in his spare time—securing peace in the Middle East.

25. Laura Briggs, *How All Politics Became Reproductive Politics: From Welfare Reform to Foreclosure to Trump* (Berkeley: University of California Press, 2017), loc. 130, Kindle. The book as a whole connects reproductive politics to neoliberalism.

26. United Nations Research Institute for Social Development, *Why Care Matters for Social Development,* UNRISD Research and Policy Brief 9, www.unrisd.org /80256B3C005BCCF9/(httpAuxPages)/25697FE238192066C12576D4004CFE50 /%24file/RPB9e.pdf.

27. See Catherine Rottenberg, *The Rise of Neoliberal Feminism* (New York: Oxford University Press, 2018).

28. See Louis Toupin, *Wages for Housework: A History of an International Feminist Movement, 1972–77* (Vancouver: University of British Columbia Press, 2018).

29. Studies of the seven million workers who lost their jobs through mass layoffs in 2004–2009 showed all the predictable effects, especially for those without a college degree: permanent reduction in wages when they find new jobs or being forced to work in the gig economy without benefits. They also are more likely to suffer from depression, marital issues, and substance abuse. See Sandra J. Sucher et al., "Layoffs: Effects on Key Stakeholders," Harvard Business School Background Note 611–028, December 2010, revised September 2014.

30. Shane McFeely and Ryan Pendell, "What Workplace Leaders Can Learn from the Real Gig Economy," Gallup, August 16, 2018, www.gallup.com/workplace /240929/workplace-leaders-learn-real-gig-economy.aspx.

31. Otto Penz and Birgit Sauer, *Governing Affects: Neoliberalism, Neo-Bureaucracies, and Service Work* (New York: Routledge, 2020), 100–101.

32. Penz and Sauer, *Governing Affects,* 111.

33. Penz and Sauer, *Governing Affects,* 111.

34. There is such an extensive literature on the fundamentals of neoliberalism that it is hard to know what to cite. David Harvey's classic *A Brief History of Neoliberalism* (Oxford: Oxford University Press, 2005) is as good a place as any to start. Ventura writes about it in *Neoliberal Culture: Living with American Neoliberalism* (New York: Routledge, 2016).

35. According to the Economic Policy Institute, "Rising wage inequality has been a defining feature of the American economy for nearly four decades." Some other findings that are significant for us here include the following:

> Since 1979, hourly pay for the vast majority of American workers has diverged from economy-wide productivity, and this divergence is at the root of numerous American economic challenges. After tracking rather closely in the three decades following World War II, growing productivity and typical worker compensation diverged. From 1979 to 2016, productivity grew 64.2 percent, while hourly compensation of production and nonsupervisory workers grew just 11.2 percent. . . . A natural question that arises from this story is just where did the "excess" productivity go? A significant portion of it went to higher corporate profits and increased income accruing to capital and business owners.

Elise Gould, *The State of American Wages 2017* (Washington, DC: Economic Policy Institute, 2018), www.epi.org/publication/the-state-of-american-wages-2017 -wages-have-finally-recovered-from-the-blow-of-the-great-recession-but-are-still -growing-too-slowly-and-unequally/#epi-toc-1.

36. Cooper, *Family Values,* 24.

37. As the law stated, "That the Father and grandfather, and the Mother and Grandmother, and the children of every poor, old, blind, lame, and impotent person, or other poor person, not able to work, being of a sufficient ability, shall at their own charges relieve and maintain every such poor person" ("1601: 43 Elizabeth 1 c.2: Act for the Relief of the Poor," *The Statutes Project: Putting Historic British Law Online,* accessed January 5, 2021, http://statutes.org.uk/site/the-statutes/seventeenth-century /1601-43-elizabeth-c-2-act-for-the-relief-of-the-poor/). In addition, see Melinda Cooper, "Neoliberalism's Family Values: Welfare, Human Capital, and Kinship," in *Nine Lives of Neoliberalism,* ed. Dieter Plehwe, Quinn Slobodian, and Philip Mirowski (Brooklyn: Verso, 2020), 98–99.

38. Cooper, *Family Values,* chapter 3.

39. Cooper, *Family Values,* 24.

40. Ventura, *Neoliberal Culture,* chapter 4. See also the 2000 Green Book Overview of Entitlement Programs, *Committee on Ways and Means, U.S. House of Representatives* (Washington, DC: U.S. G.P.O., 2000), https://aspe.hhs.gov/2000 -green-book.

41. Margaret Thatcher explained this kind of attitude in her statement against the social service state: "Once you give people the idea that all this can be done by the State, and that it is somehow second-best or even degrading to leave it to private people (it is sometimes referred to as 'cold charity') then you will begin to deprive human beings of one of the essential ingredients of humanity—personal moral

responsibility." "I BELIEVE—A Speech on Christianity and Politics," speech, St. Lawrence Jewry, City of London, March 21, 1978, Margaret Thatcher Foundation, www.margaretthatcher.org/document/103522.

42. Quoted in Seyward Darby, *Sisters in Hate: American Women on the Front Lines of White Nationalism* (New York: Little, Brown, 2020), 81.

43. Hilary Radner, *Neo-Feminist Cinema: Girly Films, Chick Flicks, and Consumer Culture* (New York: Routledge, 2010), 192.

44. On the history of zero-sum perspectives on race in the United States, see Heather McGhee, *The Sum of Us: What Racism Costs Everyone and How We Can Prosper Together* (New York: One World Press, 2021), especially chapter 1, as well as Michael I. Norton and Samuel R. Sommers, "Whites See Racism as a Zero-Sum Game That They Are Now Losing," *Perspectives on Psychological Science* 6, no. 3 (2011): 215–18.

45. Blee's chosen terminology to describe the amalgamation of white supremacist/nationalist/separatist groups, "organized racism," is akin to what we call "white power": "Organized racism is more than the aggregation of individual racist sentiments. It is a social milieu in which venomous ideas—about African Americans, Jews, Hispanics, Asians, gay men and lesbians, and others—take shape. Through networks of groups and activists, it channels personal sentiments of hatred into collective racist acts. Organized racism is different from the racism widespread in mainstream white society: it is more focused, self-conscious, and targeted at specific strategic goals." Kathleen M. Blee, *Inside Organized Racism: Women in the Hate Movement* (Berkeley: University of California Press, 2003), 3.

46. Blee, *Inside Organized Racism*, 7.

47. Blee, *Inside Organized Racism*, 115.

48. Blee, *Inside Organized Racism*, 124.

49. Barry Richards, "What Drove Anders Breivik?," 47.

50. Blee, *Inside Organized Racism*, 131.

51. Blee, *Inside Organized Racism*, 154.

52. Blee, *Inside Organized Racism,* 124.

53. Alexandra Minna Stern, *Proud Boys and the White Ethnostate: How the Alt-Right Is Warping the American Imagination* (Boston: Beacon Press, 2019), 100.

54. Steve Benen, "GOP Rep Scrambles after Thanking Trump for a Win for 'White Life,'" MSNBC.com, June 27, 2022, www.msnbc.com/rachel-maddow-show /maddowblog/gop-rep-scrambles-thanking-trump-win-white-life-rcna35451.

55. Birgit Sauer, "Authoritarian Right-Wing Populism as Masculinist Identity Politics. The Role of Affects," in *Right-Wing Populism and Gender: European Perspectives and Beyond,* ed. Gabriele Dietze and Julia Roth (Bielefeld: Transcript), 35.

56. Sauer, "Authoritarian Right-Wing Populism," 32.

57. Census Bureau data from 2018 shows that women earned, on average, just 82 cents for every $1 earned by men; comparing median wages by race and gender, white women earned 79 cents, Black women 62 cents, and Latinas 54 cents for every dollar earned by a white man. Extend that over the course of a forty-year career and those inequalities balloon: At the low end of the spectrum, Latinas earn $1.1 million less than their male counterparts. See Robin Bleweis, *Quick Facts about the Gender Wage Gap*

(Washington, DC: Center for American Progress, 2020), www.americanprogress.org /issues/women/reports/2020/03/24/482141/quick-facts-gender-wage-gap/.

But these numbers should not suggest that all men are doing well. Indeed, for men without a college degree the prospects have been poor. See Anne Case and Angus Deaton, "Mortality and Morbidity in the 21st Century," *Brookings Papers on Economic Activity* (2017): 29–32, www.brookings.edu/wp-content/uploads/2017/03 /6_casedeaton.pdf, which explores the grim life prospects poverty has created for the white working class. Such studies can be used to shore up a long-standing American narrative that implicitly assumes "working class" is a term that often connotes white people even though racial categories are not mentioned. See Sam Fullwood III, *An All-American Myth About the White Working Class* (Washington, DC: Center for American Progress, 2017), www.americanprogress.org/issues/race/news /2017/03/30/429599/american-myth-white-working-class/.

These studies provide important context for white power's rising influence. According to Elise Gould of the Economic Policy Institute in the *State of American Wages* report, when it comes to men, "Long-term trends suggest that low- and middle-wage men have fared comparatively poorly" in the neoliberal economy.

58. Penz and Sauer, *Governing Affects,* 105.

59. Penz and Sauer, *Governing Affects*.

60. Sauer, "Authoritarian Right-Wing Populism," 24.

61. Neil Davidson and Richard Saull, "Neoliberalism and the Far-Right: A Contradictory Embrace," *Critical Sociology* 43, no. 4–5 (2017): 9.

62. Davidson and Saull, "Neoliberalism and the Far-Right," 10.

63. This report was authored in part by Samuel Huntington, who later wrote the notorious *Clash of Civilizations and the Remaking of World Order* (1996) arguing that in a post–Cold War world national identity would be trumped by civilizational affinity—with the United States lumped in with Europe and Australia—as a united Western civilization. In this world, pushing for democratic reforms would be seen as a naive and dated effort.

64. Fredric Jameson, "Periodizing the 60s," *Social Text,* no. 9/10 (1984): 205.

65. Brown, *In the Ruins of Neoliberalism,* 73.

66. See Quinn Slobodian, *Globalists: The End of Empire and the Birth of Neoliberalism* (Cambridge, MA: Harvard University Press, 2018).

67. Mahnoor Khan, "Putin Claims He Makes $140,000 per Year and Has an 800-Square-Foot Apartment," *Fortune,* March 2, 2022, https://fortune.com/2022 /03/02/vladimir-putin-net-worth-2022/.

68. Christopher Caldwell, "How to Think About Vladimir Putin," *Imprimis* 46, no. 3 (March 2017), https://imprimis.hillsdale.edu/how-to-think-about -vladimir-putin/.

69. William Davies, "The New Neoliberalism," *New Left Review* 101 (September–October 2016): 132.

70. Alana Abramson, "'No Lessons Have Been Learned': Why the Trillion-Dollar Coronavirus Bailout Benefited the Rich," *Time,* June 18, 2020, https://time .com/5845116/coronavirus-bailout-rich-richer/. Indeed, the world's twenty-five

wealthiest individuals, sixteen of whom are American, saw their wealth increase by $255 billion in just the first two months of the coronavirus shutdowns.

71. Mark Hulbert, "The 'Disturbing Reality' Fueling This Bull Market," *Barrons,* August 21, 2020, www.barrons.com/articles/the-disturbing-reality-fueling -this-bull-market-51598004009.

72. Ana Maria Santacreu, "How Does US Income Inequality Compare Worldwide," Federal Reserve Bank of St. Louis (blog), October 16, 2017, www.stlouisfed .org/on-the-economy/2017/october/how-us-income-inequality-compare -worldwide.

73. Frank Ridzi, *Selling Welfare Reform: Work First and the New Common Sense of Employment* (New York: New York University Press, 2009), 37. Ridzi shows that the number of families that actually made it through the welfare support intake process dropped from nearly 80 percent in 1996 (before Clinton's reforms) to 48 percent by 2002.

74. Marco Revelli, *The New Populism: Democracy Stares into the Abyss,* trans. David Broader (New York: Verso, 2019), 11.

75. Davidson and Saull, "Neoliberalism and the Far-Right," 5.

76. Andrew Macdonald, *The Turner Diaries,* 2nd ed. (Fort Lee, NJ: Barricade Books, 1996), loc. 3102, Kindle.

77. Kenneth Molyneaux, *White Empire* (World Church of the Creator [?], 2000).

78. George Michael, "RAHOWA! A History of the World Church of the Creator," *Terrorism and Political Violence* 18, no. 4 (2006): 568.

79. H. A. Covington. *The Hill of the Ravens* (Bloomington: AuthorHouse, 2003), loc. 3420, Kindle; David Lane, *88 Precepts,* n.d., Internet Archive, August 19, 2010, https://archive.org/details/88Precepts_937/mode/2up.

80. Lane, *88 Precepts.*

81. Sindre Bangstad draws on Verena Stolcke to point out that the European far right often insinuates racism without talking about race in *Anders Breivik and the Rise of Islamophobia* (London: Zed Books, 2014), 94.

CHAPTER THREE: FAR WHITE FAMILY VALUES

1. Lisa Duggan, *The Twilight of Equality? Neoliberalism, Cultural Politics, and the Attack on Democracy* (Boston: Beacon Press, 2003), loc. 60–73, Kindle.

2. Melinda Cooper, *Family Values: Between Neoliberalism and the New Social Conservatism* (Cambridge, MA: Zone Books, 2017).

3. Fredric Jameson "Periodizing the 60s," *Social Text,* no. 9/10 (1984): 208.

4. Claire Cain Miller, "The Divorce Surge Is Over, But the Myth Lives On," *New York Times,* December 2, 2014, A3.

5. Angie Maxwell and Todd Shields, *The Long Southern Strategy: How Chasing White Voters in the South Changed American Politics* (New York: Oxford University Press, 2019).

6. Randolph Hohle, *Race and the Origins of American Neoliberalism* (New York: Routledge, 2015), 2, and *Racism in the Neoliberal Era: A Meta History of Elite White Power* (New York: Routledge, 2018), 13–14.

7. On redlining see University of Richmond's Digital Scholarship Lab, "Introduction," *Mapping Inequality: Redlining in New Deal America,* https://dsl.richmond.edu/panorama/redlining/#loc=11/41.081/-81.702&city=akron-oh&text=intro, accessed June 15, 2021.

8. Cooper, "Neoliberalism's Family Values: Welfare, Human Capital, and Kinship," in *Nine Lives of Neoliberalism,* ed. Dieter Plehwe, Quinn Slobodian, and Philip Mirowski (Brooklyn: Verso, 2020).

9. Joshua Inwood, "Neoliberal Racism: The 'Southern Strategy' and the Expanding Geographies of White Supremacy," *Social and Cultural Geography* 16, no. 4 (2015): 411.

10. Quoted in Mark Davis, "'Culture Is Inseparable from Race': Culture Wars from Pat Buchanan to Milo Yiannopoulos," *M/C Journal* 21, no. 5 (2018), https://doi.org/10.5204/mcj.1484.

11. Maxwell and Shields, *The Long Southern Strategy,* 31.

12. It is important to recognize that even Milton Friedman, the Reaganomics economist and neoliberal propagandist against the welfare state, supported some version of the welfare state in the era of the Fordist family wage. See Cooper, *Family Values,* chapter 2.

13. Robert G. Lee, *Orientals: Asian Americans in Popular Culture* (Philadelphia: Temple University Press, 1999), 53.

14. Gilbert G. Gonzalez, "The Ideology and Practice of Empire: The United States, Mexico, and Mexican Immigrants," in *A Century of Chicano History: Empires, Nations, and Migrations,* ed. Gilbert G. Gonzalez and Raul A. Fernandez (New York: Routledge, 2003), 89.

15. Quoted in Gonzalez, "The Ideology and Practice of Empire," 89.

16. E. Franklin Frazier, *The Negro Family in the United States* (Chicago: University of Illinois Press, 1939), 484.

17. W. E. B. Du Bois, "The Study of the Negro Problems," *Annals of the American Academy of Political and Social Science* 11 (January 1898): 18.

18. Gunnar Myrdal, *An American Dilemma: The Negro Problem and Modern Democracy* (New York: Harper and Brothers Publishers, 1944), iii.

19. Anne Branigin, "Southern Baptist Leaders Called Kamala Harris a 'Jezebel.' That's Not Just Insulting, It's Dangerous, Experts Say," *The Lily,* February 9, 2021, www.thelily.com/southern-baptist-leaders-called-kamala-harris-a-jezebel-thats-not-just-insulting-its-dangerous-experts-say/.

20. Office of Policy Planning and Research, United States Department of Labor, "Chapter IV: The Tangle of Pathology," *The Negro Family: The Case for National Action,* www.dol.gov/general/aboutdol/history/webid-moynihan/moynchapter4.

21. Office of Policy Planning and Research United States Department of Labor, "Chapter IV."

22. Grace Kyungwon Hong, *Death Beyond Disavowal: The Impossible Politics of Difference* (Minneapolis: University of Minnesota Press, 2015), 23.

23. Office of Policy Planning and Research, United States Department of Labor, "Chapter V: The Case for National Action," *The Negro Family: The Case for National Action,* www.dol.gov/general/aboutdol/history/webid-moynihan/moynchapter5.

24. Office of Policy Planning and Research, United States Department of Labor, "Chapter IV."

25. Office of Policy Planning and Research, United States Department of Labor, "Chapter IV."

26. Cooper's *Family Values* (35–46) makes it clear that Moynihan's report was in step with many left and left-leaning political figures at that time, including luminaries such as Martin Luther King Jr., scholars such as Francis Piven, and Black nationalist leaders.

27. Cooper, *Family Values,* 47.

28. Bill Clinton, "How We Ended Welfare, Together," *New York Times,* August 22, 2006, www.nytimes.com/2006/08/22/opinion/22clinton.html.

29. See Hohle, R*ace and the Origins of American Neoliberalism,* for an account of how "the white response to the civil rights movement inadvertently empowered the liberal business class [in the South] and set the stage for the national neoliberal turn" (2).

30. Thomas Piketty, *Capital in the Twenty-First Century,* trans. Arthur Goldhammer (Cambridge, MA: Harvard University Press), 27.

31. Joshua Inwood, "Neoliberal Racism: The 'Southern Strategy' and the Expanding Geographies of White Supremacy," *Social and Cultural Geography* 16, no. 4 (2015): 409.

32. Paul Lewis, "Obama Resists Demands to Curtail Police Militarization Calling Instead for Improved Officer Training," *Guardian,* December 1, 2014, www.theguardian.com/us-news/2014/dec/01/obama-white-house-summit-ferguson.

33. David Macdonald, "Class Attitudes, Political Knowledge, and Support for Redistribution in an Era of Inequality," *Social Science Quarterly* 101, no. 2 (2020): 960–77.

34. John B. Judis, *The Populist Explosion: How the Great Recession Transformed American and European Politics* (New York: Columbia Global Reports, 2016), loc. 95–96, 685–90, and 2229–30, Kindle.

35. Ta-Nehisi Coates, "The First White President: The Foundation of Donald Trump's Legacy Is the Negation of Barack Obama's Legacy," *The Atlantic,* October 2017, www.theatlantic.com/magazine/archive/2017/10/the-first-white-president-ta-nehisi-coates/537909/.

36. See Jonathan Metzl, *Dying of Whiteness: How the Politics of Racial Resentment Is Killing America's Heartland* (New York: Basic Books, 2019). As he argues, "White America's investment in maintaining an imagined place atop a racial hierarchy ... ironically harms the aggregate well-being of US whites as a demographic group, thereby making whiteness itself a negative health indicator" (7).

37. For an exhaustive description of concrete examples, see especially chapter 1 of George Lipsitz, *The Possessive Investment in Whiteness: How White People Profit from Identity Politics* (Philadelphia: Temple University Press, 2018).

38. Michael Bang Petersen, Mathias Osmundsen, and Alexander Bor, "Beyond Populism: The Psychology of Status-Seeking and Extreme Political Discontent," in *The Psychology of Populism,* ed. Joseph P. Forgas, William D. Crano, and Klaus Fiedler (New York: Routledge, 2020), 62–80.

39. Arlie Russell Hochschild, "I Spent 5 Years with Some of Trump's Biggest Fans. Here's What They Won't Tell You," *Mother Jones,* September–October 2016, www.motherjones.com/politics/2016/08/trump-white-blue-collar-supporters/.

40. For Foucault, see chapter 9 of *The Birth of Biopolitics: Lectures at the Collège de France, 1978-1979,* ed. Michel Senellart, trans. Graham Burchell (London: Palgrave Macmillan, 2008). For a very helpful analysis of the way various approaches to neoliberalism use affect and especially the way Hall understands affects, see Ben Anderson, "Neoliberal Affects," *Progress in Human Geography* 40, no. 6 (2016): 734–53.

41. Verónica Gago, *Neoliberalism from Below: Popular Pragmatics and Baroque Economies* (Durham, NC: Duke University Press, 2017), loc. 4817, Kindle.

42. Melinda Cooper, "Anti-Austerity on the Far Right," in *Mutant Neoliberalism: Market Rule and Political Rupture,* ed. William Callison and Zachary Manfredi (New York: Fordham University Press, 2020).

43. Alexandra Minna Stern, *Proud Boys and the White Ethnostate: How the Alt-Right Is Warping the American Imagination* (Boston: Beacon Press, 2019), 48, 52.

44. Macdonald, "Class Attitudes, Political Knowledge."

45. On white fragility see Robin DiAngelo, *White Fragility: Why It's So Hard for White People to Talk about Racism* (Boston: Beacon Press, 2018).

46. On party affiliation in this context, see Shato Iyengar and Sean. J Westwood, "Fear and Loathing across Party Lines: New Evidence on Group Polarization," *American Journal of Political Science* 59, no. 3 (2015): 690–707.

47. Margaret Thatcher, "Interview for *Woman's Own* ('No Such Thing as Society')," September 23, 1987, Margaret Thatcher Foundation, www.margaretthatcher .org/document/106689.

48. G. R. Steele, "There Is No Such Thing as Society," Institute of Economic Affairs, September 30, 2009, https://iea.org.uk/blog/there-is-no-such-thing-as-society.

49. Birgit Sauer, "Authoritarian Right-Wing Populism as Masculinist Identity Politics. The Role of Affects," in *Right-Wing Populism and Gender: European Perspectives and Beyond,* ed. Gabriele Dietze and Julia Roth (Bielefeld: Transcript, 2020), 32.

50. Nikolas Rose, "The Death of the Social? Re-figuring the Territory of Government," *Economy and Society* 25, no. 3 (1996): 327–56. See also Patricia Ventura, *Neoliberal Culture: Living with American Neoliberalism* (New York: Routledge, 2016), which argues that the erosion of the social service state is one of the key pillars of American neoliberal culture.

51. Wendy Brown, *In the Ruins of Neoliberalism: The Rise of Antidemocratic Politics in the West* (New York: Columbia University Press, 2019), 28.

52. Gago, *Neoliberalism from Below,* loc. 203, Kindle.

53. Jason Read, "A Genealogy of Homo-Economicus: Neoliberalism and the Production of Subjectivity," *Foucault Studies* 6 (2009): 25–36.

54. Sauer, "Authoritarian Right-Wing Populism," 32.

55. Ronald Reagan, "News Conference (1)," August 12, 1986, Ronald Reagan Presidential Foundation and Institute, video, www.reaganfoundation.org/ronald-reagan/reagan-quotes-speeches/news-conference-1/.

56. Maxwell and Shields, *The Long Southern Strategy,* 11 and 328.

57. Maxwell and Shields, *The Long Southern Strategy,* 11.

58. See Maxwell and Shields, *The Long Southern Strategy.*

59. Magnus E. Marsdal, "Loud Values, Muffled Interests: Third Way Social Democracy and Right-Wing Populism," in *Right-Wing Populism in Europe: Politics and Discourse,* ed. Ruth Wodak, Majid Khosravinik, and Brigitte Mral (London: Bloomsbury Academic, 2013), www.bloomsburycollections.com/book/right-wing-populism-in-europe-politics-and-discourse/ch3-loud-values-muffled-interests (emphasis in original).

60. Quoted in Inwood, "Neoliberal Racism," 415.

61. Inwood, "Neoliberal Racism," 415.

62. Brown, *In the Ruins of Neoliberalism,* 8.

63. See especially the introduction to Michael Kimmel, *Angry White Men: American Masculinity at the End of an Era* (New York: Nation Books), 2013.

64. Matthew N. Lyons, "The Christchurch Massacre and Fascist Revolutionary Politics," threewayfight, April 18, 2019, http://threewayfight.blogspot.com/2019/04/the-christchurch-massacre-and-fascist.html.

65. Christian Joppke, *Neoliberal Nationalism: Immigration and the Rise of the Populist Right* (Cambridge: Cambridge University Press, 2021), loc. 311, 432, Kindle (emphasis in original).

66. Typical of white supremacists, he cites the higher birth rates of nonwhite immigrants (contextually, he's speaking mostly about Latinx people)—which, as we've seen, supposedly contributes to the replacement of white people—and the strain they put on the social welfare state. However, he voices no apparent opposition to the welfare state in and of itself.

67. Tad Tietze, "Anders Breivik, Fascism and the Neoliberal Inheritance," in *Hayek: A Collaborative Biography: Part IV Good Dictators, Sovereign Producers and Hayek's "Ruthless Consistency,"* ed. Robert Leeson (Basingstoke: Palgrave Macmillan, 2015), 287.

68. Tietze, "Anders Breivik, Fascism and the Neoliberal Inheritance," 285–86.

69. Friedrich Hayek, *The Road to Serfdom: Text and Documents,* ed. Bruce Caldwell (Chicago: University of Chicago Press, 2007), 118.

70. Tietze, "Anders Breivik, Fascism and the Neoliberal Inheritance," 288.

71. It should be noted that a multiparty political consensus around the necessity of the social welfare function at the federal level ended two years into the Nixon era, when the United States faced a crisis of inflation (Cooper, *Family Values,* 44).

72. H.A. Covington, *Freedom's Son* (Bay City, OR: Northwestern Publishing Agency, 2011), 54 (emphases in original).

73. Covington, *Freedom's Son*, 79.

74. See the Covington section in chapter 4.

75. Andrew Macdonald [William L. Pierce], *The Turner Diaries,* 2nd ed. (Fort Lee, NJ: Barricade Books, 1996), loc. 913, 3511, Kindle.

CHAPTER FOUR: THE "FAMILY" AT THE CORE OF WHITE POWER UTOPIA

1. Chan also discusses Lane's *KD Rebel* and Covington's *The Hill of the Ravens* in "The White Power Utopia and the Reproduction of Victimized Whiteness," in *Race and Utopian Desire in American Literature and Society*, ed. Patricia Ventura and Edward K. Chan (Cham, Switzerland: Palgrave Macmillan, 2019), 139–59.

2. The term *utopia* is commonly used as a reference to a *good* place, though strictly speaking the term in its original formulation by Sir Thomas More carries a double meaning: *eu*topia (good place) and *u*topia (no place). It can also be an umbrella term for both eutopias and dystopias. For this book we are using the popular understanding of *utopia* as a good place, often set in an ideal (relatively speaking) near future.

3. For both fictional and nonfictional examples, see chapter 3 of Alexandra Minna Stern's *Proud Boys and the White Ethnostate: How the Alt-Right Is Warping the American Imagination* (Boston: Beacon Press, 2019). As she notes, Sumner Humphrey Ireland, writing as "Wilmot Robertson," helped establish the desire for a white ethnostate in modern far-right politics in the 1990s (57).

4. Andrew Macdonald [Williams L. Pierce], *The Turner Diaries,* 2nd ed. (Fort Lee, NJ: Barricade Books, 1996), loc. 3531–36, Kindle.

5. Southern Poverty Law Center, "William Pierce," Extremist Files, accessed September 23, 2020, www.splcenter.org/fighting-hate/extremist-files/individual /william-pierce.

6. J.M. Berger, "The Turner Legacy: The Storied Origins and Enduring Impact of White Nationalism's Deadly Bible," *International Centre for Counter-Terrorism—The Hague* 7, no. 8 (2016): 30.

7. Berger, "The Turner Legacy," 35.

8. Mike Levine et al., "Nation's Deadliest Domestic Terrorist Inspiring New Generation of Hate-Filled 'Monsters,' FBI Records Show," ABC News, October 6, 2020, https://abcnews.go.com/US/nations-deadliest-domestic-terrorist-inspiring -generation-hate-filled/story?id=73431262.

9. "What Is the National Alliance?," National Alliance, n.d., quoted in Southern Poverty Law Center, "William Pierce."

10. Southern Poverty Law Center, "William Pierce"; David Lane, *KD Rebel*, (N.p.: JR's Rare Books and Commentary, 2004), 83. All citations are to the PDF version that used to be available at JRBooksOnline.com, www.jrbooksonline.com

/PDF_Books_added2009–4/kdrebel.pdf. There is another version available at archive.org but it is not paginated.

11. As Joe Lockard points out, Pierce's novel shares this technique with Jack London's *The Iron Heel* (1908); "Reading *The Turner Diaries:* Jewish Blackness, Judaized Blacks, and Head-Body Race Paradigms," in *Complicating Constructions: Race, Ethnicity, and Hybridity in American Texts,* ed. David S. Goldstein and Audrey B. Thacker (Seattle: University of Washington Press, 2007), 127. Berger pushes the lineage even further to the mid-nineteenth century, particularly Edmund Ruffin's *Anticipations of the Future* (1860) in addition to a book cited by Pierce as a direct inspiration, the anonymously written *The John Franklin Letters* (1959) (Berger, "The Turner Legacy," 18, 20, 24).

12. Macdonald, *The Turner Diaries,* loc. 1119, 912, Kindle.

13. Macdonald, *The Turner Diaries,* loc. 923, Kindle.

14. Fredric Jameson, *The Political Unconscious: Reading as a Socially Symbolic Act* (Ithaca, NY: Cornell University Press, 1981), 290–91.

15. MacDonald, *The Turner Diaries,* loc. 1987, Kindle.

16. MacDonald, *The Turner Diaries,* loc. 2770, Kindle.

17. MacDonald, *The Turner Diaries,* loc. 2872–78, Kindle. Also see Bradley C. Whitsel, "Aryan Visions for the Future in the West Virginia Mountains," *Terrorism and Political Violence* 7, no. 4 (1995): 118.

18. Macdonald, *The Turner Diaries,* loc. 2891–92, Kindle.

19. Katherine M. Blee, *Inside Organized Racism: Women in the Hate Movement* (Berkeley: University of California Press, 2002), 118.

20. Macdonald, *The Turner Diaries,* loc. 504, Kindle.

21. Macdonald, *The Turner Diaries,* loc. 738, 791, Kindle.

22. Macdonald, *The Turner Diaries,* loc. 1009, Kindle.

23. Macdonald, *The Turner Diaries,* loc. 3116, Kindle.

24. We will use WCOTC for further references to this organization, which seems to be the main formation to which Molyneaux aligns himself. We should also note that the WCOTC was legally blocked from using the phrase "Church of the Creator" because of a trademark lawsuit in the early 2000s. See the Southern Poverty Law Center's chronicling of the organization, "Creativity Movement," Extremist Files, accessed September 23, 2020, www.splcenter.org/fighting-hate/extremist-files/group/creativity-movement-0.

25. Southern Poverty Law Center, "Creativity Movement."

26. Creativity Alliance, accessed July 9, 2022, https://creativityalliance.com/.

27. George Michael, "RAHOWA! A History of the World Church of the Creator," *Terrorism and Political Violence* 18, no. 4 (2006): 578.

28. Kenneth Molyneaux, "My Awakening," Creativity Alliance, accessed September 23, 2020, https://creativityalliance.com/articles/awakenings/rev-kenneth-molyneaux/.

29. This term is shared with Christian Identity and other white power groups. There is ambivalence among white power groups and individuals about whether Jewish people qualify as white or not; see especially Roof's manifesto, in which he

claims, "Unlike many white naitonalists [*sic*], I am of the opinion that the majority of American and European Jews are white."

30. Ben Klassen, *The White Man's Bible*, 2008, https://creativityalliance.com /wp-content/uploads/ebooks/HolyBooks/eBook-BenKlassen-TheWhiteMan'sBible .pdf, 58, 60-61.

31. "Sixteen Commandments," Creativity Alliance, accessed July 9, 2022, https://creativityalliance.com/home/16commandments/.

32. Michael, "RAHOWA!," 568.

33. Michael, "RAHOWA!," 573.

34. Michael, "RAHOWA!," 577.

35. Kenneth Molyneaux, *White Empire* (World Church of the Creator [?], 2000), 2. All page references will be to the PDF version of the book available at archive.org.

36. Molyneaux, *White Empire*, 2. Although the fascination with tanning in the novel might seem to deemphasize the pure white skin of the race, it is resolved by attributing it to salubrious living in the outdoors.

37. Molyneaux, *White Empire*, 45.

38. Molyneaux, *White Empire*, 2.

39. Molyneaux, *White Empire*, 3.

40. Molyneaux, *White Empire*, 3.

41. Molyneaux, *White Empire*, 3, 89, 93.

42. Molyneaux, *White Empire*, 77.

43. Molyneaux, *White Empire*, 44. On page 13 we learn the novel's chronological setting is 77 AC (or 2050 CE). "AC" stands for "After Creativity," an alternate reality whose chronology began in 1973 with Klassen's publication of *Nature's Eternal Religion*.

44. Molyneaux, *White Empire*, 14.

45. Molyneaux, *White Empire*, 15.

46. Molyneaux, *White Empire*, 24.

47. Molyneaux, *White Empire*, 29–30.

48. Molyneaux, *White Empire*, 4, 20, 25, 40, 49.

49. Molyneaux, *White Empire*, 64.

50. Molyneaux, *White Empire*, 20.

51. Molyneaux, *White Empire*, 56.

52. Molyneaux, *White Empire*, 54.

53. Molyneaux, *White Empire*, 15, 37.

54. Molyneaux, *White Empire*, 36.

55. Molyneaux, *White Empire*, 26, 42.

56. Molyneaux, *White Empire*, 35.

57. Molyneaux, *White Empire*, 28.

58. Molyneaux, *White Empire*, 37.

59. Henry A. Giroux, "The Politics of Neoliberal Fascism," *Tikkun*, August 21, 2018, www.tikkun.org/blog/2018/08/21/the-politics-of-neoliberal-fascism/.

60. David Lebow, "Trumpism and the Dialectic of Neoliberal Reason," *Perspectives on Politics* 17, no. 2 (2019): 383.

61. Molyneaux, *White Empire,* 29.

62. On the ties between neoliberalism and fascism, see Tad Tietze, "Anders Breivik, Fascism and the Neoliberal Inheritance," in *Hayek: A Collaborative Biography: Part IV, Good Dictators, Sovereign Producers and Hayek's "Ruthless Consistency,"* ed. Robert Leeson (Basingstoke: Palgrave Macmillan, 2015), 281–91.

63. *Talk Radio* (1988), an underrated Oliver Stone film inspired by Berg's life, tells the story of his on-air confrontations with white supremacists that precipitated his tragic death.

64. Southern Poverty Law Center, "David Lane," Extremist Files, accessed September 23, 2020, www.splcenter.org/fighting-hate/extremist-files/individual /david-lane.

65. David Lane, *88 Precepts,* n.d., Internet Archive, August 19, 2010, https:// archive.org/details/88Precepts_937/mode/2up.

66. Lane, *KD Rebel,* 31.

67. Lane, *KD Rebel,* 30, 9.

68. Sara Ahmed, "Affective Economies," *Social Text* 79, vol. 22, no. 2 (2004): 118 (emphasis in original).

69. C. Brandon Ogbunu, "How White Nationalists Have Co-Opted Fan Fiction," *Wired,* August 1, 2019, www.wired.com/story/white-nationalists-have-co -opted-fan-fiction/.

70. Though it is a loss for academic research, Covington's northwestfront.org website has, thankfully, been shut down as of December 30, 2020, replaced with a link to "Life After Hate," which is administered by a group of former white extremists.

71. "Neo-Nazi Leader," Idavox.com, July 27, 2018, https://idavox.com/index.php /2018/07/27/neo-nazi-leader-harold-covington-died-a-coward/.

72. Sam Thielman, "White Supremacist Calls Charleston 'A Preview of Coming Attractions,'" *Guardian,* June 28, 2015, https://www.theguardian.com/us-news /2015/jun/28/harold-covington-northwest-front-dylann-roof-manifesto-charleston -shooting. It should also be noted that Roof actually criticized Covington's Northwest Front plan.

73. Rebecca Solnit, "The American Civil War Didn't End. And Trump is a Confederate President," *Guardian,* November 4, 2018, www.theguardian.com /commentisfree/2018/nov/04/the-american-civil-war-didnt-end-and-trump-is-a -confederate-president (emphasis in original).

74. H. A. Covington, *The Hill of the Ravens* (Bloomington, IN: AuthorHouse, 2003), loc. 124–27, Kindle.

75. For the importance of Aztlán in Chicanx culture, see Gloria Anzaldúa, *Borderlands/*La Frontera: *The New Mestiza* (San Francisco: Aunt Lute Books, 2012 [1987]). For its appropriation as a symbolic threat in relation to immigration, see Lee Bebout, "The Nativist Aztlán," *Latino Studies* 10, no. 3 (2012): 290–313.

76. Covington, *The Hill of the Ravens,* loc. 1889, 1118–20, Kindle.

77. Covington, *The Hill of the Ravens,* loc. 1588, Kindle.

78. Covington, *The Hill of the Ravens,* loc. 2688, Kindle.

79. Covington, *The Hill of the Ravens*, loc. 1118–20, Kindle.

80. Covington, *The Hill of the Ravens*, loc. 3329–38, Kindle.

81. Covington, *The Hill of the Ravens*, loc. 3408–10, Kindle.

82. Covington, *The Hill of the Ravens*, loc. 320–23, 358–61, 1364, 2962–76, Kindle.

83. From the defunct Northwest Front website.

84. This also appeared on the now defunct Northwest Front website.

85. Covington, *The Hill of the Ravens*, loc. 559–68, Kindle.

86. Covington, *The Hill of the Ravens*, loc. 1160–64, 1364, 2962–76, Kindle.

87. Covington, *The Hill of the Ravens*, loc. 3455–58, Kindle.

88. Christopher Ketcham, "What the Far-Right Fascination with Pinochet's Death Squads Should Tell Us," *The Intercept*, February 4, 2021, https://theintercept.com/2021/02/04/pinochet-far-right-hoppean-snake/.

89. Randolph Hohle, *Race and the Origins of American Neoliberalism* (New York: Routledge, 2015), 223.

90. Stern, *Proud Boys and the White Ethnostate,* 59.

91. George Lipsitz, *The Possessive Investment in Whiteness: How White People Profit from Identity Politics* (Philadelphia: Temple University Press, 2018 [1998]), chapter 4; Kathleen Belew, *Bring the War Home: The White Power Movement and Paramilitary America* (Cambridge, MA: Harvard University Press, 2018).

92. For a detailed account of how this works, see especially chapter 6 of Lipsitz, *The Possessive Investment in Whiteness.*

93. Cynthia A. Young and Min Hyoung Song, "Forum Introduction: Whiteness Redux or Redefined?," *American Quarterly* 6, no. 4 (2014): 1073.

94. Roxanne Dunbar-Ortiz, "What White Supremacists Know," *Boston Review,* November 20, 2018, https://bostonreview.net/race/roxanne-dunbar-ortiz-what-white-supremacists-know.

95. For more on this new white power image, see Axel Öberg, "Meet the White Nationalist Trying to Ride the Trump Train to Lasting Power," *Mother Jones,* October 22, 2016, www.motherjones.com/politics/2016/10/richard-spencer-trump-alt-right-white-nationalist/.

96. Kiara Brantley-Jones, "False Equivalency between Black Lives Matter and Capitol Siege: Experts, Advocates," ABC News, January 17, 2021, https://abcnews.go.com/US/false-equivalency-black-lives-matter-capitol-siege-experts/story?id=75251279; Gino Spocchia, "Tucker Carlson Condemned for Bizarre Comparison between George Floyd's Death, BLM, and Capitol Riot," *Independent*, February 11, 2021, www.independent.co.uk/news/world/americas/us-politics/tucker-carlson-blm-capitol-riot-floyd-b1801017.html.

CONCLUSIONS IN STRANGE TIMES

1. Joseph E. Stiglitz, "The End of Neoliberalism and the Rebirth of History," Project Syndicate, November 4, 2019, www.project-syndicate.org/commentary/end-of-neoliberalism-unfettered-markets-fail-by-joseph-e-stiglitz-2019-11; Daniel Finn,

"Neoliberalism Has Finally Reached the End of the Road: An Interview with Cédric Durand," *Jacobin,* March 21, 2022, https://jacobin.com/2022/03/neoliberalism-state -economic-policy-monetary-pandemic-inflation; Daniel Steinmetz-Jenkins, "Has Neoliberalism Really Come to an End?," *The Nation,* April 13, 2022, www.thenation .com/article/politics/neoliberalism-gary-gerstle/.

2. Heather McGhee, *The Sum of Us: What Racism Costs Everyone and How We Can Prosper*(London: Profile Books, 2022 [2021]), 15.

3. Charles W. Mills, *The Racial Contract* (Ithaca, NY: Cornell University Press, 1999), 39.

4. Dana M. Peterson and Catherine Mann, "Closing the Racial Inequality Gaps: The Economic Costs of Black Inequality in the US," *Citi GPS: Global Perspectives and Solutions,* September 2020, https://ir.citi.com/NvIUklHPilz14 Hwd3oxqZBLMn1_XPq05FrxsZDox6hhil84ZxaxEuJUWmak51UHvYk75VKeH CMI%3D.

5. Anne Case and Angus Deaton, "Rising Morbidity and Mortality in Midlife Among White Non-Hispanic Americans in the 21st Century," *PNAS* 112, no. 49 (December 8, 2015): 15078–83, www.pnas.org/content/112/49/15078.

6. Olson quoted in Daniel Martinez HoSang and Joseph E. Lowndes, *Producers, Parasites, Patriots: Race and the New Right-Wing Politics of Precarity* (Minneapolis: University of Minnesota Press, 2019), 53.

7. Thuy Linh Tu and Nikhil Pal Singh, "Morbid Capitalism and Its Racial Symptoms," *n+1* 30 (Winter 2018), www.nplusonemag.com/issue-30/essays/morbid -capitalism/.

8. It is the top 10 percent of whites who account for the bulk of the racial wealth gap. See Matt Burenig, "The Racial Wealth Gap Is about the Upper Classes," *Jacobin,* July 5, 2020, https://jacobinmag.com/2020/07/racial-wealth-gap -redistribution.

9. See Randolph Hohle, *Racism in the Neoliberal Era: A Meta History of Elite White Power* (New York: Routledge, 2018), especially chapter 1.

10. Eddie Glaude, *Begin Again: James Baldwin's America and Its Urgent Lessons for Our Own* (New York: Penguin Random House, 2021), 7.

11. Kenton Card, "Geographies of Racial Capitalism with Ruth Wilson Gilmore," Antipode Foundation, June 1, 2020, www.youtube.com/watch?v= 2CS627aKrJI.

12. David Harvey, *A Brief History of Neoliberalism* (Oxford: Oxford University Press, 2005).

13. Zack Beauchamp, "Marjorie Taylor Greene's Space Laser and the Age-old Problem of Blaming the Jews," *Vox,* January 30, 2021, www.vox.com/22256258 /marjorie-taylor-greene-jewish-space-laser-anti-semitism-conspiracy-theories.

14. Ian Haney López, *Dog Whistle Politics: How Coded Racial Appeals Have Reinvented Racism and Wrecked the Middle Class* (Oxford: Oxford University Press, 2014).

15. Tristan Justice, "Parents Vote to Stop Critical Race Insanity in Texas's Top School District," *The Federalist,* May 3, 2021, https://thefederalist.com/2021/05/03 /parents-vote-to-stop-critical-race-insanity-in-texass-top-school-district/.

16. Tess Owen, "The Proud Boys Changed Tactics after Jan. 6. We Tracked their Activity," *Vice,* January 5, 2022, www.vice.com/en/article/z3n338/what-the-proud-boys-did-after-jan-6?utm_source=email&utm_medium=editorial&utm_content=news&utm_campaign=220105.

17. Andrew Marantz, "Does Hungary Offer a Glimpse of Our Authoritarian Future?," *The New Yorker,* June 27, 2022, www.newyorker.com/magazine/2022/07/04/does-hungary-offer-a-glimpse-of-our-authoritarian-future; Thomas J. Main, *The Rise of Illiberalism* (Washington, D.C.: Brookings Institution Press, 2022); Adam Fabry, "Neoliberalism, Crisis and Authoritarian-Ethnicist Reaction: The Ascendancy of the Orbán Regime," *Competition & Change* 23, no. 2 (2019): 165–91; Dorit Geva, "Orbán's Ordonationalism as Post-Neoliberal Hegemony," *Theory, Culture & Society* 38, no. 6 (2021): 71–93.

18. See Thomas Picketty, *Capital in the Twenty-First Century,* trans. Arthur Goldhammer (Cambridge, MA: Belknap Press of Harvard University Press, 2014).

19. Göran Therborn, "Preface: The Terrifying Convergence of the Three Worlds of the 'Social Question,'" in *The Social Question in the 21st Century: A Global View,* ed. Jan Breman et al. (Berkeley: University of California Press, 2019), ix.

20. Rooted in his reading of Bloch, Jose Esteban Muñoz argued that "utopia exists in the quotidian." *Cruising Utopia: The Then and There of Queer Futurity* (New York: New York University Press, 2009), 39.

21. Gago explores this world in *Neoliberalism from Below: Popular Pragmatics and Baroque Economies* (Durham, NC: Duke University Press, 2017), as well as in "What Are Popular Economies? Some Reflections from Argentina," *Radical Philosophy* 2, no. 2 (June 2018): 31–38.

22. Sir Thomas More's original coinage of the term "utopia" is deliberately ambiguous (and even ambivalent). "U-" (no) + "topos" (place) enacts a pun in which we can replace the prefix with the homophonic "eu-," meaning "good."

23. Tom Moylan, *Becoming Utopian: The Culture and Politics of Radical Transformation* (London: Bloomsbury, 2021).

24. Michael Hardt and Antonio Negri, *Multitude: War and Democracy in the Age of Empire* (New York: Penguin, 2004), xiii. Jameson has continued to theorize this formation in *Valences of the Dialectic* (New York: Verso, 2009), based on a reading of Paolo Virno's *A Grammar of the Multitude* (Los Angeles: Semiotext(e), 2004).

25. Ta-Nehisi Coates, *Between the World and Me* (New York: Penguin Random House, 2015), 128.

26. Mills, *The Racial Contract,* 18 (emphases in original).

BIBLIOGRAPHY

"1601: 43 Elizabeth 1 c.2: Act for the Relief of the Poor." *The Statutes Project: Putting Historic British Law Online.* Accessed January 5, 2021. http://statutes.org.uk/site /the-statutes/seventeenth-century/1601-43-elizabeth-c-2-act-for-the-relief-of-the -poor/.

Abramson, Alana. "'No Lessons Have Been Learned': Why the Trillion-Dollar Coronavirus Bailout Benefited the Rich." *Time,* June 18, 2020. https://time.com /5845116/coronavirus-bailout-rich-richer/.

Ahmed, Sara. "Affective Economies." *Social Text* 79, vol. 22, no. 2 (2004): 117–39.

Ali, Wajahat. "Deradicalizing White People." *The New York Review,* August 18, 2018. www.nybooks.com/daily/2018/08/16/deradicalizing-white-people/.

Anderson, Ben. "Neoliberal Affects." *Progress in Human Geography* 40, no. 6 (2016): 734–53.

Anderson, Carol. *White Rage: The Unspoken Truth of Our Racial Divide.* New York: Bloomsbury, 2016.

Anglin, Andrew. "What Is the Deal with WMBF Relationships?" Daily Stormer, September 19, 2016. Accessed February 15, 2022. https://archive.is/3TrgB.

Anzaldúa, Gloria. *Borderlands* / La Frontera: *The New Mestiza.* 1987. San Francisco: Aunt Lute Books, 2012.

Baer, Stephanie K. "Trump Supporters Flaunt Racist Symbols at US Capitol Coup Attempt." *Buzzfeed News,* January 6, 2021. www.buzzfeednews.com/article /skbaer/trump-supporters-racist-symbols-capitol-assault.

Bangstad, Sindre. *Anders Breivik and the Rise of Islamophobia.* London: Zed Books, 2014.

Barrouquere, Brett, and Rachel Janik. "A Gunman Opened Fire on a Synagogue in Pittsburgh, Killing at Least Eleven People and Wounding Others." Southern Poverty Law Center, October 27, 2018. www.splcenter.org/hatewatch/2018/10/27 /gunman-opened-fire-synagogue-pittsburgh-killing-least-eleven-people-and -wounding-others.

BBC News. "Munich Shooting: David Sonboly 'Planned Attack for Year.'" BBC. com, July 24, 2016. www.bbc.com/news/world-europe-36878436.

Beauchamp, Zack. "Marjorie Taylor Greene's Space Laser and the Age-old Problem of Blaming the Jews." *Vox,* January 30, 2021. www.vox.com/22256258/marjorie-taylor-greene-jewish-space-laser-anti-semitism-conspiracy-theories.

Bebout, Lee. "The Nativist Aztlán: Fantasies and Anxieties of Whiteness on the Border." *Latino Studies* 10, no. 3 (2012): 290–313.

Becker, Gary S. *A Treatise on the Family.* Enlarged edition. Cambridge, MA: Harvard University Press, 1991.

Beckett, Lois. "A History of Recent Attacks Linked to White Supremacy." *Guardian,* March 15, 2019. www.theguardian.com/world/2019/mar/16/a-history-of-recent-attacks-linked-to-white-supremacism.

Beirich, Heidi. "The Year in Hate: Rage Against Change." Southern Poverty Law Center, February 20, 2019. www.splcenter.org/fighting-hate/intelligence-report/2019/year-hate-rage-against-change.

Belew, Kathleen. *Bring the War Home: The White Power Movement and Paramilitary America.* Cambridge, MA: Harvard University Press, 2018. Kindle.

———. "There Are No Lone Wolves: The White Power Movement at War." In *A Field Guide to White Supremacy,* edited by Kathleen Belew and Ramón A. Gutiérrez, 312–24. Berkeley: University of California Press, 2021.

Benen, Steven. "GOP Rep Scrambles after Thanking Trump for a Win for 'White Life.'" MSNBC.com, June 27, 2022. www.msnbc.com/rachel-maddow-show/maddowblog/gop-rep-scrambles-thanking-trump-win-white-life-rcna35451.

———. *The Impostors: How Republicans Quit Governing and Seized American Politics.* New York: William Morrow, 2020.

Berger, J. M. "The Turner Legacy: The Storied Origins and Enduring Impact of White Nationalism's Deadly Bible," *International Centre for Counter-Terrorism—The Hague* 7, no. 8 (2016): 1–49.

"Black Power." *The Martin Luther King, Jr., Encyclopedia.* Stanford University. Accessed February 4, 2020. https://kinginstitute.stanford.edu/encyclopedia/black-power.

"Black Power." The U.S. National Archives and Records Association. Last reviewed July 7, 2010. www.archives.gov/research/african-americans/black-power.

Blee, Kathleen M. *Inside Organized Racism: Women in the Hate Movement.* Berkeley: University of California Press, 2003.

Bleweis, Robin. *Quick Facts about the Gender Wage Gap.* Washington, DC: Center for American Progress, 2020. www.americanprogress.org/issues/women/reports/2020/03/24/482141/quick-facts-gender-wage-gap/.

Bonilla-Silva, Eduardo. *Racism without Racists: Color-Blind Racism and the Persistence of Racial Inequality in the United States.* 2003. Lanham: Rowman & Littlefield, 2018.

"The Boogaloo Movement." Anti-Defamation League. Accessed March 12, 2022. www.adl.org/boogaloo.

Boren, Cindy. "Richard Sherman Frustrated by Reaction, Equates 'Thug' with Racial Slur." *Washington Post,* January 23, 2014. www.washingtonpost.com/news

/early-lead/wp/2014/01/23/richard-sherman-frustrated-by-reaction-equates-thug
-with-racial-slur/.

Borger, Julian. "Donald Trump Denounces 'Globalism' in Nationalist Address to
UN." *Guardian,* September 24, 2019. www.theguardian.com/us-news/2019/sep
/24/donald-trump-un-address-denounces-globalism.

Branigin, Anne. "Southern Baptist Leaders Called Kamala Harris a 'Jezebel': That's
Not Just Insulting, It's Dangerous, Experts Say." *The Lily,* February 9, 2021. www
.thelily.com/southern-baptist-leaders-called-kamala-harris-a-jezebel-thats-not
-just-insulting-its-dangerous-experts-say/.

Brantley-Jones, Kiara. "False Equivalency between Black Lives Matter and Capitol
Siege: Experts, Advocates." ABC News, January 17, 2021. https://abcnews.go.com
/US/false-equivalency-black-lives-matter-capitol-siege-experts/story?id=
75251279.

Briggs, Laura. *How All Politics Became Reproductive Politics: From Welfare Reform
to Foreclosure to Trump.* Berkeley: University of California Press, 2017.

Brodkin, Karen. *How Jews Became White Folks and What That Says about Race in
America.* New Brunswick, NJ: Rutgers University Press, 1998.

Brown, Wendy. *In the Ruins of Neoliberalism: The Rise of Antidemocratic Politics in
the West.* New York: Columbia University Press, 2019.

Burenig, Matt. "The Racial Wealth Gap Is about the Upper Classes." *Jacobin,* July
5, 2020. https://jacobinmag.com/2020/07/racial-wealth-gap-redistribution.

Burns, Janet. "Cut Off from Big Fintech, White Nationalists Are Using Bitcoin to
Raise Funds." *Forbes,* January 3, 2018. www.forbes.com/sites/janetwburns/2018
/01/03/cut-off-from-big-fintech-white-supremacists-are-using-bitcoin-to-raise
-funds/?sh=73a4ac6633b3.

Cai, Weiyi, Troy Griggs, Jason Kao, Juliette Love, and Joe Ward. "White Extremist
Ideology Drives Many Deadly Shootings." *New York Times,* August 14, 2019.
www.nytimes.com/interactive/2019/08/04/us/white-extremist-active-shooter
.html.

Caldwell, Christopher. "How to Think about Vladimir Putin." *Imprimis* 46, no. 3
(March 2017). https://imprimis.hillsdale.edu/how-to-think-about-vladimir
-putin/.

Card, Kenton. "Geographies of Racial Capitalism with Ruth Wilson Gilmore."
Antipode Foundation, June 1, 2020. www.youtube.com/watch?v=2CS627aKrJI.

Case, Anne, and Angus Deaton. "Mortality and Morbidity in the 21st Century."
Brookings Papers on Economic Activity, 2017. www.brookings.edu/wp-content
/uploads/2017/03/6_casedeaton.pdf.

———. "Rising Morbidity and Mortality in Midlife Among White Non-Hispanic
Americans in the 21st Century." *PNAS* 112, no. 49 (December 8, 2015): 15078–83.
www.pnas.org/content/112/49/15078.

Cashin, Sheryll. "How the Buffalo Massacre Proves There's No 'Great Replacement,'" Politico, April 21, 2022. www.politico.com/news/magazine/2022/05/21
/buffalo-massacre-great-replacement-segregation-00034177.

———. *White Space, Black Hood: Opportunity Hoarding and Segregation in the Age of Inequality.* Boston: Beacon Press, 2021.

Chan, Edward K. *The Racial Horizon of Utopia: Unthinking the Future of Race in Late Twentieth-Century American Utopian Novels.* Ralahine Utopian Studies, Volume 17. Bern: Peter Lang, 2016.

———. "The White Power Utopia and the Reproduction of Victimized Whiteness." In *Race and Utopian Desire in American Literature and Society,* edited by Patricia Ventura and Edward K. Chan, 139–59. Cham, Switzerland: Palgrave Macmillan, 2019.

Claeys, Gregory. *Dystopia: A Natural History.* Oxford: Oxford University Press, 2017.

Clinton, Bill. "How We Ended Welfare, Together." *New York Times,* August 22, 2006. www.nytimes.com/2006/08/22/opinion/22clinton.html.

Coates, Ta-Nehisi. *Between the World and Me.* New York: Penguin Random House, 2015.

———. "The First White President: The Foundation of Donald Trump's Legacy Is the Negation of Barack Obama's Legacy." *The Atlantic,* October 2017. www.theatlantic.com/magazine/archive/2017/10/the-first-white-president-ta-nehisi-coates/537909/.

Collins, Patricia Hill. *Black Sexual Politics: African Americans, Gender, and the New Racism.* New York: Routledge, 2004.

"Competing Visions of America: An Evolving Identity or a Culture Under Attack." Public Religion Research Institute, November 1, 2021. www.prri.org/press-release/competing-visions-of-america-an-evolving-identity-or-a-culture-under-attack/.

Coontz, Stephanie. *The Way We Never Were: American Families and the Nostalgia Trap.* New York: Basic Books, 1993.

Cooper, Melinda. "Anti-Austerity on the Far Right." In *Mutant Neoliberalism: Market Rule and Political Rupture,* edited by William Callison and Zachary Manfredi, 112–45. New York: Fordham University Press, 2020.

———. *Family Values: Between Neoliberalism and the New Social Conservatism.* Cambridge, MA: Zone Books, 2017.

———. "Neoliberalism's Family Values: Welfare, Human Capital, and Kinship." In *Nine Lives of Neoliberalism,* edited by Dieter Plehwe, Quinn Slobodian, and Philip Mirowski, 95–119. Brooklyn: Verso, 2020.

Covington, H. A. *Freedom's Sons.* Bay City, OR: Northwest Publishing Agency, 2011.

———. *The Hill of the Ravens.* Bloomington, IN: AuthorHouse, 2003. Kindle.

Craig, Tim. "Florida Legislature Passes Bill That Limits How Schools and Workplaces Teach about Race and Identity." *Washington Post,* March 10, 2022. www.washingtonpost.com/nation/2022/03/10/florida-legislature-passes-anti-woke-bill/.

Creativity Alliance. Accessed July 9, 2022. https://creativityalliance.com/.

Darby, Seyward. *Sisters in Hate: American Women on the Front Lines of White Nationalism.* New York: Little, Brown, 2020.

Davey, Jacob, and Julia Ebner. *"The Great Replacement": The Violent Consequences of Mainstream Extremism.* London: Institute for Strategic Dialogue, 2019. www .isdglobal.org/wp-content/uploads/2019/07/The-Great-Replacement-The -Violent-Consequences-of-Mainstreamed-Extremism-by-ISD.pdf.

Davidson, Neil, and Richard Saull. "Neoliberalism and the Far-Right: A Contradictory Embrace." *Critical Sociology* (2016): 1–18. DOI: 10.1177/0896920516671180.

Davies, William. "The New Neoliberalism." *New Left Review* 101 (September–October 2016): 121–34.

Davis, Mark. "'Culture Is Inseparable from Race': Culture Wars from Pat Buchanan to Milo Yiannopoulos." *M/C Journal* 21, no. 5 (2018). https://doi.org/10.5204/mcj .1484.

Deckman, Melissa. *Tea Party Women: Mama Grizzlies, Grassroots Leaders, and the Changing Face of the American Right.* New York: New York University Press, 2016.

DiAngelo, Robin. *White Fragility: Why It's So Hard for White People to Talk about Racism.* Boston: Beacon Press, 2018.

Du Bois, W. E. B. *Black Reconstruction: An Essay Toward a History of the Part Which Black Folk Played in the Attempt to Reconstruct Democracy in America, 1860–1880.* New York: Harcourt, Brace, 1935.

———. "The Study of the Negro Problems." *Annals of the American Academy of Political and Social Science* 11 (January 1898): 1–23.

Duggan, Lisa. *The Twilight of Equality? Neoliberalism, Cultural Politics, and the Attack on Democracy.* Boston: Beacon Press, 2003. Kindle.

Dunbar-Ortiz, Roxanne. "What White Supremacists Know." *Boston Review,* November 20, 2018. https://bostonreview.net/race/roxanne-dunbar-ortiz-what -white-supremacists-know.

Elias, Marilyn. "Sikh Temple Killer Wade Michael Page Radicalized in Army." Southern Poverty Law Center, November 11, 2012. www.splcenter.org/fighting -hate/intelligence-report/2012/sikh-temple-killer-wade-michael-page-radicalized -army.

Esposito, Luigi. "The Alt-Right as a Revolt against Neoliberalism and Political Correctness: The Role of Collective Action Frames." *Perspectives on Global Development and Technology* 18 (2019): 93–110.

Evans, Robert. "Shitposting, Inspirational Terrorism, and the Christchurch Mosque Massacre." Bellingcat, March 15, 2019. www.bellingcat.com/news/rest-of-world /2019/03/15/shitposting-inspirational-terrorism-and-the-christchurch-mosque -massacre/.

Fabry, Adam. "Neoliberalism, Crisis and Authoritarian-Ethnicist Reaction: The Ascendancy of the Orbán Regime." *Competition & Change* 23, no. 2 (2019): 165–91.

Farley, Robert. "The Facts on White Nationalism." FactCheck.org, March 20, 2019. www.factcheck.org/2019/03/the-facts-on-white-nationalism/.

Finn, Daniel. "Neoliberalism Has Finally Reached the End of the Road: An Interview with Cédric Durand." *Jacobin,* March 21, 2022. https://jacobin.com/2022 /03/neoliberalism-state-economic-policy-monetary-pandemic-inflation.

Foucault, Michel. *The Birth of Biopolitics: Lectures at the Collège de France, 1978–1979*. Edited by Michel Senellart. Translated by Graham Burchell. London: Palgrave Macmillan, 2008.

Frazier, E. Franklin. *The Negro Family in the United States*. Chicago: University of Illinois Press, 1939. https://archive.org/stream/negrofamilyintheo31737mbp /negrofamilyintheo31737mbp_djvu.txt.

Fullwood, Sam, III. *An All-American Myth About the White Working Class*. Washington, DC: Center for American Progress, 2017. www.americanprogress.org /issues/race/news/2017/03/30/429599/american-myth-white-working-class/.

Gago, Verónica. *Neoliberalism from Below: Popular Pragmatics and Baroque Economies*. Durham, NC: Duke University Press, 2017.

———. "What Are Popular Economies? Some Reflections from Argentina." *Radical Philosophy* 2, no. 2 (June 2018): 31–38.

Garamvolgyi, Flora. "Viktor Orbán Tells CPAC the Path to Power Is to 'Have Your Own Media.'" *Guardian,* May 20, 2022. www.theguardian.com/us-news/2022 /may/20/victor-orban-cpacp-republicans-hungary.

Geary, Daniel. "The Moynihan Report: An Annotated Edition." *The Atlantic,* September 14, 2015. www.theatlantic.com/politics/archive/2015/09/the-moynihan -report-an-annotated-edition/404632/#.

Geva, Dorit. "Orbán's Ordonationalism as Post-Neoliberal Hegemony." *Theory, Culture & Society* 38, no. 6 (2021): 71-93.

Gill, Rosalind. "Culture and Subjectivity in Neoliberal and Postfeminist Times." *Subjectivity* 25 (2008): 432–45.

Giroux, Henry A. "The Politics of Neoliberal Fascism." *Tikkun,* August 21, 2018. www.tikkun.org/blog/2018/08/21/the-politics-of-neoliberal-fascism/.

Glaude, Eddie. *Begin Again: James Baldwin's America and Its Urgent Lessons for Our Own*. New York: Penguin Random House, 2021.

Goldberg, David Theo. *The Threat Race: Reflections on Racial Neoliberalism*. Malden: Blackwell, 2009.

Gonzalez, Gilbert G. "The Ideology and Practice of Empire: The United States, Mexico, and Mexican Immigrants." In *A Century of Chicano History: Empires, Nations, and Migrations,* edited by Gilbert G. Gonzalez and Raul A. Fernandez, 67–96. New York: Routledge, 2003.

Gould, Elise. *The State of American Wages 2017*. Washington, DC: Economic Policy Institute, 2018. www.epi.org/publication/the-state-of-american-wages-2017 -wages-have-finally-recovered-from-the-blow-of-the-great-recession-but-are-still -growing-too-slowly-and-unequally/#epi-toc-1

"'The Great Replacement': An Explainer." Anti-Defamation League, April 19, 2021. www.adl.org/resources/backgrounders/great-replacement-explainer.

Green, Emma. "The Fight to Make Meaning Out of a Massacre." *The Atlantic,* September 29, 2019. www.theatlantic.com/politics/archive/2019/09/pittsburgh -politics-violence-gun-reform/598885/.

"Groyper Army and 'America First.'" Anti-Defamation League, March 17, 2020. www.adl.org/resources/backgrounders/groyper-army-and-america-first.

Hall, Stuart. "The Neoliberal Revolution." *Soundings* 48 (2011): 9–27.

Hardt, Michael, and Antonio Negri. *Multitude: War and Democracy in the Age of Empire*. New York: Penguin, 2004.

Harris, Cheryl I. "Whiteness as Property." *Harvard Law Review* 106, no. 8 (1993): 1707–91.

Harvey, David. *A Brief History of Neoliberalism*. Oxford: Oxford University Press, 2005.

Hayek, Friedrich. *The Road to Serfdom*. Edited by Bruce Caldwell. Chicago: University of Chicago Press, 2007.

Helm, Joe, and Lori Rozsa. "African Americans Say the Teaching of Black History Is Under Threat." *Washington Post,* February 23, 2022. www.washingtonpost .com/education/2022/02/23/schools-black-history-month-crt/.

Hill, Evan, Arielle Ray, and Dahlia Kozlowsky. "Videos Show How Rioter Was Trampled in Stampede at Capitol." *New York Times,* May 31, 2021. www.nytimes .com/2021/01/16/us/politics/videos-show-how-a-rioter-was-trampled-in-the -stampede-at-the-capitol.html.

Hill, Herbert. "Labor Unions and the Negro: The Record of Discrimination." *Commentary,* December 1959. www.commentarymagazine.com/articles/herbert-hill /labor-unions-and-the-negrothe-record-of-discrimination/.

Hochschild, Arlie Russell. "I Spent 5 Years with Some of Trump's Biggest Fans. Here's What They Won't Tell You." *Mother Jones,* September–October 2016. www.motherjones.com/politics/2016/08/trump-white-blue-collar -supporters/.

Hohle, Randolph. *Race and the Origins of American Neoliberalism*. New York: Routledge, 2015.

———. *Racism in the Neoliberal Era: A Meta History of Elite White Power*. New York: Routledge, 2018.

Hong, Grace Kyungwon. *Death Beyond Disavowal: The Impossible Politics of Difference*. Minneapolis: University of Minnesota Press, 2015.

HoSang, Daniel Martinez, and Joseph E. Lowndes. *Producers, Parasites, Patriots: Race and the New Right-Wing Politics of Precarity*. Minneapolis: University of Minnesota Press, 2019.

Huehls, Mitchum, and Rachel Greenwald Smith. "Four Phases of Neoliberalism and Literature: An Introduction." In *Neoliberalism and Contemporary Literature Culture,* edited by Mitchum Huehls and Rachel Greenwald Smith, 1–18. Baltimore, MD: Johns Hopkins University Press.

Hulbert, Mark. "The 'Disturbing Reality' Fueling This Bull Market." *Barrons,* August 21, 2020. www.barrons.com/articles/the-disturbing-reality-fueling-this -bull-market-51598004009.

Ignatiev, Noel. *How the Irish Became White*. 1995. New York: Routledge, 2009.

Inwood, Joshua. "Neoliberal Racism: The 'Southern Strategy' and the Expanding Geographies of White Supremacy." *Social and Cultural Geography* 16, no. 4 (2015): 407–23.

———. "White Supremacy, White Counter-Revolutionary Politics and the Rise of Donald Trump." *Environment and Planning C: Politics and Space* 37, no. 4 (2019): 579–96.

Ioanide, Paula. *The Emotional Politics of Racism: How Feelings Trump Facts in an Era of Colorblindness.* Stanford, CA: Stanford University Press, 2015.

Iyengar, Shato, and Sean J. Westwood. "Fear and Loathing across Party Lines: New Evidence on Group Polarization." *American Journal of Political Science* 59, no. 3 (2015): 690–707.

Jacobson, Matthew Frye. *Whiteness of a Different Color: European Immigrants and the Alchemy of Race.* Cambridge, MA: Harvard University Press, 1998.

Jameson, Fredric. "Periodizing the 60s." *Social Text* 9/10 (1984): 178–209.

———. *The Political Unconscious: Narrative as a Socially Symbolic Act.* Ithaca, NY: Cornell University Press, 1981.

———. *Valences of the Dialectic.* New York: Verso, 2009.

Jardina, Ashley. *White Identity Politics.* Cambridge: Cambridge University Press, 2019.

Jonsson, Patrik. "After Obama's Win, White Backlash Festers in US." *Christian Science Monitor,* November 17, 2008. www.csmonitor.com/USA/Politics/2008/1117/p03s01-uspo.html.

Joppke, Christian. *Neoliberal Nationalism: Immigration and the Rise of the Populist Right.* Cambridge: Cambridge University Press, 2021. Kindle.

Judis, John B. *The Populist Explosion: How the Great Recession Transformed American and European Politics.* New York: Columbia Global Reports, 2016. Kindle.

Justice, Tristan. "Parents Stop Vote to Critical Race Insanity in Texas's Top School District." *The Federalist,* May 3, 2021. https://thefederalist.com/2021/05/03/parents-vote-to-stop-critical-race-insanity-in-texass-top-school-district/.

Kelley, Robin D. G. "Births of a Nation, Redux: Surveying Trumpland with Cedric Robinson." *Boston Review,* November 5, 2020. https://bostonreview.net/race-politics/robin-d-g-kelley-births-nation.

———. Foreword to *Black Marxism,* by Cedric Robinson, xi–xxiii. Chapel Hill: University of North Carolina Press, 2000.

———. "What Did Cedric Robinson Mean by Racial Capitalism." *Boston Review,* January 12, 2017. http://bostonreview.net/race/robin-d-g-kelley-what-did-cedric-robinson-mean-racial-capitalism.

Ketcham, Christopher. "What the Far-Right Fascination with Pinochet's Death Squads Should Tell Us." *The Intercept,* February 4, 2021. https://theintercept.com/2021/02/04/pinochet-far-right-hoppean-snake/.

Khan, Mahnoor. "Putin Claims He Makes $140,000 per Year and Has an 800-Square-Foot Apartment." *Fortune,* March 2, 2022. https://fortune.com/2022/03/02/vladimir-putin-net-worth-2022/.

Kimmel, Michael. *Angry White Men: American Masculinity at the End of an Era.* New York: Nation Books, 2013.

King, C. Richard, and David J. Leonard. *Beyond Hate: White Power and Popular Culture.* New York: Routledge, 2016.

King, Mike. "Aggrieved Whiteness: White Identity Politics and Modern American Racial Formation." *Abolition Journal,* May 4, 2017. https://abolitionjournal.org /aggrieved-whiteness-white-identity-politics-and-modern-american-racial -formation/.

Klassen, Ben. *The White Man's Bible.* 2008. https://creativityalliance.com/wp-content /uploads/ebooks/HolyBooks/eBook-BenKlassen-TheWhiteMan'sBible.pdf.

Klein, Naomi. *The Shock Doctrine: The Rise of Disaster Capitalism.* New York: Picador, 2007.

Kristol, Irving. *Neoconservatism: The Autobiography of an Idea.* New York: Simon and Schuster, 1995.

Lane, David. *88 Precepts.* N.d. Internet Archive, August 19, 2010. https://archive .org/details/88Precepts_937/mode/2up.

———. *KD Rebel.* N.p.: JR's Rare Books and Commentary, 2004. www.jrbooksonline .com/PDF_Books_added2009-4/kdrebel.pdf.

Lawn, Jennifer, and Chris Prentice. "Introduction: Neoliberal Culture / The Cultures of Neoliberalism." *Sites* 12, no. 1 (2015): 1–29.

Lebow, David. "Trumpism and the Dialectic of Neoliberal Reason." *Perspectives on Politics* 17, no. 2 (2019): 380–98.

Lee, Robert G. *Orientals: Asian Americans in Popular Culture.* Philadelphia: Temple University Press, 1999.

Levine, Mike, Josh Margolin, Jenny Wagnon Courts, and Alex Hosenball. "Nation's Deadliest Domestic Terrorist Inspiring New Generation of Hate-Filled 'Monsters,' FBI Records Show." ABC News, October 6, 2020. https://abcnews.go.com /US/nations-deadliest-domestic-terrorist-inspiring-generation-hate-filled /story?id=73431262.

Lewis, Paul. "Obama Resists Demands to Curtail Police Militarization Calling Instead for Improved Officer Training." *Guardian,* December 1, 2014. www .theguardian.com/us-news/2014/dec/01/obama-white-house-summit-ferguson.

Lipsitz, George. *The Possessive Investment in Whiteness: How White People Profit from Identity Politics.* 1998. Philadelphia: Temple University Press, 2018. Kindle.

Lockard, Joe. "Reading *The Turner Diaries:* Jewish Blackness, Judaized Blacks, and Head-Body Race Paradigms." In *Complicating Constructions: Race, Ethnicity, and Hybridity in American Texts,* edited by David S. Goldstein and Audrey B. Thacker, 121–39. Seattle: University of Washington Press, 2007.

López, Ian Haney. *Dog Whistle Politics: How Coded Racial Appeals Have Reinvented Racism and Wrecked the Middle Class.* Oxford: Oxford University Press, 2014.

Lyons, Matthew N. "The Christchurch Massacre and Fascist Revolutionary Politics." *threewayfight,* April 18, 2019. http://threewayfight.blogspot.com/2019/04/ the-christchurch-massacre-and-fascist.html.

———. *Insurgent Supremacists: The U.S. Far Right's Challenge to State and Empire.* Montreal: Kersplebedeb Publishing; Oakland: PM Press, 2018.

Macdonald, Andrew [William L. Pierce]. *The Turner Diaries.* 1978. 2nd edition. Fort Lee, NJ: Barricade Books, 1996.

Macdonald, David. "Class Attitudes, Political Knowledge, and Support for Redistribution in an Era of Inequality." *Social Science Quarterly* 101, no. 2 (2020): 960–77.

Main, Thomas J. *The Rise of Illiberalism*. Washington, D.C.: Brookings Institution Press, 2022.

Marantz, Andrew. "Does Hungary Offer a Glimpse of Our Authoritarian Future?" *The New Yorker,* June 27, 2022. www.newyorker.com/magazine/2022/07/04 /does-hungary-offer-a-glimpse-of-our-authoritarian-future.

Marsdal, Magnus E. "Loud Values, Muffled Interests: Third Way Social Democracy and Right-Wing Populism." In *Right-Wing Populism in Europe: Politics and Discourse,* edited by Ruth Wodak, Majid Khosravinik, and Brigitte Mral, 39–54. London: Bloomsbury Academic, 2013.

Martinot, Steve. *The Machinery of Whiteness: Studies in the Structure of Racialization*. Philadelphia: Temple University Press, 2010.

Maxwell, Angie, and Todd Shields. *The Long Southern Strategy: How Chasing White Voters in the South Changed American Politics*. New York: Oxford University Press, 2019.

Mbembe, Achille. "Necropolitics." Translated by Libby Meintjes. *Public Culture* 15, no. 1 (2003): 11-40.

McFeely, Shane, and Ryan Pendell. "What Workplace Leaders Can Learn from the Real Gig Economy." Gallup, August 16, 2018. www.gallup.com/workplace /240929/workplace-leaders-learn-real-gig-economy.aspx.

McGhee, Heather. *The Sum of Us: What Racism Costs Everyone and How We Can Prosper Together*. New York: One World Press, 2021.

McMahon, Paula. "Nikolas Cruz Left 180 Rounds of Ammunition." *Sun Sentinel,* March 2, 2018. www.sun-sentinel.com/local/broward/parkland/florida-school -shooting/fl-florida-school-shooting-nikolas-cruz-left-180-rounds-20180302 -story.html.

Meek, Andy. "Fox News Channel Has Now Spent 20 Years in the #1 Spot on the Cable News Rankings." *Forbes.com,* February 1, 2022. www.forbes.com/sites /andymeek/2022/02/01/fox-news-channel-has-now-spent-20-years-in-the-1-spot -on-the-cable-news-rankings/?sh=1a9de06872f2.

Melamed, Jodi. "Racial Capitalism." *Critical Ethnic Studies* 1, no. 1 (2015): 76–85.

———. *Represent and Destroy: Rationalizing Violence in the New Racial Capitalism*. Minneapolis: University of Minnesota Press, 2011.

———. "Spirit of Neoliberalism: From Racial Liberalism to Neoliberal Multiculturalism." *Social Text* 24, no. 4 (89) (2006): 1–24.

Metzl, Jonathan. *Dying of Whiteness: How the Politics of Racial Resentment Is Killing America's Heartland*. New York: Basic Books, 2019.

Michael, George. "RAHOWA! A History of the World Church of the Creator." *Terrorism and Political Violence* 18, no. 4 (2006): 561–83.

Miller, Cassie. "Accusations in a Mirror: How the Radical Right Blames Rising Political Violence on the Left." Southern Poverty Law Center, June 11, 2019. www

.splcenter.org/hatewatch/2019/06/11/accusations-mirror-how-radical-right -blames-rising-political-violence-left.

Miller, Cassie, and Howard Graves. "When the 'Alt-Right' Hit the Streets: Far-Right Political Rallies in the Trump Era." *Southern Poverty Law Center*, August 10, 2020. www.splcenter.org/20200810/when-alt-right-hit-streets-far-right -political-rallies-trump-era.

Miller, Claire Cain. "The Divorce Surge Is Over, But the Myth Lives On." *New York Times,* December 2, 2014, A3.

Miller-Idriss, Cynthia. *Hate in the Homeland: The New Global Far Right.* Princeton, NJ: Princeton University Press, 2020.

Mills, Charles W. *The Racial Contract.* Ithaca, NY: Cornell University Press, 1997.

Molyneaux, Kenneth. "My Awakening." Creativity Alliance. Accessed September 23, 2020. https://creativityalliance.com/articles/awakenings/rev-kenneth -molyneaux/.

———. *White Empire.* World Church of the Creator [?], 2000. https://archive.org /details/WhiteEmpireByRev.KennethMolyneaux/page/n1/mode/2up.

Moylan, Tom. *Becoming Utopian: The Culture and Politics of Radical Transforma-tion.* London: Bloomsbury, 2021.

Mujanović, Jasmin. "Why Serb Nationalism Still Inspires Europe's Far Right." *Balkan Insight,* March 22, 2019. https://balkaninsight.com/2019/03/22/why-serb -nationalism-still-inspires-europes-far-right/.

Mullins, Luke. "Inside the Mind of the MAGA Bomber." *Washingtonian,* August 13, 2020. www.washingtonian.com/2020/08/13/inside-the-mind-of-the-maga-bomber -the-trump-superfan-who-tried-to-wreak-havoc-on-the-last-national-election/.

Muñoz, Jose Esteban. *Cruising Utopia: The Then and There of Queer Futurity.* New York: New York University Press, 2009.

Myrdal, Gunnar. *An American Dilemma: The Negro Problem and Modern Democracy.* New York: Harper and Brothers Publishers, 1944.

Neiwert, David. "Huffing about Sexual Mores, Calls the Kettle Black." *Southern Poverty Law Center*, November 18, 2010. www.splcenter.org/hatewatch/2010/11 /18/david-duke-huffing-about-sexual-mores-calls-kettle-black.

"Neo-Nazi Leader." Idavox.com, July 27, 2018. https://idavox.com/index.php/2018 /07/27/neo-nazi-leader-harold-covington-died-a-coward/.

Norton, Michael I., and Samuel R. Sommers. "Whites See Racism as a Zero-Sum Game That They Are Now Losing." *Perspectives on Psychological Science* 6, no. 3 (2011): 215–18.

Öberg, Axel. "Meet the White Nationalist Trying to Ride the Trump Train to Last-ing Power." *Mother Jones,* October 22, 2016. www.motherjones.com/politics/2016 /10/richard-spencer-trump-alt-right-white-nationalist/.

Office of Policy Planning and Research, United States Department of Labor. "Chapter IV: The Tangle of Pathology." *The Negro Family: The Case for National Action.* March 1965. www.dol.gov/general/aboutdol/history/webid-moynihan /moynchapter4.

———. "Chapter V: The Case for National Action." *The Negro Family: The Case for National Action*. March 1965. www.dol.gov/general/aboutdol/history/webid -moynihan/moynchapter5.

Ogbunu, C. Brandon "How White Nationalists Have Co-Opted Fan Fiction." *Wired,* August 1, 2019. www.wired.com/story/white-nationalists-have-co-opted -fan-fiction/.

O'Harrow, Robert, Jr., Andrew Ba Tran, and Derek Hawkins. "The Rise of Domestic Extremism in America." *Washington Post,* April 12, 2021. www.washingtonpost .com/investigations/interactive/2021/domestic-terrorism-data/.

Ormseth, Matthew, Hannah Fry, Laura J. Nelson, Colleen Shalby, Richard Winton, and Alene Tchekmedyian. "Disturbing Portrait of Gilroy Garlic Festival Shooter." *Los Angeles Times,* July 30, 2019. www.latimes.com/california/story /2019-07-29/gilroy-garlic-festival-shooting-suspect.

Owen, Tess. "The Proud Boys Changed Tactics after Jan. 6. We Tracked Their Activity." *Vice,* January 5, 2022. www.vice.com/en/article/z3n338/what-the-proud-boys -did-after-jan-6?utm_source=email&utm_medium=editorial&utm_content =news&utm_campaign=220105.

Pape, Robert. "Why We Cannot Afford to Ignore the American Insurrectionist Movement." Chicago Projects on Security and Threats, August 6, 2021. https:// cpost.uchicago.edu/research/domestic_extremism/why_we_cannot_afford_to _ignore_the_american_insurrectionist_movement/.

Pape, Robert, and Chicago Project on Security and Threats. "Understanding American Domestic Terrorism: Mobilization Potential and Risk Factor of a New Threat Trajectory." April 6, 2021. https://d3qioqp55mx5f5.cloudfront.net/cpost/i/docs /americas_insurrectionists_online_2021_04_06.pdf?mtime=1617807009.

Penz, Otto, and Birgit Sauer. *Governing Affects: Neoliberalism, Neo-Bureaucracies, and Service Work.* New York: Routledge, 2020.

Perlstein, Rick. "Exclusive: Lee Atwater's Infamous 1981 Interview on the Southern Strategy." *The Nation,* November 13, 2012. www.thenation.com/article/archive /exclusive-lee-atwaters-infamous-1981-interview-southern-strategy/.

Petersen, Michael Bang, Mathias Osmundsen, and Alexander Bor. "Beyond Populism: The Psychology of Status-Seeking and Extreme Political Discontent." In *The Psychology of Populism: The Tribal Challenge to Liberal Democracy,* edited by Joseph P. Forgas, William D. Crano, and Klaus Fiedler, 62–80. New York: Routledge, 2021.

Peterson, Dana M., and Catherine Mann. "Closing the Racial Inequality Gaps: The Economic Costs of Black Inequality in the US." *Citi GPS: Global Perspectives and Solutions,* September 2020. https://ir.citi.com/NvIUklHPilz14Hwd3oxqZBLMn1 _XPqo5FrxsZDox6hhil84ZxaxEuJUWmak51UHvYk75VKeHCMI%3D.

Picketty, Thomas. *Capital in the Twenty-First Century.* Translated by Arthur Goldhammer. Cambridge, MA: Belknap Press of Harvard University Press, 2014.

Radner, Hilary. *Neo-Feminist Cinema: Girly Films, Chick Flicks, and Consumer Culture.* New York: Routledge, 2010.

Raymond, Adam K. "The Push to Not Name Mass Shooters Is Catching On." *New York Intelligencer,* May 9, 2019. https://nymag.com/intelligencer/2019/05/the-push-to-not-name-mass-shooters-is-catching-on.html.

Read, Jason. "A Genealogy of Homo-Economicus: Neoliberalism and the Production of Subjectivity." *Foucault Studies* 6 (2009): 25–36.

Reagan, Ronald. "Inaugural Address (2)." January 20, 1981. Ronald Reagan Presidential Foundation and Institute, video. www.reaganfoundation.org/ronald-reagan/reagan-quotes-speeches/inaugural-address-2/.

———. "News Conference (1)." August 12, 1986. Ronald Reagan Presidential Foundation and Institute, video. www.reaganfoundation.org/ronald-reagan/reagan-quotes-speeches/news-conference-1/.

Revelli, Marco. *The New Populism: Democracy Stares into the Abyss,* trans. David Broader. New York: Verso, 2019.

Richards, Barry. "What Drove Anders Breivik?" *Contexts* 13, no. 4 (2014): 42–47.

Ridzi, Frank. *Selling Welfare Reform: Work First and the New Common Sense of Employment.* New York: New York University Press, 2009.

Riley, Jason. "Accused Kroger Shooter Has History of Mental Illness and Racist Comments." WDRB, October 25, 2018. www.wdrb.com/news/crime-reports/accused-kroger-shooter-has-history-of-mental-illness-and-racist/article_3dfb9159-6e5c-56db-be12-483897bd42d1.html.

Robinson, Cedric J. *Black Marxism: The Making of the Black Radical Tradition,* 2nd ed. Chapel Hill: University of North Carolina Press, 2000.

Rodríguez, Dylan. *White Reconstruction: Domestic Warfare and the Logics of Genocide.* New York: Fordham University Press, 2021.

Roediger, David R. *The Wages of Whiteness: Race and the Making of the American Working Class,* revised ed. New York: Verso, 2007.

Rose, Nikolas. "The Death of the Social? Re-figuring the Territory of Government." *Economy and Society* 25, no. 3 (1996): 327–56.

Rottenberg, Catherine. *The Rise of Neoliberal Feminism.* New York: Oxford University Press, 2018.

Ruggles, Stephen. "Patriarchy, Power, and Pay: The Transformation of American Families, 1800–2015." *Demography* 52, no. 6 (2015): 1797–1823.

Rugh, Jacob S., and Douglas S. Massey. "Racial Segregation and the American Foreclosure Crisis." *American Sociological Review* 75, no. 5 (2010): 629–51.

Said, Samira, Steve Visser, and Catherine E. Shoichet. "Houston Shooting: Nine Injured, Suspect Dead." CNN.com, September 27, 2016. https://edition.cnn.com/2016/09/26/us/houston-shooting/index.html.

Santacreu, Ana Maria. "How Does US Income Inequality Compare Worldwide." Federal Reserve Bank of St. Louis (blog), October 16, 2017. www.stlouisfed.org/on-the-economy/2017/october/how-us-income-inequality-compare-worldwide.

Sauer, Birgit. "Authoritarian Right-Wing Populism as Masculinist Identity Politics. The Role of Affects." In *Right-Wing Populism and Gender: European Perspectives and Beyond,* edited by Gabriele Dietze and Julia Roth, 23–40. Bielefeld, Germany: transcript Verlag, 2020.

Searls Giroux, Susan. "Sade's Revenge: Racial Neoliberalism and the Sovereignty of Negation." *Patterns of Prejudice* 44, no. 1 (2010): 1–26.

Senna, Danzy. "Robin DiAngelo and the Problem with Anti-Racist Self-Help." *The Atlantic,* September 2021. www.theatlantic.com/magazine/archive/2021/09 /martin-learning-in-public-diangelo-nice-racism/619497/.

Shor, Fran. *Weaponized Whiteness: The Constructions and Deconstructions of White Identity Politics.* 2019. Chicago: Haymarket Books, 2020.

Skocpol, Theda. "Resistance in American Politics: Lecture by Political Scientist Theda Skocpol." *Radboud Reflects,* October 16, 2019. www.youtube.com/watch?v =_RMHI5dmsDU.

Slobodian, Quinn. *Globalists: The End of Empire and the Birth of Neoliberalism.* Cambridge, MA: Harvard University Press, 2018.

Solnit, Rebecca. "The American Civil War Didn't End. And Trump Is a Confederate President." *Guardian,* November 4, 2018. www.theguardian.com /commentisfree/2018/nov/04/the-american-civil-war-didnt-end-and-trump-is-a -confederate-president.

Southern Poverty Law Center. "Creativity Movement." Extremist Files. Accessed September 23, 2020. www.splcenter.org/fighting-hate/extremist-files/group/creativity -movement-0.

———. "David Lane." Extremist Files. Accessed September 23, 2020. www.splcenter .org/fighting-hate/extremist-files/individual/david-lane.

———. "Hate Groups Reach Record High." Southern Poverty Law Center, February 19, 2019. www.splcenter.org/news/2019/02/19/hate-groups-reach-record -high.

———. "William Pierce." Extremist Files. Accessed September 23, 2020. www .splcenter.org/fighting-hate/extremist-files/individual/william-pierce.

Spocchia, Gino. "Tucker Carlson Condemned for Bizarre Comparison between George Floyd's Death, BLM, and Capitol Riot." *Independent,* February 11, 2021. www.independent.co.uk/news/world/americas/us-politics/tucker-carlson-blm -capitol-riot-floyd-b1801017.html.

Steele, G. R. "There Is No Such Thing as Society." Institute of Economic Affairs, September 30, 2009. https://iea.org.uk/blog/there-is-no-such-thing-as-society.

Steinmetz-Jenkins, Daniel. "Has Neoliberalism Really Come to an End?" *The Nation,* April 13, 2022. www.thenation.com/article/politics/neoliberalism-gary -gerstle/.

Stern, Alexandra Minna. *Proud Boys and the White Ethnostate: How the Alt-Right Is Warping the American Imagination.* Boston: Beacon Press, 2019.

Stiglitz, Joseph E. "The End of Neoliberalism and the Rebirth of History." Project Syndicate, November 4, 2019, www.project-syndicate.org/commentary/end-of -neoliberalism-unfettered-markets-fail-by-joseph-e-stiglitz-2019-11.

Stone, Oliver, director. *Talk Radio.* 1988; Universal City, CA: Universal Studios Home Entertainment, 2000. DVD.

Stovall, Tyler. *White Freedom: The Racial History of an Idea.* Princeton, NJ: Princeton University Press, 2021.

Sucher, Sandra J., Elana Sara Green, David Alberto Rosales, and Susan J. Winterberg. "Layoffs: Effects on Key Stakeholders." Harvard Business School Background Note 611–028, December 2010, revised September 2014.

Texas State University Advanced Law Enforcement Rapid Response Training. "The Reasons." *Don't Name Them.* Accessed February 11, 2021. www.dontnamethem .org.

Thatcher, Margaret. "I BELIEVE—A Speech on Christianity and Politics." Speech, St. Lawrence Jewry, City of London, March 21, 1978. Margaret Thatcher Foundation. www.margaretthatcher.org/document/103522.

——. "Interview for *Woman's Own* ('No Such Thing as Society')." September 23, 1987. Margaret Thatcher Foundation. www.margaretthatcher.org/document /106689.

Theen, Andrew. "Umpqua Community College Shooting: Killer's Manifesto Reveals Racist, Satanic Views." *Oregonian,* September 8, 2017. www.oregonlive .com/pacific-northwest-news/2017/09/umpqua_community_college_shoot_3 .html.

Therborn, Göran. "The Terrifying Convergence of the Three Worlds of the 'Social Question.'" In *The Social Question in the 21st Century: A Global View,* edited by Jan Breman, Kevan Harris, Ching Kwan Lee, and Marcel van der Linden, ix–xii. Berkeley: University of California Press, 2019.

Thielman, Sam. "White Supremacist Calls Charleston 'A Preview of Coming Attractions.'" *Guardian,* June 28, 2015. www.theguardian.com/us-news/2015/jun/28 /harold-covington-northwest-front-dylann-roof-manifesto-charleston-shooting.

Thompson, A. C., Lila Hassan, and Karim Hajj. "The Boogaloo Bois Have Guns, Criminal Records and Military Training. Now They Want to Overthrow the Government." ProPublica, February 1, 2021. www.propublica.org/article/booga-loo-bois-military-training.

Tietze, Tad. "Anders Breivik, Fascism and the Neoliberal Inheritance." In *Hayek: A Collaborative Biography: Part IV, Good Dictators, Sovereign Producers and Hayek's "Ruthless Consistency,"* edited by Robert Leeson, 281–91. Basingstoke: Palgrave Macmillan, 2015.

Toupin, Louis. *Wages for Housework: A History of an International Feminist Movement, 1972–77.* Vancouver: University of British Columbia Press, 2018.

Tu, Thuy Linh, and Nikhil Pal Singh. "Morbid Capitalism and Its Racial Symptoms." *n+1* 30 (Winter 2018). www.nplusonemag.com/issue-30/essays/morbid -capitalism/.

"Tucker Carlson Tonight." Fox News, April 12, 2021. https://archive.org/details/ FOXNEWSW_20210413_050000_Tucker_Carlson_Tonight.

United Nations Research Institute for Social Development. *Why Care Matters for Social Development.* UNRISD Research and Policy Brief 9. Accessed August 18, 2021. www.unrisd.org/80256B3C005BCCF9/(httpAuxPages)/25697FE238192066 C12576D4004CFE50/%24file/RPB9e.pdf.

University of Richmond's Digital Scholarship Lab. "Introduction." *Mapping Inequality: Redlining in New Deal America.* Accessed August 18, 2021. https://dsl

.richmond.edu/panorama/redlining/#loc=11/41.081/-81.702&city=akron
-oh&text=intro.

Ventura, Patricia. *Neoliberal Culture: Living with American Neoliberalism.* New York: Routledge, 2016.

Virno, Paolo. *A Grammar of the Multitude: For an Analysis of Contemporary Forms of Life.* Los Angeles: Semiotext(e), 2004.

"What Is the National Alliance?" National Alliance, n.d. Quoted in Southern Poverty Law Center, "William Pierce." Extremist Files. Accessed September 23, 2020. www.splcenter.org/fighting-hate/extremist-files/individual/william-pierce.

"White Supremacists See Hope in Obama Win." CBS News, August 8, 2008. www.cbsnews.com/news/white-supremacists-see-hope-in-obama-win/.

Whitsel, Bradley C. "Aryan Visions for the Future in the West Virginia Mountains." *Terrorism and Political Violence* 7, no. 4 (1995): 117–39.

"'Will Be Wild!': Trump Tweet Summoned Jan. 6 Mob after Advisers Refused to Back Stolen Election Claim." DemocracyNow!, July 13, 2022. www.democracynow.org/2022/7/13/trump_summoned_mob_after_unhinged_meeting.

Willis, Jay. "How Don Jr., Ivanka, and Eric Trump Have Profited Off Their Dad's Presidency." *GQ,* October 14, 2019. www.gq.com/story/trump-kids-profit-presidency.

Winton, Richard, Maura Dolan, and Anita Chabria. "Far-Right 'Boogaloo Boys' Linked to Killing of California Law Officers and Other Violence." *Los Angeles Times,* June 17, 2020. www.latimes.com/california/story/2020-06-17/far-right-boogaloo-boys-linked-to-killing-of-california-lawmen-other-violence.

Young, Cynthia A., and Min Hyoung Song. "Forum Introduction: Whiteness Redux or Redefined?" *American Quarterly* 66, no. 4 (2014): 1071–76.

INDEX

accelerationism, 13, 25–26, 30, 50, 81. *See also* civil war; race war; RaHoWa

affect, 17, 18, 21–22, 58; and citizenship, 8, 63; and family, 74, 98; and masculinity, 39, 44, 95; and neoliberalism (see *homo affectus*); and race, 74, 79, 83, 88, 94, 98; and utopia, 79, 88, 120n4; and white power, 76, 90, 93

"aggrieved whiteness," 17, 22, 44, 65, 69, 95. *See also* white victimization

alt-right, 8, 11, 23, 43, 62, 96,

An American Dilemma: The Negro Problem and Modern Democracy (Myrdal), 56

American Nazi Party, 8, 74, 89

Anderson, Carol, 2

Anglin, Andrew, 33

anti-Semitism, 11, 19, 24, 27, 28, 29, 43, 71–72, 81, 82, 90, 91, 119n68, 132n29; and capitalism, 70; and conspiracy theories, 28, 49, 70, 72, 76, 80, 84, 86, 102; and democracy, 79. *See also* ZOG

anti-society, 17, 48, 65. *See also* Thatcher, Margaret

"anti-woke acts," 21

Aryan/s, 27, 42, 43, 75, 87, 89, 91

Atwater, Lee, 18

authoritarianism, 7, 16, 50, 70, 83, 85–86, 92, 93, 103. *See also* fascism

Bannon, Steve, 75

Becker, Gary, 33

Belew, Kathleen, 8–9

Biden, Joseph "Joe"/Biden administration, 27, 48, 50, 102

Black Lives Matter (BLM), 2, 6, 21, 30, 59, 60, 67, 97, 106, 108

Black Power, 8, 36

Blair, Tony, 48

Blee, Kathleen M., 42–43, 78, 124n45

boogaloo bois, 23, 30, 119n68

Bowers, Robert, 27–28, 32

Breivik, Anders Behring, 15–17, 28, 43, 70, 79, 119n57; *2083: A European Declaration of Independence,* 15–17, 36, 50

Brown, Wendy, 23, 34, 46, 63, 69

Buffalo mass shooting, 24, 25, 28. *See also* Gendron, Payton S.

Camp des Saints, Le (Jean Raspail), 76

Camus, Renaud, 24

capitalism (white power positions against), 16–17, 52, 70, 72, 76, 79, 90, 92, 93, 120n2

Capitol insurrection/insurrectionists, 9, 10, 21, 23, 30–31, 50, 95, 102

Carlson, Tucker, 11, 24

Charleston mass shooting, 27, 89. *See also* Roof, Dylann

Charlottesville, 9, 11, 23, 43, 95, 97

Christchurch, New Zealand, mass shooting, 28, 32, 50

Christian Identity, 9, 12, 28, 58, 132n29

Christian nationalism, 30

civil rights movement, 7, 9, 11, 12, 13, 36, 49, 57, 66, 74, 95, 128n29

welfare reform, 48, 59, 126n73; Temporary Assistance to Needy Families, 41, 51, 58

welfare state, 4, 7, 10, 13, 34, 36, 53, 54, 59, 40, 62–63, 67–68, 97, 103, 104, 123n41, 127n12, 129n50, 130n66, 130n71; Aid to Families with Dependent Children (AFDC), 41

"Western chauvinist," 21

White Empire (Molyneaux), 73, 83–86

white extinction anxiety, 16, 61. *See also* "great replacement"

white extremism, 3–4, 9, 22, 102. *See also* white power

white fragility, 4, 62, 95

white genocide. *See* "great replacement"

white identity politics, 10, 13, 45, 53, 65, 81, 88, 93, 95–96, 117n35. *See also* whiteness

white minority, 96. *See also* immigration, fears of

white nationalism, 8, 73. *See also* ethnonationalism (white)

whiteness, 10, 19–20, 45, 49, 66, 68, 95, 99–100; as consciousness, 4–5, 12, 15, 69, 74, 77–79, 82–83, 94; possessive investment in, 5, 10, 18, 95, 100; as tribal family, 5, 42–43, 69, 71–72, 74, 76, 77, 79, 84, 87; as wage, 6, 17, 100–101, 116n32. *See also* family: the white family; white identity politics

white power: definition of, 8–14; music, 28, 75, 84; and neoliberal culture, 13, 97; and neoliberalism, 2–13, 14, 16–17, 33, 37–38, 50, 76, 79, 85–86, 88–89, 93–97, 98, 102–104; and patriarchy/heteropatriarchy, 1, 4–5, 6, 12–14, 18, 21, 22, 33–43, 45, 51, 54, 65, 69, 74, 79, 84, 86, 88–89, 91, 93, 94–95, 97, 98, 121n17; and social reproduction, 88–89; and Trump/Trumpism, 2, 4, 5–6, 21–23, 28, 59, 66, 94, 97, 102

white power utopia. *See Hill of the Ravens, The; KD Rebel; Turner Diaries, The; White Empire*

white privilege, 10, 72, 95–96. *See also* whiteness

white rage, 2, 45, 62, 74

white replacement. *See* "great replacement"

white separatism, 8, 73

white supremacy: as foundational to the United States, 2, 17, 34, 37, 69, 96, 103, 121n17, 128n36; in relation to white power, 1, 8, 11

white victimization, 10, 12, 65, 76, 90, 95, 102–103. *See also* "aggrieved whiteness"

"woketopian," 21, 103

World Church of the Creator, 73, 80–81. *See also* Creativity

ZOG (Zionist Occupied Government), 91

Founded in 1893,
UNIVERSITY OF CALIFORNIA PRESS
publishes bold, progressive books and journals
on topics in the arts, humanities, social sciences,
and natural sciences—with a focus on social
justice issues—that inspire thought and action
among readers worldwide.

The UC PRESS FOUNDATION
raises funds to uphold the press's vital role
as an independent, nonprofit publisher, and
receives philanthropic support from a wide
range of individuals and institutions—and from
committed readers like you. To learn more, visit
ucpress.edu/supportus.